Critical Praise for this Book

'Zillah Eisenstein, one of the most lively feminist theorists of democracy, here calls on us to question universalism, to embrace a more radical "polyversal" understanding of today's world, and, out of both efforts, to craft a more genuinely feminist democracy. As always, Eisenstein is way ahead of the curve.' – Cynthia Enloe, author of *Maneuvers: the International Politics of Militarizing Women's Lives.*

'When Eisenstein boldly declares that "the globe needs anti-racist feminist voices for peace", she speaks for us all. Embodying writing as an act of resistance in *Against Empire*, she offers a renewed politics of radical anti-colonialism centered around a constructive recognition of difference that privileges diversity as a fundamental feature of global community. Ultimately, she identifies the pursuit of justice as a common standpoint uniting us all.' – bell hooks, feminist theorist and cultural critic

'This is a powerful and provocative work, at once an autobiography of an ardent and wide-ranging activist and a critical study of the workings of empire in this time. Eisenstein shows not only how feminism can and must rise to its global challenges, but how the workings of empire are systematically related to gender. She refuses the recourse to culturally imperialist notions of "women" and the "human" and shows how each of these terms might gain a broader, emancipatory meaning within a global framework.' – Judith Butler, Maxine Elliot Professor, UC Berkeley

'Zillah Eisenstein writes with passion and commitment. She traces the complexity of the relationships between gender, class, race and religious oppression against women, links the global with the local, the West with the East, the personal with the political, the economic with the cultural. Despite the complexity of her subject, her language remains simple, illuminating and refreshing in this dark age of war and neo-imperialism.' – Nawal El Saadawi, Cairo

'Written with Eisenstein's usual lucidity, originality, and deep and wide knowledge of neoliberalism and histories of feminism around the globe, *Against Empire* is the most far-reaching and visionary argument for a radically polyversal, anti-imperialist feminism for our times. A truly courageous, provocative and eminently pedagogical book.' – Chandra Talpade Mohanty, Syracuse University, and author of *Feminism Without Borders, Decolonizing Theory, Practicing Solidarity.*

'Zillah Eisenstein takes readers with her on an exhilarating journey beyond the world of ingrained notions and policed conversations as she deflates old dichotomies and facile demonizations that divide nations, races, religions, and genders and that nurture insecurities. *Against Empire* is provocative, inviting agreement or disagreement, but above all calling for fresh and free thinking. It is a critical book for critical times.' – Margot Badran, Northwestern University

About this Book

Zillah Eisenstein, one of North America's most eminent and politically engaged feminist thinkers, continues her unrelenting critique of neoliberal globalization and its capture of democratic possibilities in *Against Empire*. She is deeply critical of President George W. Bush's headlong recourse to the use of war, the neocon embrace of American empire as something positive for humanity, and the accelerated imposition on the rest of the world of the most negative aspects of American capitalism. Zillah Eisenstein urgently asks that we build a global anti-war movement to counter US power.

She believes that it is essential to see beyond the distortions inherent in mainstream presentations of history, and to detect the silencing of racialized, sex/gendered and classed ways of seeing. At the heart of her book is the insistence that the so-called West is as much fiction as reality; as much appropriation as originary; as exclusionary as it is promissory. Eisenstein contends that the sexualized black slave trade was an early form of globalization. The West and western feminisms have no monopoly of authorship; we need to pluralize the understanding of feminisms as other-than-western. The West has debts to places elsewhere, as much as places elsewhere have debts to the Enlightenment. Black America, India, the Islamic world and Africa envision unique conceptions of what it is to be fully, 'polyversally', human.

Professor Eisenstein gives her readers a rich picture of women's activism across the globe today. If there is to be hope of a more peaceful, more just and happier world, it lies, she believes, in the understandings and activism of women today.

This book is written for all people who wish to examine more deeply what the West really is, how it is seen by the rest of the world, and the hidden histories that make up human complexity and diversity below the waterline of conventional narratives.

About the Author

Zillah Eisenstein is Professor of Politics at Ithaca College in New York. She has written feminist theory in North America for the past twenty-five years. Her writing is an integral part of her political activism. She writes in order to share and learn with, and from, others engaged in political struggles for social justice. She writes about her work building coalitions across women's differences: the black/white divide in the US; the struggles of Serb and Muslim women in the war in Bosnia; the needs of women health workers in Cuba; the commitments of environmentalists in Ghana; the relationship between socialists and feminists in union organizing; the struggles against extremist fundamentalisms in Egypt and Afghanistan; the needs of women workers in India.

Throughout her career her books have tracked the rise of neoliberalism both within the US and across the globe. She has documented the demise of liberal democracy and scrutinized the growth of imperial and militarist globalization. She has also critically written about the attack on affirmative action in the US, the masculinist bias of law, the crisis of breast cancer and AIDS, the racism of patriarchy and the patriarchal structuring of race, the new nationalisms, and corporatist multiculturalism.

Her most recent books include:

- **Hatreds: Racialized and Sexualized Conflicts in the 21st Century** (New York, Routledge, 1996)
- **Global Obscenities: Patriarchy, Capitalism and the Lure of Cyberfantasy** (New York, WU Press, 1998)
- **ManMade Breast Cancers** (Ithaca, Cornell University Press, 2001)

Against Empire

Feminisms, Racism, and the West

Zillah Eisenstein

Spinifex Press
MELBOURNE

Zed Books
LONDON & NEW YORK

Against Empire: Feminisms, Racism, and the West was first published in 2004 by
Zed Books Ltd, 7 Cynthia Street, London N1 9JF, UK and
Room 400, 175 Fifth Avenue, New York, NY 10010, USA
www.zedbooks.co.uk

Published in Australia and New Zealand by
Spinifex Press, 504 Queensberry Street, North Melbourne,
Victoria 3051, Australia
www.spinifexpress.com.au

Copyright © Zillah Eisenstein 2004

The rights of the author of this work have been asserted by her
in accordance with the Copyright, Designs and Patents Act, 1988

Cover designed by Andrew Corbett
Typeset in 10/12 pt Bembo
by Long House, Cumbria, UK
Printed and bound in Malta
by Gutenberg Press

Distributed in the USA exclusively by Palgrave Macmillan, a division of
St Martin's Press, LLC,175 Fifth Avenue, New York, NY 10010

All rights reserved

A catalogue record for this book
is available from the British Library

US Cataloging-in-Publication Data
is available from the Library of Congress

ISBN Hb 1 84277 394 1
Pb 1 84277 395 X

In Australasia
ISBN Pb 1 876756 53 5

Contents

Acknowledgements

My debts are great to my friends, family, and colleagues who surround me with their wisdom, their love and their generosity. I could not write, nor would I want to write, without them. It is with enormous gratitude that I thank each and every one of them.

Thanks to my parents, Morris Eisenstein and Fannie Price Eisenstein for always demanding that I look to know more and wonder endlessly, even when I was too young.

Thanks to my devoted friends who always read my writing and talk with me about it whenever I need them to: Miriam Brody, Susan Buck-Morss, Rosalind Petchesky, and Patty Zimmermann. So much of this book has been a dialogue with them, about bodies and wars, for decades. Ros's own writings have deeply impacted on my thinking here.

Thanks to my readers and their critical comments on early drafts and murmurings of this book: Sandra Greene, Mary Katzenstein, Anna Marie-Smith and Margaret Washington. Miriam read everything I threw at her and pressed me for clarity. Susan continued with me through to the end, convincing me that I could do this. Ros, Patty, and Carla Golden read sections and gave elaborate comments.

Thanks to Chandra Talpade Mohanty for her intellectually nurturing friendship. We spoke out against the wars of/on 'terror' together. Thanks to Isaac Kramnick and Martin Bernal who spoke with me at length as I began this book. Their caring suggestions are deeply appreciated. Thanks to Naeem Inayatalluh who read and talked with me about the colonial eye and its construction of difference. His friendship deeply touches upon my conversations here. Thanks to Asma Barlas for profoundly affecting my thinking about religion and the democratic possibilities of Islam. I am deeply grateful to her for our decade-long dialogues. Thanks to my friend and colleague Tom Shevory for being both of these to me. Thanks to Nawal El Saadawi for her writing and Sherif Hetata for welcoming me to their home.

Thanks to Leila Ahmed, Margot Badran, Miriam Cooke, Adrienne Davis, and Roxanne Euben for their writings, and for their correspondence with me. Each has been sustaining and enormously helpful to me. Thanks to Mindy Peden and Jim Meyer for their research assistance which was immeasurable. Thanks to Provost Peter Bardaglio for financial and collegial support. Thanks to Sarah Dean for her secretarial assist. Thanks to my editor Barbara Clarke at Zed who was always encouraging and to Robert Molteno for seeing production through to the end, along with Anna Hardman, Julian Hosie, Anne Rodford and Rosemary Taylorson. Thanks to Ros for suggesting Zed Books.

Thanks to my students in my theory courses "Marxism and Liberalism on Slavery and Patriarchy", "Feminist Conversations", and "Feminisms 2003" for allowing me to explore unconventional ideas with them. Thanks to Rebecca Riley, and Ellen Wade for their lifetime friendships. They are a part of everything I do. Thanks to my sister Julia Price Eisenstein for her unflagging spirit. Thanks to Bernie Wohl for bonds deeper than blood. Thanks to the women's movements in Cairo, Egypt; Hyderabad and Mumbai, India; Accra, Ghana; Havana, Cuba; Seoul, Korea; to name just a few, where I have learned so much and beyond. Thanks to my daughter Sarah Eisenstein Stumbar who buoys my spirit and allows me to believe that we can make the world better. It is particularly special to me that she commented on much of the manuscript. Thanks to Richard for knowing how to soothe my soul.

And my profoundest thanks to the anti-war movements in the US and places elsewhere.

for Richard
and his anti-war heart

Preface

I started writing this book long before September 11, 2001, and its aftermaths in Afghanistan and Iraq. These events have become a part of my story because the historical record demands this. This book would have been crafted and framed differently if these moments had not happened. I have no other justification for some of the particular sites I have chosen than that they have demanded my attention. I hope it will become clear how I think every political moment is informed by a series of *befores* and *alreadys*. There are histories to expose in any contemporary moment, be it September 11, 2001, or the US wars of/on 'terror'. This book is about exposing these silenced and misrepresented histories.

If power is to dominate effectively it must not reveal itself fully to others. The seeing and knowing of power is therefore always partial and incomplete. My purpose here is to uncover the relations and histories of power more fully, in order to see and know as much as possible. Ultimately this book is an attempt to see more, to know more about how differences and rich variety are silenced in the authorized narratives of history. My purpose is to move towards a more inclusive viewing of humanity by looking for absences, listening for silences, and imagining beyond my own limits.

This writing takes threads of different established stories and cautiously tries to sew them together in new form. So there is no one theme that simply summarizes my attempt to envision the polyversal humanity that inhabits truly democratic theory. But at the heart of my discussion is the insistence that the so-called West is as much fiction as real; as much appropriation as originary; as exclusionary as it is promissory. I also offer the idea that the West and Western feminisms have no monopoly of authorship and that alternative feminisms have long thrived 'elsewhere' in multiple fashion. As well, I sometimes see the misuse of women's rights discourse in imperial form as extraordinarily problematic for women living outside the West. These thoughts set the frame for looking at Black America, India, the Islamic world and Africa in order to see their unique conceptions of inclusive democratic possibility; and at the slave trade as a sexualized economy determined by race. I argue that the sexualized black slave trade was an early form of globalization that still frames power today. These are connected thoughts with no simple narration.

Instead I offer a rethinking of sex, and race, and class in order to rewrite universalized rights for polyvocal needs. I use the human body as my inclusive site for humanity in order to dislocate the West/non-West divide in order to encourage the strength and vision to change ourselves and the world for the better of us all. And my argument unravels in strange ways.

A few caveats before I begin, so to speak. Although there are no simple starts to anything, I start the book with the US wars on Iraq. Language itself has become part of the problem of these wars. I will not use the Bush rhetoric of "war on terrorism" because war itself is terror-filled; because the US creates more terror than it receives; because the word 'terrorism' has become a reactionary tool for mobilizing blind patriotism, smothering dissent, and enforcing silence. This does not mean that I do not think that extremist fanatics create misery for everyone, everywhere, and that I am not committed to ridding the world of this enormous pain.

By the time you are reading this book there will be a new set of moments to understand. Much of what you will read will already be part of the befores. There are no simple beginnings or endings. President Bush declared victory over Iraq on May 1, 2003 and yet the war continues. On August 27, 2003, 'post'-war GI deaths exceeded the number of deaths during the official war.

I am trying to think and see beyond the sites that are put in view. I am writing from the US in summer 2003, where Bush and Cheney, Rumsfeld, Powell and Rice, Wolfowitz and Perle are in charge of us. Millions protested against the 2003 war in Iraq, but it began and proceeded despite an active anti-war movement at home and abroad. Supposedly the US intervened in Afghanistan and Iraq to bring freedom and democracy 'elsewhere'. In both these instances women's bodies were key to these war fantasies. In the first, Afghan women were clad in the enforced burqa; in the second US women prisoners of war were symbolized in freely chosen khaki. Yet, these interventions have not brought freedom, nor democracy.

The rest of the world viewed a war that we did not see here. Russell Smith says that "the coverage of this war in the press and on television has been disgusting".[2] Our so-called voluntary military is shrinking so the Marines enforce a 'stop-loss' order and the Army declares an "involuntary extension" on those who might choose to retire.[3] It is disproportionately our working class of color, many of whom are reservists, who fight for the US abroad. This is not just, nor fair, nor democratic. The rich and powerful will become richer and more powerful from this war; and the poor will become poorer.

The US wars of/on 'terror' were in process before the massacre of September 11, 2001. The Gulf War of 1991 never really ended. The wars on/of 'terror' have longstanding agendas with complicated histories. We must remember to remember how the present is structured by its distant and closer past: the slave trade, the nuclear bombing of Hiroshima, the CIA-led coup in Chile against Allende, the war in Afghanistan. Each is layered and silenced into the present.

I start with the aftermath of September 11, 2001 and this is not truly the start. I look to find the *befores* and *alreadys* and *afters*. I work backwards to the slave trade, and across to Mahatma Gandhi and Aurobindo Ghose and W.E.B. DuBois and Ida B. Wells who tell the stories of resistance, and forward to Afghanistan and Iraq and the next 'elsewhere'. I am in this moment of a "war on terrorism" and see wars of 'terror'. This book, then, goes back and forth between the terror of the West from before and the wars of/on 'terror' now.

We need to remember and keep remembering, as Kenzaburo Oe asks of us, to use shame and humiliation as weapons in the movement against nuclear arms, and militarism, and global imperialism.[4] Besides remembering I also try to create a memory of the racialized and sexualized sites of women's specificity within these befores and alreadys. And I want to build context for seeing this present moment. Each and every life lost on September 11 was a horrible, horrific loss. And, yet, the AIDS pandemic also that means 2.3 million deaths occurred in 2001 in sub-Saharan Africa which means the deaths of two September 11s happened each day of that year.[5]

In writing this book I sometimes use my own personal stories as a way of locating myself within the larger parameters of the globe. I feel more keenly than ever that I must try to voice earnestly the privileges and the blinders that go with living in the US as it becomes a more singular dominating global force. Tales of my personal life locate me and expose my limitations simultaneously. The personal begins to tell the political as the local also involves the global. My hope is that each domain elucidates the other.

I interrogate my starting points contextually and then seek to take them into my discussions of Gandhi and Malcolm X. It is significant that I now, again, choose to re-read and remember W. E. B. DuBois and Ida B. Wells in order better to envision struggles for democracy. It is also enormously important that I wonder again about the originary locations of feminisms, and see more variety and complexity than I did two decades ago. My critique is in part of myself as of the West and much of the journey of the book is defined by this personal path. Many of my sites are only understood by seeing my own limitations as part of the story. And, there are also always other sites to visit and uncover.

If I am right in believing that context always matters and is constraining, then this is a difficult time in which to create openings for seeing more. Neoliberalism has trumped the globe. The Bush administrations have orchestrated the corruption, deceit, and exploitation of ordinary folk by corporate America. Enron, Tyco, World Com., Xerox: all falsify the records of billions of dollars of profits in order to satisfy insatiable greed.

I read in the *New York Times* of a young boy who is abused and killed in a foster home while the overworked social worker has too many cases to be able to check on him regularly. Later that day I go to the airport and see fifteen federal workers standing around monitoring the new surveillance equipment. I am thinking how wrong this all is: spending money on building a police state while so many other critical human needs are ignored. People are losing jobs, cannot keep or get health insurance, pantries are empty of food long before new deliveries arrive, kindergartens are being closed for lack of funds, and billions are spent on war. Across the globe more than 75 percent of the people are poor, while in 2001, 826 million were starving, and millions of children were dying of preventable diseases.

The Bush 2003 tax cut proposal continued this neoliberal agenda: downsize all governmental responsibility except for war-making. Meanwhile 32 percent of the tax cut benefits will go to society's richest 1 percent. Most families' tax decrease will be less than $800 while those families averaging over $1 million a year will get tax breaks of about $80,000. Eight million people, mostly low-income taxpayers, will receive no benefit at all from the tax revision.

A class war is being waged in the US while all eyes look abroad. This war is not new to the US or the needs of global capitalism. The 1980 presidential election of Ronald Reagan authorized the windfall for the upper class. Since this time, neoconservative/neoliberal, Republicans and Democrats alike, have allowed an assault on the gains made by the civil rights and women's movements in the US. This neoliberal war, fought against the role of publicly responsible government, has successfully dismantled the social-welfare state and put in its place a security-military complex better suited for empire building.

The US is a battlefield of sorts, with affirmative action, abortion rights, discrimination law all under severe attack. Instead of challenging the racist divisions of labor and class privilege, President Bush uses Colin Powell and Condoleezza Rice to represent a diversity that equalizes the multiple forms of discrimination, prejudice and exclusion that are found in multiracial and pluricultural societies.[6] It will be no surprise, as my story unfolds, that the greatest struggles of resistance are located with antiracist feminisms against empire. It is these feminisms – historical and contemporary – that remain silenced and invisible to much of the world.

As I write, the remilitarized US state is proceeding with new abandon towards unilateral empire. The downsizing and restructuring of the US economy through the 1980s and 1990s has now been accompanied by a restructuring of the CIA, FBI, and Pentagon into a centralized Department of Homeland Security, headed by Tom Ridge. The Department has a budget of $37 billion and employs 170,000. This new security nation-state monitors and conducts surveillance in the name of democracy. But many have become too accustomed to what Slavoj Žižek calls sanitized and unreal lives. People wish to believe that the malignant qualities of life can be removed from their content: coffee without caffeine, cream without fat, beer without alcohol, war without casualties, democracy without its messiness and freedoms.[7]

I have written this book, which is messy, in order to move beyond the constraints of US imperial global policy. It is my humble contribution to the struggle to see and know more in order to resist domination and create a healthy, peaceful, justice-filled world.

Notes

1. In this book I depart from my longstanding practice of not capitalizing countries or ethnic/racial identities. In the past I have not used capitalization to emphasize the fluidity and lack of clear borders of these constructions. I have changed this practice at the request of my editors who think that this will not translate well for a wide-ranging international readership. However, I continue not to capitalize 'white' in the hope of destabilizing its silenced privileging as not being a color.
2. Russell Smith, "The New Newspeak", *New York Review of Books*, vol. L, no. 9 (May 29, 2003), p. 19. See also in the same volume Michael Massing, "The Unseen War", pp. 16–19.
3. John Gregory Dunne, "The Horror is Seductive", *New York Review of Books*, ibid., pp. 23–5.
4. Kenzaburo Oe, *Hiroshima* (New York: Grove Press, 1981 [1965]), pp. 13, 83.
5. Gilbert Achcar, "The Clash of Barbarisms", *Monthly Review*, vol. 54, no. 4 (September 2002), pp. 17–30.
6. Sueli Carneiro, "A Blood Debt", in Lucy Garrido, ed., *Your Mouth is Fundamental, Against Fundamentalism* (Montevideo, Uruguay: Cotidiano Mujer, 2002), p. 39.
7. Slavoj Žižek, *Welcome to the Desert of the Real* (New York: Verso, 2002), pp. 10, 11.

1 Unilateral Empire: The United Nations of America[1]

The US at present is not what a democracy looks like. Neither is feminism one and the same with the Bush administration's appropriation of women's rights talk on behalf of Afghan women, or women in the US military. Controversy over the meanings of democracy and feminism is hardly new. But my attempt at seeing and thinking through these issues today has a compelling newness, especially for many of us living in the United States.

Much of what makes this moment new is the unilateral stance of the US. Our leaders are so giddy with their power that they arrogantly and inadvertently reveal their imperial plot for most of the world to see. US empire building Americanizes the globe in its particularly racialized and masculinist form. The Bush administration continues to plaster its version of neoliberalism on to the rest of the globe. People I speak with 'elsewhere' think they should be able to vote in US elections given that they are expected to live according to US design.

I use the term 'elsewhere/s' to pluralize my viewings and my sitings for thinking about other-than-Western democracies.[2] I use these places outside the US as sites to radically pluralize my viewing of humanity's complex understanding of democracies and feminisms. Radical pluralism requires a displacement of the US as the privileged site of modernity, democracy, feminism, and so on, and demands an accounting from places 'elsewhere'.

This project is risky as I span the globe historically, and comparatively. I try to avoid the East/West, traditional/modern, secular/religious divides and know that I am only sometimes successful in doing so. I look for multiple and incomplete starts and fissures, rather than originary locations, in order to see the most innovative democratic and antiracist feminist dialogues possible. This requires a public and intellectual space large enough for all of us. Sadly, this public space is shrinking and narrowing.

The present is always shifting, yet at any given moment it is also the surrounding in which we live, so it is both history and the present, simultaneously. Thinking and seeing *before* the moment – its history – and *after* – its future possibilities – demands complex knowing.

Global Capital and Empire

My inquiry starts here: that Western democratic theory has appropriated all the experience it chooses, as its own, locating the West as the originary home of democracy. This starting point is not simply the well-known critique that Western democracies were exclusive at their core of indigenous peoples, non-propertied men, all women, and African slaves but rather that the ideas of individuality and human freedom also come from these excluded people, from their acts of resistance. The West has in part learned what democracy means from the Haitian revolution, and from women's anticolonial struggles in Egypt, Algeria, Argentina, Chiapas, and Chile. As such, Western democracy, as well as Western feminism, was never simply Western: it grew out of global struggles of resistance, at multiple sites, like the slave trade. Equality and freedom are early on envisioned by those punished by and excluded from Western notions of freedom.

The flows between 'East' and 'West' go each way; from West to East; and East to West. And, these very constructs are exactly that – constructs that are as much symbolic as real. Therefore, I use the terms while at the same time I hope to open and complexify them. Because these labels reify the very hierarchies I wish to displace, much of the historical record I seek does not exist. Silences and exclusions form the erasure. Yet, there is more than one conception of democracy and freedom, and the Western brand is not simply of the West, nor the best.

In the twenty-first century, the West means the US more than Europe, as well as the globalized forms of cultural capitalism which no longer have any one geographical location. The flows travel from global capital to sites everywhere; yet there still are flows traveling in reverse against these developments from the anti-globalization demonstrations in Seattle, Washington, and Johannesburg, South Africa. Given the relations of power, flows both ways are absorbed by power-filled discourses which appropriate and silence subversive variety.

Global capitalism parades as globalization. Globalization holds out the probability of world poverty worsening along with repressive measures against those who suffer most. It also holds out the possibility of resistance against these forces. Growing criticism of global capital and its culture of domination has taken hold in places like Seattle, Paris, and Barcelona. At the same time Coke and McDonald's are known throughout the world and people line up for miles to enter a new McDonald's in Kuwait. In China the owners of Noodle King say that they have learned everything from McD's, but that they offer a "traditional menu in an untraditional setting". Yet, they wonder if they must give up the "human touch", in the end, for what is considered modernity.[3] Being modern means downsizing labor because labor is too costly. Coke, McDonald's, Kentucky Fried Chicken represent the West, while the US is more and more dependent on other countries to do our work. Dell computers are built in Tijuana; 90 percent of the world's scanners and most computer motherboards are manufactured in Taiwan.[4]

Bourgeois culture is seductive and captivating *and* it is oppressive and isolating. Monitoring is needed and, most of all, the US needs to surveil more and more of the globe in order to protect its own needs which extend well beyond its own territorial borders. So the US builds empire for itself and the globe be damned. The US votes against the Kyoto Treaty, women's rights initiatives, the banning of land mines, etcetera. Well-known capitalists like George Soros recognize that the US is the major obstacle to building international initiatives that endorse a sense of global community, responsibility, and cooperation.[5]

In the US many progressives feel powerless and helpless. The Bush administration presses on with its "homeland security" agenda while destroying civil liberties at home, and protecting tyrannies abroad. In media and politics, language emptied of meaning has become triumphant. Terms championing the human struggles of people around the world have been recontexualized for a global economy that is diverse and plural, but not equal nor equally free. The meanings of color are shifting slowly and contradictorily given the new slaveries of the globe.

Color, and its cultural and political naming in terms of race, has no one meaning. The slave trade designated a new context for seeing Black skin; today the exclusion of most African countries from the cybertech world renews this context in historical form. Yet, colors continue to mix, and Yellows and Browns have more visibility in the global cyber economy. Columbus 'invented' the Indian; the Indian was something else before he 'discovered' them. Afterwards, they were hung, and burned with unspeakable rage and cruelty but the Spanish slaughters and violence destroyed much of these traces.[6]

Yet meaning is always sluggish and complex. Aimé Césaire writes that Hitler was seen as a monster, not because of the crimes themselves that he was responsible for, but because he used these crimes to humiliate the white man. He used against Europeans the European colonialist practices that had formerly been "reserved exclusively for the Arabs of Algeria, the 'coolies' of India, and the 'niggers' of Africa".[7] This reflects in part the fact that Hitler did not see Jews as white; nor did many Europeans.

Language is the only means we have to name what we see, and it also gets emptied of meaning. Each word is filtered through the concentrated power of our times, which selfishly captures meaning for itself. The world becomes indecipherable and as Jean Baudrillard says, 'undecidable'. When little is expected of language it no longer has effective meaning. Instead, image becomes the operating mode; reality is disconnected from itself and we are left with "radical uncertainty". Digitality only re-encodes these modes of exchange: artificiality replaces the real.[8]

However, people retain their human capacity to know pain or to feel jubilation. The 1991 Gulf War happened, even if the US pretends it did not; our president does not know much and is probably one of the least educated rich men of the world even though we pretend he leads. The children of Iraq continue to suffer and die whether this is named or not.

Seeing and being seen, Islamic and Muslim culture is rediscovered by political and economic forces. Once again the ascendency of Islam returns, even if this time it is from a marginalized positioning. As such, feminisms and women's resistance in Islam, which are not new, but are being newly uncovered once again, allow us to see more of the history and presence of women's struggle for liberation as central to the globe. So much is said to be new, when most of everything is almost always also old.

I, a woman born in the US of communist and atheist parents, wonder anew about my identity. Raised as an atheist, I have never known God as an explanation for what people do, or for what happens to them. I was brought up to believe in people: that people make the world through their struggle and pain. Others enter the world 'believing'. We each share the point of entry which initiates us to a way of seeing and thinking. Jew, Muslim, atheist, Christian, Hindu – each starts with a before … with some shared explanations of beginnings. There are too many kinds of religious belief and ways of believing, and too many kinds of nonbelieving for there to be any simple divide between secular and religious. Bush speaks of good and evil in biblical terms, is said to see no moral ambiguity when he decides to drop bombs on Iraq, and yet is said to lead a secular state. Meanwhile, others, in Islam, are defined as religious fanatics.

The wars in Israel and Palestine and Rwanda and between Hindu and Muslim in Gujarat, and white and Black in South Africa speak intractability. But the struggles of secular Muslims in Iran against the Khomeini regime also bespeak human struggles that move beyond neat divides. Yet our politicians have no interest in opening our language or our thinking or our seeing. Progressives standing against all forms of fundamentalist extremism – capitalist, Muslim, Christian – must make a new clarity possible for seeing a shared humanity.

Israel, initially founded on the idea of freedom for Jews, is also an apartheid state practicing racism against Palestinians. That is why Israel is seen as the new South Africa in much of the world outside the US. This reminds me of how bigoted and reactionary so many of the middle-class Jewish communities – in Atlanta, Georgia, and Columbus, Ohio – were to my family as my parents actively took part in the Civil Rights Movement in the 1960s. These communities wanted nothing to do with us, making it impossible for us to move into their neighborhoods; and we were not interested in their synagogues.

How do oppressive moments get appropriated as supposedly democratic? Who gets to claim the meaning of democracy and for whom is it claimed? White propertied men used colonialism and imperialism to appropriate democracy for themselves. The Enlightenment articulated the language of democracy in spite of its dependence on the slave trade. Haitian revolutionaries were silenced by the revolutionaries of the American colonies. India is said to be a democracy yet Gandhi does not stand alongside Jefferson in US history books because Gandhi was an anti-Western/anti-materialist democrat. Democracy that looks different from Western individualism is dismissed as something else, from 'elsewheres'. This power of naming affects all viewing and seeing. It even gives feminism to the West, when struggles for women's freedom have existed always, and everywhere. And while it does this, many progressive feminisms which have existed within the West are also denied.

My 'always' and 'everywhere' assume I know more than I do. But right now I must think subversively which means seeing comparatively. The larger the sweep, the better the understanding of *similarity* as partial and incomplete. Similarity is not the same as sameness; and yet a simple notion of difference will not do because any one site has its multiple meanings which are not fully knowable. The big sweep is no more incomplete than the small local site. It just feels safer.

I was brought up by my communist parents to believe that I should never endorse a way of being or living that I would not be willing to embrace myself. I have used this as my democratic guide – always to imagine myself in the situation before giving my support for it. But I now wonder if this is too limiting, that it assumes that we must be willing to exchange each other's lives, when all I need to do is to understand another person's choice. Do not misunderstand this stance as liberal pluralism, or cultural relativism.

My radically plural standpoint requires that humanity be respected and allowed self-determination, but in cacophonous voices. This polyversal humanism locates the feminist promissories of this book. My radical pluralism does not allow for suicide bombers, no matter their gender, because this involves indiscriminate killing. Nor does it allow any form of racialized or gendered exclusion of any person from the right freely to choose their path in life. I move beyond the liberal/Western notion of diversity which accepts out of necessity, rather than choice, that people will differ. This means seeking out cultural differences in order to deepen understanding by sharing and decentering the self with a newly fulfilling complexity.

Being direct and open with each other allows us to try and subvert the cultural constructions that continually confront us and keep us from knowing what someone else is thinking. I must ask questions in order to know. But subtle webs of silence – be it about lovers, or dreams, or family sadnesses – are defined as private. Privacy, as a veil for secrecy and fantasy, can often disable and disengage. Many cultures, including those of the West, think silence is better than openness. Yet Westerners are said to be too open, too brash, too noisy about private tales. Just look at our tv shows. But it is as though the more that is revealed publicly – from Bill Clinton's affairs to the sexual abuses of the Catholic priests – the more silences operate privately. I find the silences, rather than more talk, deafening.

Thinking is done best by borrowing, dialoguing, mirroring, exchanging, arguing. This means that modernity, secularism, terrorism, the West, Islam, globalization, feminisms – all need clarification. The difficulty of speaking in power-filled discourses is that we reproduce them at the same time as we challenge them. The term 'slavery' itself is a homogenized abstraction that silences the incredible individualized lives of the slaves themselves. Yet slavery must be named for its crushing inhumanity. I interrogate and challenge the very idea of the West, and yet find myself using and replicating it too much of the time.

The present scourge of terrorism disallows, from above, a careful hearing of whose terror the US is concerned with. The so-called "war on terrorism" is used across the globe to silence human rights activists. Whereas the US has often in the past authorized human rights rhetoric, today it authorizes anti-terror legislation allowing governments here and elsewhere to equate human rights dissidents with terrorists.

US security guidelines now require Arabs and Muslims from Iran, Iraq, and Syria who enter the US to be fingerprinted and photographed, although Saudis are exempt. Arrests and threats of deportation plague most Arabs and Muslims throughout the US. Since September 11, 2001, more than 40 percent of Pakistanis in Brooklyn have been detained. Families are leaving the US for Canada and elsewhere in order to avoid the constant surveillance and fear.[9] Houman Mortazavi, who emigrated from Iran, says of the US: "I've been seriously thinking of moving somewhere civilized, where I will not be prosecuted for who I am."[10] Another Iranian says the US is plagued by a new cesspool of racial conservatism.[11]

There seems to be little consistency in and reason for many of the violations of civil rights. Saudis are often exempt, yet several Saudis were on the planes that destroyed the peace and quiet of so many on 9/11. Similarly, none of the initial 598 detainees suspected of Al Qaeda connections who were held at Guantanamo Bay came from Iraq. Yet the war of/on 'terror' was directed against Iraq. Bush repeatedly used

Saddam's "weapons of mass destruction" (WMD) as justification for war. Bush declared Saddam an "imminent threat", declared that he would pass on WMD to Al Qaeda if left in power. Yet, no weapons have been located; and more and more information has surfaced to show that this threat was more made up than real. This kind of misinformation, deception, and lying makes it almost impossible to think.

The Wars of/on 'Terror'

Right-wing "war on terrorism" rhetoric in the US distorts and deceives. Along with many progressives, Noam Chomsky points out that the bombings of Afghanistan and Iraq were massacres rather than 'wars'. Furthermore, 'terrorism' has become a catch-all term for the enemy who challenges US imperialism. Viewed by the likes of George Bush, Donald Rumsfeld, and Paul Wolfowitz, terrorism is the activity of terrorists; and terrorists are not us, nor are they like us – terrorists are those who hate 'our' freedom/democracy, modernity/secularism, and hard-won success. 'Terrorism' has now fully replaced communism as the globe's scourge. 'Our' enemies, the enemies of democracy and freedom, exist everywhere and anywhere. Yet much of the rest of the world thinks that President Bush is more of a threat to the world than Saddam Hussein. More on all this later.

The political aftermaths of September 11, 2001 were in motion before that day. A neoliberal/imperial agenda, already firmly in place, took advantage of the deep emotionalism tied to that day. The Bush administration has nurtured this fear and used it to dismantle democracy further. Bush and Cheney feed the US public a constant litany of retribution and defense, while people in South Africa and Rwanda struggle, even if not always successfully, to find reconciliation.

Antiterrorism rhetoric fits well with global capitalism. Today 'terrorism' – whether it is Al Qaeda's or the imperial state's – is deployed and scattered globally, much like capital itself. There is no single country that houses terrorism … or capitalism. Both are networked transnationally. The needs of capital to thrive globally conflict with US desires for unilateral control. Terrorism becomes a convenient justificatory cover for US interventionism. Anti-'terrorism' rhetoric then protects US empire building while creating the very conditions that spawn true terror and terrorists.

Do not misunderstand me. I very much wish to stop terror-filled moments across the globe. However, the Bush administration is not addressing this terror and cannot with its present imperial policies. The US wishes to articulate a unilateral dominance in global terms, a wish that expresses a contradiction between US nationalism and global capitalism. Hence, the need for a strong militarist presence. Noam Chomsky writes that '9/11' was not a statement against globalization, but a statement against US foreign policies in Israel, Guatemala, and so on.[12] Yes, but our foreign policies are about maintaining an imperial kind of globalization. The US wants it both ways here: unilateral nationalism and transnational capitalism.

John Ashcroft, Condoleezza Rice, and Dick Cheney oversee from the top this process of nationalizing US global strategies. Bush tries to keep up with what is going on. Military tribunals are legitimized as fair treatment for the enemy. Detainees held at Guantanamo Bay are not classified as prisoners of war and therefore do not have the rights that the enemy has in conventional warfare. Which combatants count as human, with legal rights, is no longer clear.[13] Reports from Guantanamo Bay say that the conditions of prisoners are unconscionable – that they are treated like animals, crouching naked on the ground. As a result, many of the detainees have attempted suicide.

In the US, the FBI's counterintelligence program (COINTELPRO) has been reactivated for the monitoring and detention of suspected terrorists. Every Muslim is a possible target. A recent initiative prohibits non-citizens from working as airport screeners even though nearly 30,000 immigrants were working as airport screeners at the time the initiative was announced. Forty percent of these screeners at Los Angeles International airport and 80 percent at the San Francisco Bay Area airport were immigrants who have permanent legal residence.

The US defense budget increases exponentially; billions of dollars are promised for securing security for the homeland, and gripped in fear the US authorizes the privatizing and conservatizing of US politics. The purpose of the state becomes reduced to policing and surveillance. This reductionism is reminiscent of the Hobbesian state of war: the best any government can do is provide self-preservation. The US PATRIOT Act – PATRIOT being the acronym for Providing Appropriate Tools Required to Intercept and Obstruct Terrorism – sets out the new agenda of a police state for monitoring its internal borders. Documents like the Defense Planning Guidance report, originally written in 1992 and brought out again in 2002 with little change by Wolfowitz, Cheney and Colin Powell, focus on the global need for pre-emptive strikes for monitoring across external borders.[14] Pre-emptive strikes bespeak the priority given to absolute and complete domination over all potential enemies.

The Bush administration took the September 11, 2001 attacks and manipulated them to its own purposes for empire building. Its goal is singular domination of the globe. In its arrogance, it has become the bully on the block who lies, and cheats, and kills, as documented in the administration's own internal reports. We – the imperial 'we' – are a 'terror' state overseeing the new warfare with laptops and modems.[15] This network-centric warfare (NCW) uses unmanned aerial vehicles and writes off collateral damage. It is a war that denies the established, institutional and international law regulating war. It demands "total war" which cannot be constrained and restrained by human rights rhetoric.[16] The consequences are devastating as war is thought of like an arcade game and 'tactical' nuclear weapons are discussed. All human rights succumb to this disembodied militarist directive. The Bush administration thinks nothing of targeting and killing suspected Al Qaeda members without judicial process. Bush boldly and brashly told the whole world that the US government was a willing assassin in the hunt for Saddam.[17]

The 'security' state rewrites the rights of the dissident. At the start of the bombing of Iraq, antiwar marchers were readily denied a permit to march through the streets of New York City. Antiwar activists were/are charged with anti-patriotism. The 'security' state is itself also being restructured. The Pentagon downsized and streamlined the State Department while placing the final version of the Iraqi emergency supplemental appropriations bill under its own central control. Continued conflicts between the CIA, the Pentagon, and the State Department have also created much confusion and greatly damaged reconstruction efforts in Iraq. The power grab within the Bush administration exists both inside and outside this restructuring process.

Although it would be wonderful to end the actions of fanatical extremists in Israel, Bali, Nigeria, and India, or stop those who damaged the SS *Cole* and embassies in Africa, the US will never be able to do so by itself perpetrating acts of violence and violation.[18] The US will first have to stop its disrespectful cultural imposition on places elsewhere.[19] And the US will have to start abiding by the same international standard with respect to human rights that is expected of other countries. It might help if we were finally to sign the Convention on the Rights of the Child, and the Convention on the Elimination of All Forms of Discrimination Against Women. It is telling that the US is so often unwilling both to sign covenants that simply recognize liberal democratic rights and to be held accountable to them. Yet well-known columnist Thomas Friedman assumes that the US sets the standard of democracy; that although the US makes mistakes, nothing much good happens without us. He writes that more than at any other time, "the world has come to accept the Western values of peace, democracy, and free markets".[20]

Rhetoric like Friedman's is much of the problem. The US appropriates 'democracy' for its own global agenda, and displaces 'terrorism' to others elsewhere. I agree that terrorism is immoral, but as Baudrillard says, globalization is immoral as well; and terrorism is defiant of imperial globalization. Baudrillard points out that if Islam were dominating the world, terrorism would rise up against Islam too because "the globe is resistant to globalization".[21] Global capitalism persists through extreme exploitation. There are all kinds of 'terror' – homelessness, starvation, disease, bombs. US prisons are filled, public schools are crumbling, millions of people have lost jobs, over forty-two million people do not have health insurance. All this is also terrifying. It is why people around the world need to globalize resistance. Security for the wealthy few is not the answer. Truly global democratic discourses and vibrant societies are needed. Instead of spending upwards of $3 trillion on US wars of/on 'terror', poverty and repression must be fought against wherever they exist.

The Gulf Wars, 1991, 1998, 2003

The newest US face of power has become more excessive than earlier forms, to match the current excesses of wealth and greed. The US does what it wants despite world opinion. When more than eight million people in London, Prague, New York, San Francisco, Melbourne, Paris, Jakarta, Karachi, and elsewhere said no to a war on Iraq, the US went ahead anyhow. They could make this war alone, without any other authorization, without even that of the United Nations. US unilateralism – with a bit of British assist – was key to this moment.

The US war against Iraq preceded the post-September 11, 2001 "war on terrorism". It has been a more-than-decade-long war with three noted episodes: Desert Storm, in 1991, orchestrated by Bush Sr; the renewed bombing of 1998 designed by Bill Clinton and Madeleine Albright; and the "war on terrorism"/Operation Iraqi Freedom of 2003 led by Bush Jr and Donald Rumsfeld. Economic sanctions were in place this entire time, devastating the country as a whole, while Saddam amassed incredible wealth for himself. Through the sanctions, the US blocked shipments of milk, yogurt, printing equipment for schools, dialysis and dental supplies, chlorine for purifying water, and textbooks for medical schools. Children suffered the most: hundreds of thousands died of malnutrition and radiation poisoning.

The '91 episode ended with the US declaring victory but pulling out before an incursion into Baghdad. Saddam Hussein remained in power but the war was said to be over anyway. In '98, US bombing was renewed to pressure Saddam to allow UN weapons inspections again. The US declared war on Saddam, again, in 2003. One more time, the US declared victory while Saddam was still on the loose. Now, even although Saddam has been captured and is under arrest, the war in Iraq rages on.

In order to rally support for the '03 war the Bush administration lied to the American people. The administration said that in order to fight 'terrorism' Saddam had to be deposed: otherwise he would supply weapons of mass destruction to Al Qaeda. Even our own CIA said there was no known connection between the two. The triple lie – that the terrorism of September 11 was connected to Iraq, that Saddam and Osama bin Laden were cohorts, and that Saddam had available WMD was used to deceive and mobilize the US for war. This mobilization was then further justified by talk about the necessity of regime change, towards democracy.

The US wages war on Iraq and says it is a "war on terrorism."[22] But terrorism is transnational and the Iraq war was nation-based. Maybe this is what it means to say that the good generals always fight the last war; that they are always one war behind. They did not know how to fight a transnational war of/on 'terror' so they made a "war on terrorism" with a knowable territorial site. The war on Iraq has put US power in gross view. This differs from the more usual clandestine power that defined earlier US interventions – in Chile, in Nicaragua, in the Congo. War appears to be the foreign policy of choice for post-1989, post-Soviet times.

The Iraq war plan was titled "Shock and Awe". It is telling that this initiative was written in 1996, six years before the sadness of September 11, 2001. This policy underwrites the importance of using "overwhelming and decisive force" and makes quite clear that "deception, confusion, misinformation and disinformation, perhaps in massive amounts, must be employed". And it concludes that it "seeks to impose (in extreme cases) the non-nuclear equivalent of the impact that the atomic weapons dropped on Hiroshima and Nagasaki had on the Japanese".[23]

As the US public awaited President Bush's decision to go to war, Bush kept demanding that the UN assure him on the threat from WMD. It was all too clear that the US was going to war and that the only question to resolve was *when*. The full truth was less clear: that the US had been at war with Iraq since 1991 and that this last episode would simply be what Perry Anderson has called the 'asphyxiation' stage.[24]

Just short of three weeks into the war, a military victory was declared. We were told that Baghdad was controlled by "coalition forces" – meaning the US with British assist – even though intermittent fighting continued in several cities, unrest and disquiet filled the streets, and fear of suicide bombers was still high. Very shortly after victory was declared, reports of mass looting filled the news media. Rumsfeld said this was all being overblown. The country was gripped by violent rioting. There was no law or order. There was no electricity or clean water. "The streets of Baghdad are a swamp of crime and uncollected garbage."[25] The mayhem continues a year later. Rumsfeld says that freedom is messy.

Rumsfeld conveniently never mentions to the US public that he repeatedly met with and supported Saddam during the Iran–Iraq war, and was fully aware of Saddam's use of chemical weapons during this time.[26] When asked by journalists why no WMD have been found, he responded that this does not matter, that the true reason for war was to bring freedom to Iraq. He says this despite the wartorn and miserable situation most Iraqis face.

Rhetoric is key to this war. Victory was declared in Iraq but US troops still are in battle, anxious and weary, facing new missions.[27] US troops look more and more like occupiers than liberators to the people of Iraq and to themselves as well. Journalists describe these conditions and feelings and refer to a 'postwar' Iraq while doing so. This level of deception – by the administration and its discourse – is commonplace. There are more US ground troops (150,000) in Iraq after victory has been declared, than at the start (70,000). And, even though the deception and lies are revealed by some journalists, it seems as though this simply naturalizes and normalizes the lying as part of politics itself. The more some of the lies are exposed, the more they reign as truth.

Bush's deception and hypocrisy seem to know no bounds. Just at the moment that troops were being deployed overseas to Iraq, he cut federal school aid for the children of men and women in the military. Bush did this by substantially reducing the funding for Government Impact Aid which financially assists school districts that have a shortfall in taxes because of the large number of military families in their district. Payments to the Virginia Beach schools, which are home to many military children, were targeted to be cut in half. This was done just at the time that the needs of children with deployed parents–for counseling and tutoring–increased exponentially.[28]

People in the US do not really know much about the costs of this war. An awful lot of schools and hospitals could be built with this war money in both the US and Iraq. Some estimates cite the cost of the Iraq war at $2 billion a month. Other estimates assume that it will cost close to $2 trillion at its end. But there was and is little outcry within the US because so many seem to think that this spending is necessary if the "war on terrorism" is to be won. And Bush continually reiterates this deceit. Speaking from the aircraft carrier Abraham Lincoln on its way back home to the US Bush stated that the victory in Iraq was a victory "against terrorism and Al Qaeda that began on September 11, 2001, and still goes on". He continued to call Saddam "an ally of Al Qaeda" and recommitted the US to avenge the deaths of loved ones: "with those attacks, the terrorists and their supporters declared war on the United States. And war is what they got."[29]

Before the war had even officially ended, the spoils of war were being promised to US corporations. Both Bechtel Corporation – which former Secretary of State George Shultz had ties to – and Halliburton and its subsidiaries – which Cheney, a former chief executive officer, had ties with – were already in line for contracts to rebuild Iraq. Bechtel landed contracts upwards of $680 million for reconstruction work. James Woolsey, former CIA director and also a part of Paladin Capital Group, a venture capital firm that specializes in domestic security, has played an early role in the 'postwar' occupation. According to Bob Herbert of the *New York Times*, power brokers like these immediately homed in on $100 billion worth of postwar reconstruction contracts.[30]

This corporate power grab is expected and accepted as the simple spoils of war, much like the privatization and marketing of Iraq as a whole. Supposedly, the only hope for Iraq is successful corporate investment.[31] However, the real problem remains that there is no game plan for reconstruction other than this power grab. Both the people of Iraq and US ground troops are caught in this horrid and failed peace.

It is unconscionable that the rich will make out like bandits while the war is not being fought by rich kids. Instead the US military is disproportionately made up of our multiracial working class. And many of these working class soldiers, since the ending of the draft, are now women, who make up 15 percent of the military. Many of these women are single parents who joined the army as a new job opportunity and as a way of paying for their children's education. It is also the case that significant numbers of US fighting forces are not even US citizens, but newly arrived immigrants who enlist in order to waive the waiting period for citizenship. This is borne out by the number of American casualties in Iraq who were not born in the United States.[32]

Operation Iraqi Freedom is a pseudonym for US empire building. Empires build grief and disorder, not democracies. Soon enough Iraq will become like Afghanistan. Desperate times will continue in both places but the US gaze will be on new sites 'elsewhere'. As a cab driver in Kabul says of the warlords in 'postwar' Afghanistan: "These men were here before the Taliban. Then they became Taliban. Now they support Karzai. But they will always be thieves." Only the bravest of women walk without their sky-blue burqas. The situation in the country is getting worse and worse. It is still in critical need of roads, and schools, and jobs. Foreign aid workers are held up at gunpoint and are unable to do their jobs. Yet Bush no longer speaks about the reconstruction of Afghanistan. Although the Afghan war is said to be over, US troops remain there on high alert.[33]

Osama bin Laden is still missing. US troops will continue to hunt the Taliban, and to attempt peacekeeping in Iraq. Meanwhile an interim regime in Iraq initially headed by retired Lieutenant-General Jay Garner oversees the flow of oil, which does not bode well for democracy. Saddam may be gone, but US corporate interests and designs have just fully arrived.

Humanizing Militarism

US imperialism attempts to humanize this extremist militarist phase of global yet territorial corporate building.[34] Enter women. Although women have become a significant presence in the military, their presence has not regendered the military democratically.[35] Yet women have been used symbolically to humanize and democratize war-making: we are told that mothers now fight alongside fathers; women alongside men.[36] The gendered role of a masculinized warrior is now filled by either males or females. But there is little equality to be seen here between men and women either inside or outside this hierarchy.

Why else would so much attention be paid to the 'rescue' and recovery of Private Jessica Lynch? Because she is a woman, and not a man. She was a POW – blonde and young and feminine, a symbol representing the nation's virtuous identity to itself. Initially she was said to be the tough soldier – "I kept shooting until I was out of bullets" – but also vulnerable and feminized by her injuries.[37] However, despite everything, she still needed to be rescued. Images of her rescue were shown over and over to the world. The facts surrounding the 'rescue' were more difficult to get: first we were told that she had gunshot and stab wounds, then we were told she didn't; then we were told she had been mistreated by Iraqi doctors, then we were told they befriended her and donated their own blood for her transfusions; then we were told that her 'rescue' was not quite that, that she had been in a hospital with no guards. Next we were told that the entire account we had been given of her alleged capture was a mistake: based on wrong information, etcetera. She had been injured in a humvee accident, rather than a firefight. Next, we were just expected to forget the confusions and not ask further questions.

It is not insignificant that so much of the presentation, at home, of the initial war was with a woman's face. Humanize the war by showing us a lot of single moms and young women fighting it. But do not democratize the war too much; remind us at every chance that women are more fragile, more open to sexual abuse by the enemy, not quite able to fight the war by themselves. Women personalized the war and made it feel more intimate while it remained completely distanced. To remind us that nothing about gender had drastically changed, we were also told that Jessica wanted to be a grade school teacher.

Gender supposedly operates to humanize the US in foreign eyes as well. Nicholas Kristof of the *New York Times* writes that one of the best modern weapons of the Western arsenal is 'Claire' – and she carries a machine gun. Apparently Kristof thinks that Iraqi soldiers are squeamish about shooting female soldiers so we should let their "chauvinism work for us". He argues that the US should use coed military units because they look less menacing, and not like rapists who will do harm to civilians. So women are good for fighting wars in Islamic countries because of "foreign chauvinism". It is more than a little bit ironic that this is Kristof's argument for re-examining the ban on women in the front lines, as well as "equality for all".[38]

Returning POWs other than Lynch were also a part of the rescue scenario needed to cover over the mixed and ambiguous rescue that was delivered to the people of Iraq. Six men, somewhat demasculinized by virtue of their capture, and one Black woman, Shoshana Johnson, a single mother of a two-year-old, were miraculously found, and able to return home. I too celebrated their wonderful luck and the kindness of their captors. I had been quietly watching for word about Specialist Johnson once I heard of her disappearance. She was an unlucky cook whose group made a wrong turn in a sandstorm and was captured. My heartstrings, too, were pulled wondering if her young daughter would ever get to see her again. For many days no one was sure if she or the others were alive. But the focus on their stories, and the jubilation that dominated several days of tv reporting upon their return were misplaced. Too many other Americans would not return. Too many Iraqis had already died. So much of the war that we saw was not about the real suffering and pain. The war was about Lynch and other POWs because this made people in the US feel better about war, and about gender too.

Women fly F18s, launch TomaHawk missiles, and are on the front lines of intelligence units. There are 200,000 active-duty women.[39] Most of them join the military to better themselves in a world with few options for them. Private first class Lori Piestewa, a Hopi Indian killed in the same ambush as Lynch, represents the multiracial identities of women in this war. These women, in particular, symbolize to the rest of the world the equality of women in the West. The symbolic is in part true, and in part not. Women in the US are thought to be treated equal: to be modern and free. Yet most middle-class and wealthy women are not found in the military. Private Lynch is West Virginia working-class poor. She is the age of Bush's twin daughters, both attending college, far away from this war. Johnson and Piestewa, both single moms, were in the military in order to go to school. Necessity, more than equality seems to be the guide here. More often than not, inequity and sexual harassment, rather than sexual equality, is the mark of the US military.

While the US makes war, the US Air Force, stands charged with multiple counts of rape. By February 2003 upwards of fifty women had finally come forward to speak out publicly against a decade's worth of unfair treatment at the Air Force Academy. Several documented their rapes, their failed attempts to have their complaints acted upon, and the stone walls they encountered in trying to do so. One woman, Debra Dickerson, told her story of being raped, on Christmas Day, 1981. She pressed charges, her rapist confessed, and then the military blamed her. She says she was born poor and Black, and escaped poverty in large measure by enlisting in the Air Force. She became their golden girl, but in the end she wrote that: "It was infinitely more difficult to be female in uniform than to be black."[40]

Yet women in khaki[41] are juxtaposed against women 'elsewhere', even though these women elsewhere – as in Iraq – are also trying to scrape together a life for themselves and their loved ones. It is a tricky scenario to clarify. Women in military garb bespeak new gains for women who are trying to build a life of economic independence; but this is a track that is raced and classed by inequities already existing in their lives. Arab women from across Egypt said no to war in Iraq and were in the front lines calling for peace and the protection of the environment and natural resources of the area. They condemned the cost of a multi-billion-dollar war when billions of people across the globe have no access to potable water or proper sanitation. Given this context, the incursion of women and people of color into a military hell bent on empire building is one of the saddest contradictions of these times.

This irony may affect the women in Iraq the most cruelly. Although Saddam Hussein was no friend to women, during most of his regime they worked and studied with few restrictions compared to women in many other Muslim countries. Middle-class women were part of the professional class. They could vote, and they could maintain custody of children after divorce. These rights began to be challenged in the last years of Saddam's rule as he sought support from Islamic extremists against the US. Women were newly required to travel with a male relative. Now, in post-Saddam Iraq, women are fearful that if Islamic Shiite extremism takes hold, they will lose more freedoms.[42] But it is already clear that no one in the Bush administration is watching, or cares, what happens to women in Iraq.

Bush's Crusades

The description of capitalism as modern and democratic is a misappropriated version of history set in place by those in charge. As well, the modern bourgeois state is often identified with secularism. Secular is equated with Western, and the West with modernity, and then religion is positioned as nonmodern. Yet Bush pushes his faith-based initiatives and deploys his religiosity to advance his right-wing agendas. Public religiosity was already very much in vogue in the 1992 presidential election, with Joseph Lieberman declaring his religious faith to be central to his moralism.[43] Tax monies go to religious schools more and more frequently. US money bears the legend: "in God we trust". Yet, politicians and commentators in the US often reduce the politics of Muslim countries to Islamic religious meanings, while distinguishing bourgeois culture from Christianity.

The cover story of *Newsweek*, on February 11, 2002 was headlined: "The Bible and the Qur'an",[44] and with it the appropriation of religion for politics was authorized. The media contains much discussion calling for a recognition of theological liberalisms and non-liberal secularisms, while recognizing the need for nuance and modesty.[45] A distinction however is drawn between allowing religious values in public life, and following divine direction in policy making.[46]

Bush often uses visions of good and evil to characterize his presidency, defining these visions in unambiguous terms. Supposedly he is doing God's will and work. In his 2003 State of the Union address he said: "the liberty we prize is not America's gift to the world, it is God's gift to humanity."[47] His use of religion in defining goals for the secular state problematizes both and should alert us to his right-wing manipulation of each as a result.

Bush interprets evangelical Christianity for his own purposes. Although he has a multiracial cabinet and has many women in his administration, his presidency bespeaks other commitments. His end election scenario hinged on intimidation and disenfranchisement of Black voters in Florida. He backs challenges to affirmative action law and his administration filed briefs on behalf of the white plaintiffs seeking redress from the University of Michigan over affirmative action. He insists that affirmative action imposes quotas, and he says that quotas racially discriminate against whites. He continues to appoint federal judges who have racist histories.

Bush can easily be described as a zealot and extremist when it comes to issues related to women's freedom of choice. He imposes a Christian theocracy on issues tied to women's bodies. He says that embryos are a "sacred gift from our creator", and rejects stem cell research as a result. When asked to think about his positions related to abortion he often will say, "I'll pray on this." He is proud not to see ambiguity because of his "all-knowing God".[48]

Bush appointed David Hager to head the Food and Drug Administration (FDA) Reproductive Health Drugs Advisory Commission, which makes decisions on matters relating to drugs used in obstetrics, gynecology, pregnancy termination, and contraception. Hager is a practicing ob/gyn who in his book *As Jesus Cared for Women* describes himself as pro-life. He refuses to prescribe contraceptives to unmarried women. He says that given his religious beliefs he will try to revoke the approval for mifespristone (RU-486) used for early abortion. This is dangerous zealotry for a secular state; in fact, most in Bush's inner circle now speak of the US as a Judeo-Christian country.

Anti-abortion politics, whether couched in religious rhetoric or not, also dominates Bush's agenda for increased AIDS funding for Africa. He has disallowed any AIDS funding for programs where sex education or abortion are allowed. That is, he continues to use his anti-sex-awareness policy and anti-abortion beliefs in formulating policies that are not directly connected to these issues. He does this when millions of people's lives and deaths are at stake.

To conclude, in order to begin: it is sadly true that innocent people died on September 11, 2001. There were innocent people in the Towers and the Pentagon, but also in Hiroshima, and Afghanistan, and Iraq. So we must start seeing, really seeing.

When we hear of jihad we must be careful not to 'other' all Muslims as fanatics. Suicide bombers are not all that different from any other warrior. They kill innocents and themselves. More normalized war kills innocents, but not necessarily the perpetrators. Roxanne Euben asks us not to treat jihad as pathological or fanatical, but rather as the struggle with oneself in the world to find meaning and wholeness. As currently popularized, the word 'jihad' connotes "an idealized Western public sphere in which reasoned arguments and nonviolent practices largely prevail" and becomes a repository for "contemporary anxieties about death, the irrational religious" and othering. We need to recognize that there are many jihads, and many democracies. Jihad, at its best, and in its meaning for most Muslims the world over, is the struggle to find justice, equality, and freedom for the internal and external self. "Human beings must change themselves so that they may change the world." A virtuous Muslim must realize human freedom for all.[49]

Palestinian suicide bombers – men and women alike – are juxtaposed against the Israeli army as part of the US campaign against terrorism, and for Israel. And Israel stands as the US arm of democracy in the Middle East. But democracy in Israel is illusory today. Gruesome devastation has been normalized for all the world to see. If not clarified soon, the Palestinian struggle will also turn into something other than liberatory.

I write against empire building in its exploitative, racialized, masculinist, militarist forms. I can see more inclusively when I look to find these complex webs. I ask you to look for them, and to destroy them. Anti-racist feminisms are needed in all parts of the world to build an insurgent people's movement of struggle, to humanize the globe, and to guide political resistance against masculinist terror-filled wars.

I now link backwards to find the silences that have been constructed by the West, for the West, in order that the imperial 'we' may be exposed for its terrorizing deceptions.

Notes

1. I am indebted to Tariq Ali for the phrase. See his "Recolonizing Iraq", *New Left Review*, 21, (May–June, 2003), p.7.
2. See Carol Quillen, "Feminist Theory, Justice and the Lure of the Human", *Signs*,

vol. 27, no. 1 (Autumn, 2001), pp. 87–122, for the phrasing 'other-than' in pluralizing feminisms beyond liberalism.

3. Jianying Zha, "Learning from McDonald's", *Transition*, issue 91, vol. 12, no. 1 (May 2002), pp. 18-39.
4. Barry Lynn, "Unmade in America", *Harper's*, vol. 304, no. 1825 (June 2002), pp. 33–42.
5. George Soros, *On Globalization* (New York: Public Affairs, 2002), pp. 66, 159.
6. Scott Malcomson, *One Drop of Blood: The American Misadventure of Race* (New York: Farrar Straus Giroux, 2000), pp. 68, 91, 98.
7. Aimé Césaire, *Discourse on Colonialism* (New York: Monthly Review Press, 1972), p. 36.
8. Jean Baudrillard, *Impossible Exchange* (New York: Verso, 2001), pp. 14, 15.
9. Andrea Elliott, "In Brooklyn, 9/11 Damage", *New York Times*, June 7, 2003, p. A9. Also see Rachel Swarns, "More Than 13,000 May Face Deportation", *New York Times*, June 7, 2003, p. A9.
10. Quoted in Azadeh Ensha, "Undoing the Dream", *Color Lines*, vol. 6, no. 2 (Summer 2003), p. 15.
11. Quoting Guiti Lami, who left Iran in 1978 for the United States. See: "Undoing the Dream", p. 15.
12. Noam Chomsky, *9–11* (New York: Seven Stories Press, 2001).
13. Judith Butler, "Guantanamo Limbo", *The Nation*, vol. 274, no. 12 (April 2002), pp. 20–24.
14. David Armstrong, "Dick Cheney's Song of America", *Harper's*, vol. 305, no. 1829 (October 2002), pp. 76–83.
15. Bruce Berkowitz, *The New Face of War* (New York: Free Press, 2003).
16. Rosalind Morris, "Theses on the Questions of War: History, Media, Terror", *Social Text*, 72, vol. 20, no. 3 (Fall 2002), p. 152.
17. Seymour Hersh, "Manhunt", *New Yorker*, December 23/30, 2002, pp. 66–74.
18. Judith Butler, "Explanation and Exoneration, or What We Can Hear?", *Social Text*, 72, vol. 20, no. 3 (Fall 2002), pp. 177–88.
19. A. G. Noorani, *Islam and Jihad* (New York: Zed Books, 2002), p. 11.
20. Thomas Friedman, "Going Our Way", *New York Times*, September 15, 2002, p. wk15.
21. Jean Baudrillard, "L'Esprit Du Terrorisme", *Le Monde*, November 2, 2001, p. 18. Also see his *The Spirit of Terrorism* (New York: Verso, 2002).
22. Paul Virilio, *Ground Zero* (New York: Verso, 2002).
23. Harlan Ullman and James Wade, *Shock and Awe* (Washington, DC: NDU Press, 1996), p. 4.
24. Perry Anderson, "Force and Consent", *Harper's*, vol. 306, no. 1832 (January 2003), p. 21.
25. Naomi Klein, "Downsizing in Disguise", *The Nation*, vol. 276, no. 24 (June 23, 2003), p.10.
26. See detailed verification of Rumsfeld's negotiations with Saddam Hussein during the 1980s in The National Security Archive. www.gwu.edu/~nsarchiv/NSAEBB/NSAEBB82

27. Steven Lee Myers, "Anxious and Weary of War, GIs Face a New Iraq Mission", *New York Times*, June 15, 2003, p. A1.
28. Bob Herbert, "A Strange Budget Cut", *New York Times*, February 20, 2003, p. A31.
29. David Sanger, "Victory in a War on Terror", *New York Times*, May 2, 2003, p.A1.
30. Bob Herbert, "Spoils of War", *New York Times*, April 10, 2003, p. A27.
31. Tim Shorrock, "Selling (Off) Iraq", *The Nation*, vol. 276, no. 4 (June 23, 2003), pp. 11–16.
32. David Halbfinger and Steven Holmes, "Military Mirrors a Working-class America", *New York Times*, March 30, 2003, p. A1.
33. Scott Baldauf, "Letter from Afghanistan", *The Nation*, vol. 276, no. 16 (April 28, 2003), pp. 24–8.
34. For an important discussion of gender and militarism see Cynthia Enloe, *Does Khaki Become You?* (Boston: South End Press, 1983); and her *Bananas, Beaches and Bases, Making Feminist Sense of International Politics* (Berkeley: University of California Press, 1989).
35. Jodi Wilgoren, "The New War Brings New Role for Women", *New York Times*, March 28, 2003, B1.
36. Jim Lacey, Cath Booth Thomas, *et al.*, "An American Family Goes to War", *Newsweek*, vol. 161, no.12 (March 24, 2003), pp. 26–34.
37. Melani McAlister, "Saving Private Lynch", *New York Times*, April 6, 2003, p. wk13.
38. Nicholas D. Kristof, "A Woman's Place", *New York Times*, April 25, 2003, p. A31.
39. Jodi Wilgoren, "A New War Brings New Role for Women", *New York Times*, April 2, 2003, p. B1.
40. Debra Dickerson, "Rallying Around the Rapist", *New York Times*, March 18, 2003, p. A33.
41. I am indebted to Cynthia Enloe for this phrasing.
42. Nazila Fathi, "Iraqi Career Women Ponder A Future Under Shiite Rule", *New York Times*, May 25, 2003, p. A19.
43. Ellen Willis, "Freedom from Religion", *The Nation*, vol. 272, no. 7 (February 19, 2001), p. 16.
44. Kenneth Woodward, "The Bible and the Qur'an", *Newsweek*, February 11, 2002, pp. 51–7.
45. William Connolly, *Why I Am Not a Secularist* (Minneapolis: University of Minnesota Press, 1999), pp. 10, 19.
46. Isaac Kramnick and Lawrence Moore, *The Godless Constitution* (New York: W.W. Norton, 1996), pp. 12, 14.
47. Howard Fineman, "Bush and God", *Newsweek*, March 10, 2003, pp. 22–31.
48. Richard Brookhiser, "Close-Up: The Mind of George Bush", *Atlantic Monthly*, vol. 291, no. 3 (April 2003), pp. 55–69.
49. Roxanne Euben, "Killing for Politics", *Political Theory*, vol. 30, no. 1 (February 2002), pp. 5, 8, 19, 22.

2 Thinking to See: Secrets, Silences, and 'Befores'

Once I see that interpretation is *already* embedded in the very process of thought I recognize that there is a *before* that I cannot completely ever know or recover. The very idea of history itself is destabilized as a process of storytelling with different storytellers. I then wonder not which story is more truthful than the next but rather which viewings are inclusive of the tale of humanity at the start. There is no exact start because the start has already been lost. Discourses of and about the eighteenth century simply confound this. I therefore need to know whose story I am reading, who is telling the story, and from what timebound lens it is being told.

The 'I' here is significant. I am from the United States at a time when it is viewed by most of the world as imperialist and believing itself to be above the law. I have been formally educated in this country through a lens of privilege and the dismissal of other cultures. My skin is white although I was brought up in the Civil Rights Movement by two parents who had been active in the Communist Party. So the blind spots I reveal here are a mix of those of an antiracist feminist who grew up in the margins of this society and those of a dissidence still threaded through power-filled viewings from the West.

One more caveat. I reject the view or assumption that there is a coherent geographical location of the West, not only today, but also before. And I also use the phrase the West as a constructed political identity that has enormous resonance and power. So there is a built-in tension to my writing: I disclaim the authoritative voice of the West, as simply Western, and I also write as though there is a West. This bespeaks the power-filled meanings of language as a completely politically invested construction, which is simultaneously real and unreal.

History is never just simply the 'past'. Nor is history simply its official rendering. There is also the unknown history of what Sandra Greene calls "things not said", moments not remembered, statements made only in whispers and conveyed in secret.[1] History resonates in the present even if unconsciously. So the present is also always rooted in its earlier forms. And people continue these beginnings in and through daily life. History is made while old histories are simultaneously reproduced, without most of us ever owning the story told.[2] And we also remember and forget and never know.

If there is always an *already* in place, and there is always a *before*, there is no obvious start of anything. So I look thickly – in as complex a fashion as possible – so that I can imagine a politics for 'us all'. This is a challenge in these splintered, globalized times when neoliberalism has no commitment to including 'everybody'. A politics for everybody embraces Christian, and Jew, and Hindu, and Muslim, and Dalit, and Arab, and Black, and Brown, and Yellow, and women and men, and girls and boys, rich and poor. Allow everyone their multiple identities and allow them to thrive. Yet the world is filled with Enron executives, and bin Laden, and Sharon, and Rumsfeld and Bush, and Blair, and Saddam.

I consider an inclusive viewing of humanity, for its totality and its democratic potentiality. Yet the world is dominated by the privileged powerful who fight for their own narrowed, exclusive visions of neoliberalism. In spite of this unholy totalizing of oppressions that so many of the world's people have suffered, fissures exist out of which the disempowered speak. I learn from these fissures, these sites of resistance, that a thicker and more complex vision of humanity is urgently needed.

The current moment of extreme distortion, that oppositions the West against Islam, unsettles the truthfulness of the divide itself. With 'other-than' Western stories of democracy to tell, the divide self-destructs. The expressions of democracy that are 'other-than' liberal individualist in form, trace notions of human freedom to before the eighteenth century.

The themes of this moment – the aftermaths of September 11, 2001 – are the themes of power and oppression; the injustices of colonialism and the disregard for people's cultures around the world; the desire of people for a better life; the love of freedom and creativity; the downtrodden lives that millions live while looking on at the glitz of the world's rich. Women's place in all this is central to life's rhythms. Women wear their cultures and their nations on their bodies. The chador, or burqa, or khaki uniform, or miniskirt symbolize the Western/Islamic divide. Women in the West are supposedly modern, democratic, and free. Women in Islam are 'not'.

Meanwhile President Bush mobilized his "war on terrorism" against the forces of evil. He tells us we will be at war for a very long time. And without remembering, it is too easy to forget that Bush lost the popular national election and won in Florida only thanks to an incredibly racist set of circumstances. The US public pretends that Bush was elected fairly, even those of us who voted against him. He is inept but retains the confidence of many Americans. But this is about the here and now and I need to go back first to my own personal history; and then to before the West.

My Local Beginnings

I think I began to see race in its power-filled meanings while I grew up among Blacks, and some whites, in the Civil Rights Movement. My father always used to say that only by seeing colors could you refuse their politicized meaning; that racism meant that you had to deal with the constructions of race on a conscious level, not silence them. He used to tell my sisters and I stories of his childhood; how he was often beaten up by anti-Semites in his neighborhood. He shared stories of World War Two with us to make sure we knew how in the army he was punished for being both a Jew and Communist. He was made a forward observer – his task was to go ahead and secure a combat area – and an MP (military police). Both jobs were often given to Jews as a way of isolating them. I grew up knowing that my father had one of the yellow stars worn by a Jew in a concentration camp he helped liberate sitting in the top drawer of his clothes dresser. His identity was as a political Jew. He never wanted to forget to fight against bigotry of any sort. Now, the yellow star hangs on the wall in my home to help me also remember.

My sisters and I were brought up as atheist Jews. Being an atheist just meant that God was never used as an explanation of anything. Being a Jew meant that we would never allow someone to be punished for their identity. It seemed quite ordinary that both my parents were totally involved in the Civil Rights Movement, and therefore so were we. When we were all still very young our usual Saturday morning was to get dressed and join the picket line in front of Woolworth's. In these early years, race was at the center of my life; the Civil Rights Movement created our sense of family and home. My childhood and my friendships were entirely interracial. Inside our home and in the movement itself, I was at peace. But this was not true at school, or walking through the neighborhoods near where we lived.

When my father taught at Atlanta University in the mid-sixties and we lived in faculty housing – and ate in the dorms until our home was ready to move into – our whiteness in the Black community was not of much note. Public schools had just begun the process of desegregation and I was not allowed to enroll in the Black school, close to where we lived. When I arrived at my white working-class school, called Brown High, I was keenly aware of my whiteness because everyone else was white, except Clemsy Wood who was the only Black at school. He was the first student to be bussed over from my neighborhood, the Black neighborhood. The day I met Clemsy he was on crutches. In the football game the weekend before he had been taught the lesson that he was not wanted on the field again. Clemsy couldn't carry his books and use his crutches at the same time so I picked up his books and we walked down the hall together. I became a "white traitor" the day I carried his books. Soon it was known throughout the school that my dad taught at the 'Nigger' school and that I lived in the 'Nigger' neighborhood. I was lonely.

My parents couldn't help me because they were a part of the problem. They had uprooted me from my life to come to Atlanta and do what their lives demanded of them. But I now felt that their choices demanded too much from me. Meanwhile my sisters Giah and Julia were doing better than I was. Although they were routinely taunted and physically assaulted at their white grammar school, they remained brave and forthright. I retreated into anger and sadness although I continued to carry Clemsy's books.

At fifteen, having white skin and not being thought of as white, so to speak, by other whites, but also not being Black, I withdrew into myself. For a while in Atlanta I just tried to hide. I never invited anyone home. I had little to say to my parents. In order to get to school I walked through my working- and middle-class Black neighborhood into a white working-class and poor section which surrounded Brown High. I sometimes would get stares at the start of my walk, but by the time I was close to school I would be bullied. I painfully remember hating my life then. I never blended in. Nothing was easy, not even a simple walk. I refer back to these moments to remember the meaning of white privilege for my friends who are Black.

In the early 1970s, in response to the Civil Rights Movement, there was government funding for summer programs for Black inner-city kids. My father ran several interracial summer programs outside of New York City in these years. I worked with him for several summers. Dad believed deeply in what he long ago called the "richness of difference". He thought that differences create conflict and the conflict is good – not to be smoothed over, but good. He thought that conflict uncovers the realities of power and we learn more about ourselves from this conflict. For him, differences should make us uncomfortable with the narrowness of who we are – to the point that we grow and expand to create new relationships through the discomfort. He used to say that the only way we change is if we think we have to. I often think that my father would be enormously critical of today's neoliberal accommodation and manipulation of difference.

Racism and themes of difference have defined much of my life as a white girl and woman. And as a woman with white skin I have struggled to become an antiracist feminist. I am sure my early life is why I continue to open my viewing of humanity's inclusivity and try to refigure how my white skin and privilege get in the way of my doing this. My whiteness says things about me that are both true, and not. For many people of other colors, my whiteness speaks racism. For some whites, my whiteness speaks a shared supremacy. My skin is colored white and it speaks a racial privileging that I do not believe in. My whiteness inhibits me; my racial site is less inclusive than other colors, and if I wish to, most other whites allow me to forget this.

Colonized Bodies and Seeing

Colonization allows the colonizers to view the world from their standpoint. From this site false universals are concocted and the colonizers' positions of power allow this deception, and enforce the falsity as truth. The colonized not only know themselves, but also are forced to know those who have done the colonizing. Native Americans were already here; their culture comes before Columbus. Those Blacks who were slaves knew themselves within their particular African origins before they became captives, of other Africans, or whites. To survive, they had to come to know the white slavemasters and slavemistresses. This 'deep' way of viewing is not necessary for the powerful.

The writings of Gandhi, who spoke against colonialism, and Malcolm X, who spoke against racist imperialism, reflect a knowledge of the oppressed and also of the oppressor. This does not mean that colonizers do not hire anthropologists and linguists in order better to know the colonized, but this viewing is done for different reasons, and from a position of power. The colonizers' concern with domination structures what they seek to know and how they know it.[3]

I know myself as female and I also must know the colonizing male world. But this colonizing world is white, and so am I. So there is a complexity to be sorted through; there is also this complexity in the system of slavery itself, which is a system of racial *and* sexual horror for slave women, but never simply this. Identity is multiple and so are differences. The more multiple, the more possibility for partial connections which are similarly different and differently similar. I have come to think of this as our polyunity – that all people are connected as human but in diverse ways. And the site of polyversality – that our variety traverses through our unity – requires rethinking our thinking. Instead of simply thinking about a past and a present I need to find the already and before.

People think and see through language but language is also a barrier. West/non-West; white/Black; people of color/white women; savage/civilization; enlightenment/slavery; Christianity/Islam; terrorism/democracy, and on and on. When geographies, and cultures, and identities are each pluralized to their real meanings then how shall 'we' speak. And the 'we' here may just be simply what Susan Buck-Morss describes as the "'we' who may have nothing more nor less in common than sharing *this* time".[4] This time connects individual selves beyond a hopeless individualism.

Sharing this time means sharing the heritage of eighteenth-century Enlightenment. This notion of bourgeois radicalism presents those of us living today with grand distortions. Writers like John Locke and John Stuart Mill represent liberal democratic theory while Black and Brown slave bodies are shipped from Africa. J. J. Rousseau is termed a radical egalitarian while he groups all women with children and cripples, and slavery remains a metaphor for white man's dependency on others. We are told that we live in global times in a global village, while girls and women of color toil away in *maquiladora* factories. Seeing anew means subverting the distortions of before with a willingness to be deeply uncomfortable with the self. A polyversality of timeless values must be used to unsettle and realize the human self.

Inclusivity requires seeing the multiples of knowing that are embodied within any notion of identity. This means imagining beyond the power-filled knowledges of the day. President Bush claims to have an inclusive cabinet because different colors of flesh appear. But this singularizes inclusivity to the realm of color. His cabinet represents a rainbow vision of right-wing wealth. We live in difficult times which hijack the notion of racial diversity for a homogeneous global capitalist class.

I travel back in time, from this reactionary moment, to think about before. I need to construct a site from which I am able to see more complexly. My site is before the present-day construction of the Black/white divide. My site must be the free Black African alongside the Black slave body so that Africa is not reduced to its counter-image always defined by the West.

Africa must be recognized as an enormously diverse continent and not homogenized as "starving masses", which is often the imaginary provided by and to Westerners.[5] I write of Africa and slavery knowing that both terms wrongly homogenize complexity, more than they reveal individual stories. Slavery as a term is filled with contradiction. It calls attention to an unspeakable degradation of Black people, and it also silences, and hence violates, the humanity that existed and persisted within it.

Slaves must be specified for the individuals they were. Slave bodies were often female, sometimes a young child, always with a history deriving from the African continent. The body and its sexual raciality is a formidable place from which to know more thickly. This site of the body's oppression: its torture and rape; its ill-treatment, sexual abuse and exploitation; its unwitting labor, demands that we see the human struggle for democracy from within slavery. From this site of bodily specificity, the false universalizations of colonization and globalization can be exposed.

Slaves fought slavery because each slave was a human being. This struggle can be seen, so to speak put in view, against Enlightenment discourse which promised humanity to all. But democracy cannot be found simply in these promissory words of individual freedom. It is rather in the struggle for this promissory, in the in-between space between the promise and the claims made by slaves, that the Enlightenment finds substance.

Black slave women fought and survived and created a world and this is a rich location for democratic practice and theory. This history of resistance while claiming the discourse of human rights does not simply derive from Western discourse, nor is the claim for one's human dignity simply of the West. Enlightenment values embracing a humanism that depends "on the identification of each of us with all" authorized an inclusive view of 'everybody' while excluding many. The ideals were not actualized; only promised. And the idea that each human life is equal in value to each other life derives from what it means to be human, not merely Western. There is a "universal wrongness of inhumane coercion", but universalism is not simply derivative of the West or the Enlightenment.[6] There are whisperings elsewhere.

Slave bodies compel a polyunified reading of humanity. The body's needs speak to its humanness and its variety. The body's needs speak beyond imperial/colonial categories. The body is not bounded and boarded up into its slave viewings. Yet the colonized relation already binds us to a narrowed view of the oppressed Black body. But bodies are also more porously open and complex than our ways of seeing.

The site of the slave trade is one of connectivity to the lives of Native Americans who came before the African slave trade, and to other colonial moments of oppression and exploitation which carve stories on people of color's bodies. The body demands and articulates in polyvalent ways the meaning of humanity across geographical and cultural spaces. Colonialism denies exclusive geographic categorization because it has always traveled across these divides. One need not wait for twenty-first century global capital in order to recognize the multiplicity of location of brutality. Conquest – using sexual and racial brutality – was as much a part of the West as anywhere 'elsewhere'. Not until the brutality of so-called civilized societies is recognized "can we freely revel in the distinctive genius of each human culture".[7]

Capital has always traveled and dominated. And the domination has not meant real erasure but simply enforced erasure by the power-filled dialogues that create secrets, silences, and lies. Domination is never just one-sided. It is always something else for the dominated. Domination always has a dynamic, a process, another side. It is what the dominated possess that is sought by the dominator. Africa has become the periphery and the US the center in part through the occlusion by imperialist language of the body. Seeing the world as white and Western disallows seeing much else 'elsewhere'.

My point of origin, then, for thinking about democracy is the body. The body, or our bodies, locate humanity itself. It is from this place of the body that desire, sex, reproduction, labor, creativity, are derived. It is the body's claim on each of us that connects us one to another. So I follow human bodies to 'elsewheres' to find a polyversal humanity rather than locate the promise of universality within any one location.

I trace the body as the site of humanity while trying not to use the languages of colonialism which name geographical places as though they were simple realities. Words like 'West' and 'East' distort the mix and flows that are a part of each. There are aspects of life that cannot be embraced by the relation to the West. Yet, in the power-driven world of global capital, there is a West, even while it distorts the complexities of its own origins with its imperial gaze. The US was anticolonialist at its start, yet while being so, used and allowed the slave trade. Today's 'West' was racist before.

The ideas of freedom, equality, and justice originate from the human body, not with any one geographic or cultural location. Specific historical meanings of freedom take on different imaginings in particular times. The practice of inclusive democracy is not found more readily in the eighteenth century, although particularly individualist formulations are articulated then. Because slavery and patriarchy are embedded in the same historical moment, a 'practice' of democracy is not to be found at this site. A lived democracy is only to be found by going inside the resistances and expressions of humanity.

Ideas that are said to be of the West are often initiated and located elsewhere. Terming democracy as of the West already gives too much credit to the West. Such naming reflects an imperial capture of ideas from 'elsewhere'. Expressions of eighteenth century democratic theory derive as much from the slave revolts in Haiti as from Europe, as much from the demands of the slaves' humanity as from Western ideas of freedom. The story that is told exists because Europeans were positioned to write history.

The silencing of the Haitian revolution within the dominant discourses of the Enlightenment allows a partial story to be told: one of non-slave rebellion. Knowledge of the Haitian revolution unsettles the constructs of democracy by disclosing its particularist and exclusionary formulations. Haiti demands a move beyond white 'Western' universalism. And this move should not be reduced to a bourgeois expression of human rights but rather recognized as another vital site from which democratic practice is formulated.[8]

Genes and their body types are already cultural – there is always a before here. So although colonialism and imperialism and global capitalism – which are all of one process – are imbricated inside and outside bodies, bodies always are also readied to demand their needs. Capital may not recognize the need for a living wage, but that does not deny the hunger of a hungry body. The wished-for monoculture of global capital exploits people everywhere in each geographical space. This is an inverted notion of unity which binds together an emerging class of people across racial and sexual lines in their homogenized forms of 'difference'.

Because colonialism was global in form, at the start it needed and exploited different cultures. Today's globalization of capital seeks a more unified, non-national/cultural artifice called the West – and everything else becomes the 'rest'. So, given global capital, the West as such is everywhere, and loses its specificity. It – the so-called West – becomes the universal in and of itself; and colonialism and imperialism evaporate into globalization. But, as this has been in process since the early 1970s, it is culminating in the twenty-first century in a more unilateral singular form. The West has become the US because no other country can compete with US militarism at this time.

US military might breeds anti-Americanism among Europeans, Latin Americans, Asians, and so on because the US flaunts power, and ignores all restraints. The US is seen as "intolerant of competing world-views" and "its clout and its cocksuredness makes it as great a threat to democratic values as any despot in a multicultural context".[9] Even Salman Rushdie, who embraces much of the dichotomy between Islam and the West, warns the US after the war in Afghanistan: "This is not the time to ignore the rest of the world and decide to go it alone. To do so would be to risk losing after you've won."[10]

In this process the rest of humanity become the polyglot of diversity, supplying the unity of capital. This is hardly an embrace of multiplicity but rather a corralling of it for a problematic unity of exploitation. Real democracy cannot exist here.

On Western Universalism

The West has never simply been the West. Ideas, along with the dialogue surrounding them, have always traveled across place and time. According to Janet Abu-Lughod, the institutional prerequisites for capitalism were in place in the Islamic world before the Europeans arrived. China was the most advanced economy of the medieval world. Europe developed out of the pre-existent systems of the thirteenth century; it was facilitated by a world economy which it then restructured to its liking. When it reached out, "it found riches rather than empty space". Europe came as an "upstart peripheral". According to Abu-Lughod, the turning point came when the Middle East linked the eastern Mediterranean with the Indian Ocean between 1250 and 1350, when East and West became roughly balanced. The story of European hegemony conceals the story of the old world core of the Middle East, India, and China. At this time Europe lagged behind; it caught up and gained the upper hand only in the sixteenth century.[11]

Edward Said was very important in exposing the Orientalism of the West; yet at present the concept distorts as much as it reveals.[12] The language of 'Orient' itself is a construction, and is also more than a collection of lies. The Orient has its meaning in relation to the West. If you give up the simplicity of one, the other falls with it.

There are important influences impacting on the West that create intriguing crossover dialogues. Then democracy becomes a discussion of diverse ideas about social justice and inclusion; disparate views speak with and to each other, and mutual debts are recognized within this diversity. Roxanne Euben argues that the West is not a civilization with homogenous roots or clearly delineated historical or contemporary boundaries.[13]

At present, globalization presents itself as though everything good originates in the West. Images move from West to East; even when democracy thrives in the East, globalization presents it not as a local event, but as part of the global West. This is done often by using Western ideas to "articulate already existing demands and allowing them to find an international audience".[14] As such, the local values of the West are universalized and fixed as though they are global, not local; so the (local) West parades globally. This establishes the West as the standard while dismissing variety and denying a radical pluralism as the standard for democracy itself.[15]

Amartya Sen argues persuasively that the origins of ideas are seldom pure or singular. Math, which was initially a mix of Indian, Arabic, Mayan and European discoveries, is called "Western math". The West is equated with individual freedom and political democracy, but Sen questions the extrapolation backwards. He says the West exists spottily in Asia in the writings and politics of Ashoka and Akbar. Whereas Plato and Aristotle made their exclusions to universal citizenship, Ashoka in the third century BC insisted on a complete universalism. Sen asks us to see variety and incompleteness in both 'our' and 'their' cultures.[16]

The ideas and embrace of diversity are not of the West; but rather derive from the complexity of humanity itself. There is no one way to interpret these meanings. Twentieth century Bengali theorists fighting colonialism articulate a creative dialogue with and against the West. Historically the reality of Bengali diversity stood against the onslaught of colonial cultural imperialism; today, however, the global West utilizes and steals the construct of diversity for the needs of global capitalism. Then, when people look for solace from the indignities of global capital, Eastern spiritualism is marketed to the West, by the West as a balm for the competitive ruggedness of the market.[17]

There is a humanity to be discovered and it cannot be found by universalizing the West's notion of 'the' universal. Instead this polyversal humanity must be specified by thinking about the *before* of colonialist language and deceit. The point is to turn over and around the way we see universality – which means theorizing the specific as the means of allowing a polyunity to emerge. We should recognize that democracy existed in North America before the colonies, before the Declaration of Independence, before the Constitution. Democracy has been a collaborative process, even if not between peoples of equal power.[18] If the start is always already a moment of combination and befores, we need a way of being "respectful of different social and economic paths of development". Capitalist Eurocentrism should be named for its narrowness of interest and not falsely universalized, especially not as democracy. Samir Amin says: "No Great Wall separates the center from the periphery in the world system. Were not Mao, Che and Fanon heroes of the progressive young people of the West at one time?"[19]

Just like there are many democracies, there are many notions of individual rights, and these are not just 'Western' conceptions. Of course, many people outside the West already know this pluralism exists. Abdullahi A. An-Na'im and Jeffrey Hammond reject the accepted "exclusive Western authorship of human rights". At the time of the drawing up of the United Nations Universal Declaration of Rights in the late 1940s, most of the signatories possessed African colonies. They identify human rights with "a long history of struggle for social justice" rather than with a particular location. But in order to see variety within human rights discourse one must be respectful of cultural differences and see them as possibilities, rather than just difficulties.[20] This requires, as Martin Chanock asks, a rethinking of the usual equation of the West with individualism, and of Africa with communalism. As well, it demands reviewing the idea that the West's notion of rights makes it more cordial to feminism than non-Western notions of individualism.[21]

If the body is a site for knowing more, then the global must be interrogated from this local site. No two bodies are identical and all bodies share basic needs or they die. This sharedness is too subversive, so political discourses distance us from this knowing and become a tool for obeying rather than seeing.[22] Constructions of universal life flatten out too much of the life that is happening. The word 'global', itself, is so vast and big that no one can fully grasp its meaning. I can know the meaning of 'global' only from a particular localized site, yet there is no *local* anymore; just supposed 'glocal' constructs.

When I denaturalize a body – as a site of power, as a place of political conflict, and as an attempt at control – it requires an unpacking of hierarchical individuals.[23] By starting with a female slave's body, I am acknowledging memory and history which is both oppressive and potentially creative. A female slave's body speaks of her power and her oppression simultaneously. Oppressors only enslave what they want, fear, and need. Otherwise, they would just leave her alone, or give her away. But if these women had been set free, they would have used their creative power to make a different world.

Although the body can be viewed in abstracted form, I purposely use it as the place from which to see nuance. The body localizes power and it also diffuses it[24] without regard to controls of language. Considering the body as porous allows us to search for a notion of cultural sharing that can displace a Western notion of origin and replace it with a historical practice of democracy. Bodies always speak their passionate humanity even though in inseparable fashion from other networks of meanings. The body cannot announce its meanings in some kind of unmediated way, yet it can open us to a polyversal reading of humanity.

About Thinking

I wonder why 'we' see what we see when we see it; and why we do not see when we don't. The 'we' here is me, and the 'we' is also me in the West. I am thinking *particularly*, locally and globally: 'glocally'. My viewing cannot be universal because the layerings of power and its privileges impact the contours of thought. Seeing from the West I try to leave the imperial gaze behind. There are too many languages I need to know; and there are too few translations in my homeland.

Cultural viewings are in and of themselves fraught with hierarchical notions of what is cultural to begin with. Ordinariness and everydayness are what I use to think about cultural meanings: ordinariness and everydayness and the way people live their everyday lives.[25] But any one culture is already a "bundle of relationships" as is the name given to mark any one thing, such as race, or gender, or nation.[26] So the final statement of power just "may be its invisibility". For Michel-Rolph Trouillot, history is necessarily a distortion of "historical facts" which "are not created equal".[27] He poignantly argues that silences are integral to knowing "because any single event enters history with some of its constituting parts missing". The record is always incomplete because "historical facts are not created equal". The process by which a historical 'event' becomes 'a fact' is a complex process of politics. As such, history should allow for new discovery, if one is looking for newness.[28]

Cultures and their histories, if read and seen as such, become open to the unexpected rather than to universalized narratives. Knowledge reconfigures the universalized naming of any location or structural system. I wonder about the term 'capitalism' and why it is used to name a power system that tells stories other than the tale of the exploitation of labor. Given that capitalism (class) was simultaneously webbed with slavery (racism), why call attention to only a single central narrative? 'Globalization' describes today's world's system as economic when it is as much a racialized and gendered hierarchical system of power. The naming of power continues to silence the whiteness and maleness of labor, while distorting the 'bundled' realities of the proletariat.

Marcus Rediker and Peter Linebaugh express similar thoughts. They write of the early proletariat as diverse: "poor women serving the state by bearing children", and as 'multitudinous' and "motley and multi-ethnic in appearance". The proletariat was male and female of all ages, terrorized, transatlantic, landless, and so on.[29] A particular kind of "racial optics" has people using Marx's notion of proletariat.[30] The language of otherness and difference became naturalized as the empire's continents become dark, and races become savage.[31] There is a colonialist history to this becoming. Capitalism is the story of colonial conquest, of the Americas, and then of Asia and Africa.[32] And this conquest is part and parcel of an imperial masculinity which fantasizes the protection of white femininity.[33] Dominance and domination are white and male. Colonialism simply presents itself as civilization and attempts to naturalize theft, rape, and dehumanization. Yet colonialism, like imperialism, does not bring all the facts to the fore.[34]

This unraveling of the facts and false universals takes K.N. Chaudhuri to Asia itself. He argues that the term 'Asia' is essentially a Western construction with little accuracy. There is too much complexity in 'Asia' for one term to hold it. 'Asia' speaks a continental unity that does not exist. 'Asia', before Europe existed, meant Arab, Indian, Malay, Thai, Chinese, Japanese. Later, 'Asia' becomes a construct of non-European identity.[35] Today some of us in the West are seeing more inclusively. But so much of the language I must use binds me to established histories and established critiques. And critiques are bounded by some of the same narrowed contours as the systems of power they seek to dismantle.

Silences and secrets are not exactly the same. Silences are absences with often no known record. Secrets are known and then not told. So there is a consciousness to a secret even though it may just appear as a silence. But it is also much messier than this because exclusions, invisibility, misrepresentation, repression, and lying are usually embedded in silences and secrets. These are difficult spaces to inhabit. I wonder how today's openings arise to allow me to know that I do not know enough; or to tell me that what we know is incorrect or piecemeal, with little regard for the totality of meaning.

The diversity of humanity is not new, although it is in clearer view at new sites in the West than at other times. North America was Red, Yellow, Brown and Black from the start; so why must the West recognize this today, and not then? Many whites are beginning to see that there are many other colors; that they are not the universal. But, although the meanings of color are shifting for global capital, white racial privilege has not been dislodged. The multiracial visibility of today's labor has been opened but without much restructuring of white racialized power.

The Enlightenment was able to silence its own contradictions to the globe, even though not to the slaves in Haiti. Today, global capital's monoculturalism is challenged by real-world multiculturalism but re-encodes the powerful unity of transnational racism through local market sites. This new/old revision of racism differs from the lynching motif of the 1890s which solidified the unity of whiteness for the new nation.[36] Today the "war on terrorism" rewrites racism for the twenty-first century globe.

New routes to seeing are needed to lay bare the power structures that cover over history. This is a process of uncovering and recovering the present along with the denials and the repression of the colonized. This process is one of decolonizing the thought that is used to uncover colonialism itself. The tools of thinking are always in part tied to the repressive regimes they wish to challenge. I therefore continue to look for what I do not already know. But each colonial visor is wrapped and already embedded.

It is extraordinarily hard to think about what we see and don't see when progressive ways of thinking are continually being stolen and redeployed for the purposes of preserving power systems. Oppression and repression, deception and silences, stunt our viewings of the present, with no before or after. The artist Carrie Mae Weems in her 'Hampton Project' asks us to see and think about what happened *before*: "Before the past and before the future … Before Columbus and the invention of the New World … Before Manifest Destiny ... Before the Trail of Tears ... Before the Middle Passage ..."[37] The before pushes us to learn something else than what is established as known; it pushes us to see a non-official history of formation and creation. Given that the US currently colonizes Afghanistan and Iraq while democratizing oppression so that no one can escape, and given that imperialism knows no boundaries, it is harder than ever to think with a past and a future.[38]

Creating Comas and Sameness

The problem is not only that we are asked not to think about before, but also that we are asked to have little or no memory at all. We are asked to forget that Saddam Hussein was the problem now that he has been arrested and the war has worsened. If we are asked to look backwards, it is within a framework of nostalgia, where the past has been sanitized and mass-marketed, like with Holocaust films. In this First World colonized domain, the tools for thinking backwards and forwards are stolen from most of us. People live in the moment in cybertech readiness. Quickness and speed seep into how we eat and live daily life. Bill and Hillary told their lies and called their lies secrets. President Bush pretends that he is compassionate about conservatism, and the public pretends with him.

Because nothing is quite real, there is no beginning or end. Nothing, according to Jean Baudrillard, is ever over, or done with, which makes it impossible to see beyond the present. The horrid consequence is that prediction, as the memory of the future, diminishes right along with a memory of the past. Interestingly, Baudrillard likens all this to cloning – the ultimate fantasy of reproducing the 'same' which allows us to forget death. Amidst all the chatter about diversity and a fear of it, all people wish for is to "reconstruct an homogeneous and uniformly consistent universe", a clone, "an identical copy of our world".[39]

But if totality requires extensive multiplicity, I desire a way of connecting heterogeneity to form a "collective assemblage". I do not mean an assemblage that speaks a unity which is simply a "power-takeover of the multiplicity". Nor do I mean that there is a simple origin and a simple end. But I want to think through to see variation without conquest.[40] The universal is not an abstraction of the totality but rather a specification of it through a series of meandering differences. This demands an opening of what Paul Gilroy and others call "official history". This is no easy activity because categories "reassert themselves even in the moment of their supposed erasure".[41]

Gilles Deleuze, in part, assists me in clarifying my meaning when he says that "abstractions explain nothing; they themselves have to be explained". He claims there is no such thing as a universal, no transcendent unity. Instead there are "only processes, sometimes unifying, subjectifying, rationalizing, but just processes all the same. These processes are at work in concrete 'multiplicities'; multiplicity is the real element in which things happen."[42] For me, the unity is not transcendent but it can be culled from specified moments.

I resist a totalizing view and wish more to multiply the potentialities of seeing. Deleuze sees multiplicity as freeing up "unitary paranoia" while proliferating disjunction without pyramids of hierarchy and subdivision. He privileges difference over uniformity, fluidity over unities and the nomad's wanderings over the sedentary life.[43] The same specifying of unity – its polydimensional meaning – must be done for difference itself. One needs to remember that "difference in itself lacks its own identity". There is a variety to multiplicity which also must be carefully thought through and seen.[44] Thought should not be subordinated to the abstractness of language, with its static imagery, even though the constraints are power-filled.

The problem is one of 'completeness'. Fredric Jameson names the difficulty as trying to see the "concrete whole of reality". This requires being able to think about pre-existing thought.[45] But we are faced with pseudo-concrete images, Žižek's "plague of fantasies" which blur our viewings. Because of the irrepresentability of the 'real' there is just surplus-obedience; we obey rather than confront. For Žižek, such obedience becomes internal to survival.[46] So the US government goes to war and its public offers its obedience. The only whisperings of democracy are where anti-war murmurings are voiced.

Deterritorializing the View

For Deleuze, the surface reflects on itself, and although "nothing is hidden ... not everything is visible".[47] So I focus on the not-so-easily visible; I must release my thought to be able to do new things.[48] Believing that humanity demands a sense of polyversality I must find a way of seeing sharedness rather than sameness. This means seeing without the imperial, or colonial, or globalized gaze which flattens out surface appearances. And I have to be ready to lose parts of myself in this process.

The Sarajevan poet Ferida Durakovic writes in "Every Mother is a Wunderkind" of her glorious mother who keeps her wanting to be alive, even though death surrounds her. "Early in the afternoon she lights the oil lamp and leaves it in the stairway, so that people see what they are bumping into. She leaves the apartment door open, so the neighbors grope more easily in the skyscraper dark. She leaves matches by my bed, on shelves, on tables. She wakes up at night and lights the oil lamp again in the corridor. She doesn't sleep at all, but all night listens attentively across the whole town, on four sides, with her crazy, motherly, hearty ear. Are we breathing? Are we warm? Do we have bad dreams? Is something hurting us?" Durakovic's mother is ashamed of bringing her into such a world. "If I knew, she says, that I must die for the war to end, I swear to God I would lie down and die. Just for my children and grandchildren to live."[49] My friend Aida does not know if this translates well enough into English; and I think this is my mother as she sits by my side through chemotherapy after losing Sarah and Giah to breast cancer. These are different kinds of terror and death; and "Every Mother is a Wunderkind", even though every mother is not.

I look for intelligible connections and threads and follow them. I see stunning variety within our humanness. But I must be cautious that I do not allow the idea of our humanity to blind me, to allow me make up things that are not really-real. Deleuze and Guattari say: "Don't be one or multiple, be multiplicities."[50] I might say build a polyunity. I am not traveling through a radical pluralism to find monism but rather denying their separability.[51]

I insist on holding onto the idea of humanity, because without it, I cannot find my way. The thought of Delueze and Guattari is close to my own here. "We constantly lose our ideas. That is why we want to hang on to fixed opinions so much."[52] But an idea survives only if you can use it; it only retains appeal if it "forms some kind of alliance with what we do".[53]

If absolutes are "illusions of reason", then "crack open words" to allow them their real meanings.[54] If there is no formal essence of a thing, but instead only "temporary stabilizations", or "open-ended unity", then creativity disorients simple knowing of the already established.[55] Maybe I will displace liberty, equality, and justice with desire, creativity, and multiplicity.[56] Invention and formulation must be scrutinized along with the imperial gaze only to accept that no idea can pull itself outside of its history. Critical thought demands the unofficial stories that go into naming.[57] Difference must be embraced as an 'opportunity' rather than as a problem. Foreignness must be recognized "on behalf of democracy", rather than outside it.[58]

This writing is an act of resistance. According to Foucault, people write "to struggle to resist; to write is to become; to write is to draw a map ..."[59] Writing pushes me to find a more careful language to explore with; it demands a better historical memory from me. When I write, I see the pretense of meaning more starkly. Writing uncovers chaos. I look at the words. When I am just thinking I do not see the words in the same way. Words carve out the borders and contours of thinking. Ideas need the words to create visibility. But this is not just about words; it is also about their meanings. Made-up status has to do with the power relations of seeing. If power stands still, so does the possibility for newly resistant thought.[60] If nothing is "immediately visible", or "directly readable", then writing is political at its core. Nothing escapes invention, interpretation, or subversion.

Deleuze privileges investigation more than knowing which displaces wondering about origins with wondering about what happens after and in between.[61] As 'we', in the West, learn about after and in between, we can find out what we think happened before. Thinking about before is very different than knowing what actually happened. Originary starts are already made-up and stolen. So, it is better to start, so to speak, knowingly in the middle, rather than fantasizing a knowable beginning.

As power shifts, so do the disciplinary sites of normalization.[62] As knowable starts come into question, as the ideas of natural and normal fluctuate, cracks develop which allow shreds of uncertainty. Then the very idea of 'civilization' can be revealed as an invented universalized idea that structures all else; much like the notion of 'savage', which derives from the Latin connoting woods and forest and nature, outside history. 'Others' get made up to deal with the fear of not-knowing. Creating the savage, or slave, or woman, or Arab allows made-up certainty rather than honest complex variability and unknowability. This distancing is necessary to the process of 'othering'. As Claude Lévi-Strauss says: "One cannot fully enjoy the other, identify with him, and yet at the same time remain different."[63]

Cannibalizing the 'Other'

Knowing is already colonized by its male privilege and its racialized and classed meanings. As such, the language we inherit for seeing is already an instrument of racialized masculinist empire. Seeing more inclusively means that a layer of repressed vision is removed. The best we may be able to do is what Peter Hulme advises: to read speculatively, recognizing that the story can never be fully recovered, and that that which has been recovered is often distorted and manufactured. For Hulme, much of recorded history is fanciful; and this is especially so for the record of Columbus and cannibalism; John Smith and Pocahontas, and Robinson Crusoe and Friday. These versions of the encounter between clothed Europe and naked America obscure the real history. America is supposedly found and we do not ask what was lost. This "gesture of 'discovery' is at the same time a ruse of concealment".[64]

The "man-eating savages" who Columbus encounters have little to do with the real discovery of the nation. But this aspersion puts Native Americans at the "very borders of humanity". They cleverly are not made inhuman – like animals – because then no outrage is possible. As cannibals they become the opposite of civilized: they become savage and forbidden. To take their nation from them becomes an act of civilization, rather than of savagery. The myth of Pocahontas – of cultural harmony through romance – allows the fantasy that she chooses John Rolfe and British superiority over her own father. The story of Robinson Crusoe allows for another colonial romance of total devotion and subjugation which speaks choice rather than slavery. The rescued Caribbean Amerindian Friday performs the tale of radical individualism right alongside slavery. The cannibal residue on the island reminds us to call up our false memories of savagery. Hulme makes clear that Crusoe allows for the unspeakable negotiation "between the violence of slavery and the notion of a moral economy".[65]

Once history becomes the stringing of political tales romanticizing the colonization and brutalizing of Native American and African slave men, women and children, the present looks more romantic too. But Europeans who immigrated to the colonies upon discovering the Iroquois League wrote home to say that "a mighty nation existed here". Several historians credit the Iroquois with the notion of federation which Ben Franklin adopted for the colonies.[66] Bruce Johansen argues that until one gives up the polarity of civilized/savage one cannot see the intellectual contribution of American Indians to European and American thought; that American Indians are as significant as the Romans and Greeks to democratic theory. After all, colonial leaders were searching for alternatives to European tyrannical class rule. It is why they came to America.[67]

Ideas like federalism, checks and balances, popular nomination, and women's suffrage are found early on in the Iroquois League. Both Jefferson and Franklin admired Indian democratic thought and have a debt to it – although the debt is usually forgotten. But Native Americans embraced liberty and freedom and were critical of hierarchy and excessive wealth.[68] Women's standing was defined matrilineally, although much of their status was lost as the kinship structure was shattered by encounters with the white man.[69]

Discovering Difference in the Imperial Gaze

Words like 'race' and 'gender' and 'slavery' bespeak a neatness of categorization that both does and does not exist. There is no race – just colors – before it is socially constructed, and yet the globe is inhabited by different races today. As Simone de Beauvoir states, "one is not born a woman", one becomes one; and yet the gendered construct of woman is both stable and always shifting. Race and gender are said to bespeak difference, and yet are only constituted in their differences. There is much blurring and bleeding within each construction, and between them.[70] Identities breed closure and essentialism and also their undoing.

If we have already forgotten to think historically, as Fredric Jameson claims, there is no interest in finding our way through the different illusory illusions. This makes it nearly impossible to think about what we think we see and don't see. When I think back to the 'invention' of America, I need to destroy the divisions of savage and civilization, of periphery and center. These divisions are not true today; but never were.

The idea of difference has always been distorted. Its recent history speaks the stories of Columbus, and Pocohantas, and Friday. The unitary difference is constructed, and out of made-up life and history. To recognize the embrace of 'difference' today as part of this history is to see the needs of global capital's embrace of diversity. Today's tolerance of 'difference' is what Jameson calls the "result of social homogenization and standardization and the obliteration of genuine social difference in the first place". Difference is celebrated in order to eliminate it. This involves erasure and deceit, silences and lies. As such, the very concept of difference has been 'booby-trapped' from the start.[71] There is a *before* already in play.

Patricia Williams says that the "hard work of a non-racist sensitivity is the boundary crossing, from safe circle to wilderness ... to travel from the safe to the unsafe".[72] Instability, mutability, translatability become the methods for seeing democratically. Paul Gilroy demands that we work "against the closure of categories" and towards "inescapable hybridity" and intermixture. He cautions against "overintegrated conceptions of pure and homogeneous culture" but also warns against an "overintegrated sense of cultural and ethnic particularity". Gilroy sees the ships in motion between Europe, America, Africa and the Caribbean in order to indict enslaved Africans, slaughtered Indians, and indentured Asians. In order to build an "intercultural and anti-ethnocentric" set of place locations he connects and particularizes the histories over again. The cultural fusion will be embedded in intermixture; not dilution or universalization.[73]

AIDS and People's Humanity

Global capital positions the rest of us to look at AIDS in Africa and to cannibalize Africa yet one more time through this lens. AIDS has been 'spreading' to Africa and now the rest of the world worries that it may travel once again back to the West. Flows are not insignificant here and neither are the way that they are viewed.

Drug companies make medicines that are too expensive for most of the world's people, and several of the countries in Africa, especially South Africa, have said the drug companies must devise policy that can allow them to better face their health crisis. India and Brazil are producing AIDS drugs for sale much more cheaply than the transnational pharmaceuticals, which are being pressured into lowering their prices. Pharmaceutical companies are fighting against this intrusion into their billion-dollar industry as they try to protect their patents from being circumvented by poor countries.[74] The US, along with the World Trade Organization, filed a formal complaint against Brazil, saying Brazil was violating international trade rules. Yet Merck was forced to agree to cut prices on two AIDS medicines in Brazil.[75] Black bodies are once again paraded as victims to the world and yet they are also a site from which democratic struggle and social justice can be written.

There are many epidemics within AIDS, and many different reasons impacting its spread, involving racism, patriarchal hierarchies, and poverty.[76] The vision of hypersexualized and multipartnered Africans is offered as an explanation when poverty and malnutrition better explains much of the particularity of the epidemic which cuts across continents.[77] After all, young gay and bisexual Black men are also at huge risk in the US. One in every fifty Black men in the US is infected with HIV.[78]

AIDS is, then, a site from which democratic struggle can be launched for this century. Black bodies are the site for this politics and AIDS has become the new anti-apartheid movement demanding drugs and health for all.[79] Sick and dying bodies are the sign of our greedy times, when wealthy nations exploit others; but the homelands of these afflicted people are also fighting back. Affordable drugs for the masses and limits on pharmaceutical companies like Pfizer are a rallying site for a new anti-racist democratic politics. Henry Louis Gates asks that reparations for slavery be paid in the form of AIDS funding. If the US gives no less than $2 billion annually to fight AIDS, that will amount to $1,750 for each person taken from Africa and brought to the New World.[80] This could be a new democratic beginning of sorts.

The US could look 'elsewhere' – to Africa – to learn how to build a democratic politics. This is a politics which rejects global riches at the expense of people's health and bodies. AIDS deaths in sub-Saharan Africa in 2000 totaled 2.4 million out of 3 million worldwide. AIDS has been globalized, but disproportionately to poor local sites. AIDS is a new form of global apartheid despite the language of racial access and multiculturalism. The World Health Organization finds that 44 of the 52 countries in which life expectancy is less than fifty years are in Africa.[81] Ninety percent of AIDS deaths are within Africa; in Zimbabwe 750 people die each week, and 25 percent of all Zimbabwean adults may be infected.[82] Race and place still matter.

AIDS exposes the racialized masculinist forms of existence today, the racialized coding of global capital. It puts in full view the racialized/sexualized exclusionary meanings of humanity which defined the slave trade. Meanwhile President Bush rallies support for his racialized "war on terrorism". He silenced all discussion of US racism in his State of the Union 2003 address and instead tried to humanize his neoliberal right-wing agenda with his AIDS proposal for Africa. Bush's AIDS proposal was his attempt to articulate a humanitarian internationalism consistent with his "compassionate conservatism".

In 2003 Bush announced his intention to triple US spending on AIDS in Africa to $15 billion over the next five years, even though this amount remains seriously inadequate to the task. According to a United Nations estimate, approximately $10.5 billion will be needed each year to address the crisis.[83] Shortly after the State of the Union address, Bush was criticized for misrepresenting his effort: his plan created parallel and redundant funding. He was also criticized for imposing restrictions on AIDS funding according to whether the programs were abstinence-based despite the fact that unprotected heterosexual sex is the leading factor in HIV transmission throughout the world. He also requires that family planning clinics do not provide abortions to AIDS patients and has suggested restrictions on these agencies if they are receiving HIV funding.[84]

It is sad that Colin Powell seems to have forgotten that before "the war on terrorism" he declared that AIDS in Africa was a "national security issue for the US". Even supercapitalist Jeffrey Sachs states that it is a moral imperative that the US provide sufficient funding to address the crisis which means $5 billion each year for the next five years.[85] Kofi Annan asks that the world recognize that AIDS poses the main challenge for the health of the globe. And he asks that AIDS policies directly address the women of Africa because their health secures the glue for their communities. Annan believes that it is women who know how to cope and build the necessary networks to save their communities. The U.N. must build a "partnership with the African farmer and her husband". To save Africa "we would do well to focus on saving Africa's women".[86]

With women being half of those infected worldwide, preventive methods against the spread of AIDS are needed, not Bush's religious wars and crusades against reproductive health programs which are already in place and easily accessed for preventive care. But instead of a creative AIDS proposal for the globe, we are handed more neoliberalism.

In the South African film *Long Night's Journey Into Day* I was introduced to the "truth and reconciliation" trials. The mothers of murdered teenage anti-apartheid activists think they will be able to suffer their tragedy better if they can at least know who killed their sons and daughters, and why. In order to face their horrific pain and loss they need to know about the deaths more than they need to punish the killers. Listening to these mothers I heard a different reckoning with the concept of justice, one without retribution and punishment. Given the punishing times we live in, I think we need less retribution. And it should not be forgotten that these slain anti-apartheid activists had been labeled terrorists by their white apartheid government.

Notes

1. Sandra Greene, "Vibrant Culture of Whispering: Alternative Narratives Refusing to be Forgotten", *Africa Today*, (forthcoming), pp. 2, 3.
2. Eric Foner, *Who Owns History?* (New York: Hill and Wang, 2002).
3. Thanks to historian and friend Sandra Greene for the double-sided meaning of colonial knowing.
4. Susan Buck-Morss, *Dreamworld and Catastrophe* (Cambridge, MA: MIT Press, 2000, p. 68.
5. Michael Maren, *The Road to Hell* (New York: The Free Press, 1997), p. 2.
6. Thomas de Zengotita, "Finding Our Way Back to the Enlightenment", *Harper's*, vol. 306, no. 1832 (January, 2003), pp. 3, 40.
7. Richard Trexler, *Sex and Conquest: Gendered Violence, Political Order, and the European Conquest of the Americas* (Ithaca: Cornell University Press, 1995), p. 180.
8. Much of my thinking here was clarified at the workshop "Haiti and Universal History: An Interdisciplinary Workshop on Silence and Power", September 14–16, 2001, convened by Susan Buck-Morss, Cornell University, Ithaca, New York.
9. Mahmood Mamdani, "Introduction", in Mahmood Mamdani, ed., *Beyond Rights Talk and Culture Talk* (New York: St Martin's Press, 2000), p. 3.
10. Salman Rushdie, "America and Anti-Americans", *New York Times*, February 4, 2002, p. A23.
11. Janet L. Abu-Lughod, *Before European Hegemony* (New York: Oxford University Press, 1989), pp. 12, 13, 20, 66, 224, 361.
12. See Edward Said, *Orientalism* (New York: Vintage, 1979), and a discussion of this book in Patrick Williams and Laura Chrisman, eds., *Colonial Discourse and Post-colonial Theory* (New York: Columbia University Press, 1994), pp. 132–71.
13. Roxanne Euben, *Enemy in the Mirror* (Princeton: Princeton University Press, 1999).
14. Dennis Altman, *Global Sex* (Chicago: University of Chicago Press, 2001), p. 125.
15. David Theo Goldberg, *Racist Culture* (Cambridge: Blackwell, 1993), p. 33.
16. Amartya Sen, *Our Culture, Their Culture* (Calcutta: West Bengal Film Centre, 1996), pp. 18– 20, 26.
17. Vijay Prashad, *The Karma of Brown Folk* (Minneapolis: University of Minnesota Press, 2000).
18. Bruce Johansen, *Debating Democracy, Native American Legacy of Freedom* (Sante Fe,

New Mexico: Clear Light, 1998), p. 150.

19. Samir Amin, *Eurocentrism* (New York: Monthly Review Press, 1989), pp. 150, 151.
20. Abdullahi A. An-Na'im and Jeffrey Hammond, "Cultural Transformation and Human Rights in African Societies", and Abdullahi A. An-Na'im, "Introduction", in Abdullahi A. An-Na'im, ed., *Cultural Transformation and Human Rights in Africa* (London: Zed Books, 2002), pp. 7, 19.
21. Martin Chanock, "Human Rights and Cultural Branding: Who Speaks and How", in Abdullahi A. An-Na'im, ed., *Cultural Transformation and Human Rights in Africa*, pp. 43, 46.
22. Gilles Deleuze and Felix Guattari, *A Thousand Plateaus*, translated by Brian Massuni (Minneapolis: University of Minnesota Press, 1987), p. 76.
23. Gilles Deleuze, *Foucault*, translated by Sean Hand (Minneapolis: University of Minnesota, 1988), p. xliii.
24. Ibid., p. 26.
25. Joseph Bristow, *Empire Boys: Adventures in a Man's World* (New York: Harper Collins, 1991), p. 6.
26. Eric Wolf, *Europe and the People Without History* (Berkeley: University of California Press, 1982), p. 3.
27. Michel-Rolph Trouillot, *Silencing the Past* (Boston: Beacon Press, 1995), pp. xix, 49.
28. Natalie Zemon Davis, *Slaves on Screen* (Cambridge: Harvard University Press, 2000), p. 133.
29. Marcus Rediker and Peter Linebaugh, *The Many-headed Hydra: Sailors, Slaves, Commoners and the Hidden History of the Revolutionary Atlantic* (Boston: Beacon, 2000), pp. 332, 333.
30. Alys Eve Weinbaum, "Reproducing Racial Globality", *Social Text*, vol. 19, no. 2 (Summer, 2001), p. 22.
31. Joseph Bristow, *Empire Boys*, pp. 1, 2.
32. Samir Amin, "Imperialism and Globalization", *Monthly Review Press*, vol. 53, no. 2 (June 2001), pp. 6, 7.
33. Laura Chrisman, "The Imperial Unconscious? Representations of Imperial Discourse", in Williams and Chrisman, eds., *Colonial Discourse and Post-colonial Theory*, p. 501.
34. Aimé Cesaire, *Discourse on Colonialism* (New York: Monthly Review Press, 1972).
35. K.N. Chaudhuri, *Asia Before Europe* (New York: Cambridge University Press, 1990), pp. 22–8.
36. Lisa Duggan, *Sapphic Slashers* (Durham: Duke University Press, 2000), p. 40.
37. Carrie Mae Weems, *The Hampton Project, 2000*, installation at the Williams College Museum of Art, Williamstown, Massachusetts, March 4–October 12, 2000. The photographs and narrative are also available in book form as *The Hampton Project*, from Aperture Press.
38. Chela Sandoval, *Methodology of the Oppressed* (Minneapolis: University of Minnesota Press, 2000), p. 36.

39. Jean Baudrillard, *The Vital Illusion* (New York: Columbia University Press, 2000), pp. 8, 37.
40. Deleuze and Guattari, *A Thousand Plateaus*, pp. 8, 21, 34.
41. Paul Gilroy, *Against Race* (Cambridge, MA:Harvard University Press, 2000), pp. 12, 220.
42. Gilles Deleuze, *Negotiations*, translated by Martin Joughin (New York: Columbia University Press, 1990), p. 146.
43. Deleuze, *Foucault*, p. xii.
44. Patrick Hayden, *Multiplicity and Becoming* (New York: Peter Lang, 1998), pp. 35, 38.
45. Fredric Jameson, *Marxism and Form* (Princeton: Princeton University Press, 1971), pp. 308, 312, 341.
46. Slavoj Žižek, *The Plague of Fantasies* (London: Verso, 1997), p. 1.
47. Jean-Clet Martin, "The Eye of the Outside", in Paul Patton, ed., *Deleuze: A Critical Reader* (Oxford: Blackwell, 1996), p. 18.
48. Paul Patton, "Introduction", in Patton, ed., *Deleuze*, p. 14.
49. Ferida Durakovic, "Every Mother is a Wunderkind", in *Heart of Darkness* (Fredonia, NY: White Pine Press, 1998), pp. 97, 98.
50. Deleuze and Guattari, *A Thousand Plateaus*, p. 24.
51. Jean-Michel Salanskis, "Idea and Destination", in Paul Patton, *Deleuze*, p. 60.
52. Gilles Deleuze and Felix Guattari, *What is Philosophy*?, translated by Hugh Tomlinson and Graham Burchell (New York: Columbia University Press, 1994), p. 201.
53. Philip Goodchild, *Deleuze and Guattari* (Thousand Oaks: Sage, 1996), p. 211.
54. Ibid., 12, 22.
55. Patrick Hayden, *Multiplicity and Becoming*, pp. 95, 97.
56. Ibid., p. 73.
57. Deleuze, *Negotiations*, p. 2.
58. Bonnie Honig, *Democracy and the Foreigner* (Princeton: Princeton University Press, 2001), p. 9.
59. Deleuze, *Foucault*, p. 44.
60. Ibid., p. 59.
61. Deleuze, *Negotiations*, pp. 121, 139.
62. Ibid., pp. 173, 174.
63. Claude Lévi-Strauss, *The View from Afar* (New York: Basic Books, 1985), pp. 24, 26.
64. Peter Hulme, *Colonial Encounters* (New York: Metheun, 1986), pp. xiii, 2, 3, 12.
65. Ibid., pp. 14, 81, 137–42, 176, 187, 208–9, 222.
66. Edmund Wilson, *Apologies to the Iroquois* (Syracuse: Syracuse University Press, 1959, 1991), pp. 47-51.
67. Bruce Johansen, *Forgotten Founders* (MA: Gambit, 1982), pp. xiii, xv, 20.
68. Ibid., pp. 10, 40, 118, 119.
69. J. Hewitt, 'status of Woman in Iroquois Polity Before 1784", in W.G. Spittal, ed., *Iroquois Women, An Anthology* (Ontario: Iroqrafts, 1990), pp. 61–8. Also see Sally Roesch Wagner, "The Root of Oppression is the Loss of Memory", *Iroquois*

Women, pp. 223–30.
70. Jane Flax, *The American Dream in Black and White* (Ithaca: Cornell University Press, 1998), p. 2.
71. Fredric Jameson, *Postmodernism* (Durham: Duke University Press, 1995), p. 341.
72. Patricia Williams, *The Alchemy of Race and Rights* (Cambridge: Harvard University Press, 1991), p. 129.
73. Paul Gilroy, *The Black Atlantic* (Cambridge, MA: Harvard University Press, 1993), pp. xi, 2, 31, 144.
74. Editorial. "AIDS and Profits", *The Nation*, vol. 272, no. 14 (April 9, 2001), p. 3.
75. Melody Petersen and Larry Rohter, "Maker Agrees to Cut Price of 2 AIDS Drugs in Brazil", *New York Times*, March 31, 2001, p. A4.
76. Sheryl Gay Stolberg, "In AIDS War, New Weapons and New Victims", *New York Times*, June 3, 2001, p. A24.
77. Eileen Stillwaggon, "AIDS and Poverty in Africa", *The Nation*, vol. 272, no. 20 (May 21, 2001), pp. 22–6.
78. Bob Herbert, "A Black AIDS Epidemic", *New York Times*, June 14, 2001, p.A17.
79. Mark Gevisser, "Comment: AIDS, The New Apartheid", *The Nation*, vol. 272, no. 19 (May 14, 01), pp. 5–6.
80. Henry Louis Gates, "The Future of Slavery's Past", *New York Times*, July 28, 2001, p. wk, p. 15.
81. Saleh Booker and William Minter, "Global Apartheid", *The Nation*, vol. 273, no. 2 (July 9, 2001), p. 11.
82. Michael Specter, "Doctors Powerless As AIDS Rakes Africa", *New York Times*, August 6, 2001, p. A6.
83. Rachel Swarns, "Africans Welcome US Help on AIDS", *New York Times*, January 30, 2003, p. A23.
84. Jodi Jacobson, "Women, AIDS and the Far Right – The Dis-Integration of US Global AIDS Funding", Tacoma Park, Maryland. Center for Health and Gender Equity, February 2003. Available at: www.genderhealth.org
85. Jeffey Sachs, "The Best Possible Investment in Africa", *New York Times*, February 10, 2001, p. A15.
86. Kofi Annan, "In Africa, AIDS Has a Woman's Face", *New York Times*, December 29, 2002, p. Wk.9.

3 Humanizing Humanity: Secrets of the Universal

Thinking without our skins and with our bodily desires and needs promises a possibility for recognizing human connectedness. Once one recognizes the human claims of one's own bodily needs for food, shelter, love, privacy, and sexual autonomy they subvert the isolated self. These are shared meanings of what it is to be human. Each body demands food and can experience hunger. According to K.N. Chaudhuri, "food is a category recognized by all human minds".[1]

Meanings of the body are culturally diverse and yet shared across cultures. Any body can suffer rape or torture or sexual pleasure. There is no simplistic homogeneity here, nor simple complexity. And because today the notion of bodily rights has cross-pollinated in multiple and complex fashion, the belief that bodily rights is a construct of the West distorts the multiple sites for understanding its meaning. Western hegemony has stolen much that is not uniquely its own: both from before and now.

It is imperialist for Westerners to think that bodily rights, or democracy, or humanity are singularized ideas, explicated the most fully by the Enlightenment, or the West. Although there are Westernized forms of each belief, these ideas are way too polymorphous to be reduced to their Western/ imperial form. The body's wish for autonomy flows from the polyversal meaning of humanity. No matter how multiple this articulation of bodily autonomy is, the desire to protect one's body from harm does not have to be learned. The body is one's own, however many ways 'ownership' may be conceived.[2] Propriety over one's body traverses across multiple dialogues and has no one simple location or meaning. The seductiveness of the very idea of humanity is that it takes us each to our bodily rights. Rights discourse may be power-filled by the West, but rights are cross-culturally human, not simply Western liberal in origin, even though the hegemony of the discourse often treats them as such.

The polyversal pull of the idea of humanity derives from the way bodily needs criss-cross across huge distances of the globe. The very notion of an inclusive humanness – which spans this global variety – is best viewed at sites where humanity can be seen through differences of color, location, and culture. Envisioning humanity in a nonexclusionary way requires that one takes the Western promissory of democratic freedom and release it from the power-filled meanings of colonialism, imperialism, and global capitalism. Such a counter-hegemony demands a truthfulness from Western democracy that it cannot deliver. The authorization of and by Western discourse of all things democratic and laudable must be revealed in its other locations so the polyvocal meanings of democracy can be discovered. These meanings are much like the double-sidedness of slavery that Harriet Jacobs speaks of: "My master had power and law on his side; I had a determined will. There is might in each."[3]

Abstract Universals and Their Exclusions

Emptied universals must always be specified in order that humanity does not become an abstraction of itself. Particularist, exclusionary standpoints are destabilized by being named. Then the Greeks can be viewed as establishing a colonizing democracy or as democratizing imperialism.[4] A citizenry – minus slaves and other women – bespeaks imperialist abstractness, not democratic universalism.

Equality calls attention to the possibility of resemblance and equivalence between people. In this rendering, differences are not problematized as such; they are not seen as negative. The challenges are profound because power-brokers try to tame difference in order to make it livable and thinkable – the press on each of us is to try and find the univocal and smother the rest; as though the truth is more accessible this way.[5] Anthony Appiah wrestles with this issue of identities when he says we must "recognize *both* the centrality of difference within human identity *and* the fundamental moral unity of humanity".[6] Or as Patricia Williams writes: "...that my difference was in some ways the same as hers, that simultaneously her difference was in some ways very different from mine, and that simultaneously we were in all ways the same."[7] Paul Gilroy writes of the "overwhelming natural and biological unity of the human species" while also recognizing the enormous "cross-over dynamics" of what he sees as "diaspora dispersal".[8] Local stories, in diverse languages, allow for a translocal imagination rich in a reciprocity that divulges the multiplicity of the ways humanity is expressed. The tension between sameness and difference remains while a polyversal voice for seeing is explored.[9]

Chaudhuri writes of this complexity while discussing the basic simplicity of food. He says that while food habits differ, food itself in its generalized form is a "constant through time". Foods differ, but share the categories of raw, cooked and preserved; of rice, bread and cereal. Porridge and stew have been the food of the poor across enormous cultural variety.[10] Hunger is knowable through the shared experience of eating.

Amartya Sen asks us to see unity but not as an imagined uniformity. Unity instead must be expressed through the multiplicities of diversity. Universality then becomes the "unitary significance of our diverse diversities".[11] Sen admires the filmmaker Satyajit Ray because he attempts to reveal a universal pattern to people's uniqueness. He shows the deep heterogeneity of local cultures in order to build intercultural communication. He then embraces a global dialogue while celebrating the "persistence of heterogeneity at the most local level". Ray does not fear dialogue as polluting, nor does he fear external influences from the West. Instead he seeks critical openness. Sen embraces these initiatives and has become an important voice in the global democratic dialogue as he reveals not only the misnaming and misrepresentation of Asia's diversity but also its commitments to human rights, freedom, and toleration.[12]

The mixing of diverse identities and their shared meanings unsettles the simple divides which presuppose uniformity on either side. Afro-Jamaican writers bring the Chinese diasporic experience to the Caribbean: Chinese workers – the other middle passage – were brought to the Americas in the holds of European and American ships. *Kuli* in Chinese means "bitter labor"; from Hindi, *kuli* means bonded labor. There is a Chinese history in Jamaica to discover.[13] These histories and the meaning of multi-ethnicities mean that Latinos, Blacks, and Asian-

Americans do not "occupy distinct social geographies or isolated political economies".[14] Gary Okihiro argues that "yellow is a shade of black, and black, of yellow"; that coolieism meant that Chinese were sold as and likened to 'pigs'. As such, Yellow is more Black than white.[15] There are the shared experiences and realities, like the Chinese slave labor in Cuba during the nineteenth century, which is both unique and similar to the Black slave trade. The West colonized and conquered Asia and Africa. The struggle for equality and democracy is a shared history between dispossessed peoples.

African-Americans make up more than 25 percent of all poor people in the US when they are only about 12 percent of the population. Latinos compose about 23 percent of people below the poverty line; immigrants are 50 percent more likely to be poor than native-born; and US prisons have become warehouses for the poor and unemployed of racialized minorities.[16] The mix of racist meanings and their histories connect and also smash the unique richness of the varieties of these groups of people. Important expressions of diversity are reduced to an enforced uniformity which disallows a more human unity in diversity.

In the catalogue to a wonderful art exhibition at the Canadian Museum of Civilization titled "Canadian Artists of Arab Origin", Nancy Huston writes that "we are all two, each of us, at least two – it is only a matter of knowing it". Liliane Karnouk says of her art: "I choose to create furniture that bridges the gap between my Islamic carpets and my computer table." Her exile has allowed her to use her sense of distance and multiplicity. Another artist, Camille Zakhal-ia, uses collage to represent the fragmented identity he inherits from Lebanon, Greece, Turkey, and Bahrain. All the artists express the exchange and mixture of cultural borrowing and inventing. The cultural intermixing is continual and creates new culture/s. In her installation, "Mirror, Mirror, 2000", Laila Binbrek presents a two-sided vanity table with one mirror in the middle. The mirror is absent, and only the wooden frame remains. One side of the table is filled with perfumes, make-up, and fashion magazines from Saudi Arabia and Egypt. The other side is filled with the same items but from the US and England. The open mirror represents the flow between her two selves; the items present the facades that she uses to face the world.[17]

I run the risk of homogenizing exactly what I wish to see in its uniqueness because there are different local human ways of being that cannot be grasped by abstract notions of inclusivity. Although it is true that "humanism is consistent with the desire for global homogeneity" this need not be the end purpose of this project. I reject the "deadening urge" to create 'uniformity', but I also reject the deadening urge to see only difference, and then to kill it.[18] The real story of universal humanity is its polyversal history and present. This means that there are "difficult generalizations" to be discovered and translated. But of course, this is better than the uninteresting, and unbelievable fossilized universals that cohere today. We need careful articulations by which to see, not a made-up "war on terrorism" with its disingenuous abstracted oppositions of good and evil, us and them.

Truths and Reconciliation

Universals explain nothing but instead must themselves be explained.[20] This explanation is made very difficult given the fabrications and the inventions of the *before*. Mahatma Gandhi, leader of the Indian movement for independence, wrote in order to see and organize 'all' Indians, including the untouchables. He led the movement for self-liberation which embraced the "identification of the individual with the universal". The self in Hindu thought is one with a larger unity which expresses true *swaraj* (self-rule). Self-knowledge opens the freedom to discover one's human unity. In this construct of humanity there is no Western/liberal antagonism of the self and others. Instead there is a cooperative sharedness. For Gandhi this is expressed through "unity in diversity". The European/Western style of 'self-realization' meaning 'self-aggrandizement' undercuts the connectivity of Gandhi's notion of self. Diversity and unity are not in opposition for Gandhi. He demands the emancipation of the self as part of the process of emancipating the nation from the British. His anticolonialist thought demands an embrace of diversity within unity that colonialism does not.[21]

Wole Soyinka speaks of the African world "as an equal sector of a universal humanity". He looks beyond apartheid to find a reconciliation of the races in South Africa that can allow for "the healing of a bruised racial psyche". Both victim and violators are locked together in discovering the truths that can allow them to be set free. Truth is a prelude to such reconciliation. Such healing demands the recognition of the 'unthinkable'. The end process is "social harmonization" which can allow for justice. For the millennium, Soyinka offers us a healing triology motif of truth, reparations, and reconciliation, which is embedded in the unbelievable pain of colonialist racial hatred. Out of the 'difference' that color made he remains committed to uncovering the human strains that tie one to another. Soyinka, speaking on behalf of the formerly oppressed, seeks to reconcile and build new connection; meanwhile, the Bush administration more often than not speaks of war.

It is those who fight hard against inhuman suffering who create the strongest voice for finding human unity. Paul Robeson pleaded with Blacks to speak with one voice despite their great differences. He nurtured the unity he could find, "a unity in which we subordinate all that divides us, a unity which excludes no one, a unity in which no faction or group is permitted to impose its particular outlook on others". For him, all political views must be represented if the movement is to be really unified. Robeson's belief in unity did not erase his strong identification and identity as Black; but neither did he lose sight of the "oneness of humankind".[23]

Malcolm X, who was called a separatist by those who feared his call for racial justice, also embraced humanity at the root of his revolutionary stance. In his own words: "I'm for truth, no matter who tells it. I'm for justice, no matter who it is for or against. I'm a human being first and foremost, and as such I'm for whoever and whatever benefits humanity *as a whole.*"[24] Near the end of his life, Malcolm X argued relentlessly that he was not fighting for integration or segregation but rather for recognition as 'human'. He was not fighting simply for civil rights, but rather for human rights.[25]

This tension between racial justice and the inclusivity of humanity twists itself in absurd fashion. It seems particularly poignant that the horror and sadness of the massacres of Tutsis and Hutus in Rwanda expressed the hatred towards difference, while the name Rwanda means "the universe". Today Rwandans are left wondering whether they can find justice after genocide; or whether they will remain a hopelessly divided nation. In the reconciliation court one person sadly stated: "We were told that it is those who colonized us who taught us to be enemies."[26] It is more often the case than not that colonialism itself is responsible for what the West claims as 'backward' in Africa.

Mahmood Mamdani believes that the Rwandan genocide can only be understood in terms of what happened before, during colonialism's manufacturing of the native/settler divide in specifically racialized ethnic form. The Rwandan genocide speaks a kind of race branding that was constructed through the colonial differentiation of Hutu and Tutsi. Upwards to one million Tutsi died. Colonial discourse set up the Tutsi as alien, foreign, a settler; the Hutu as native. This racializing was used to fragment and "disperse the colonized majority into minorities". The genocide was a "racial cleansing of an alien presence".[27] Instead of seeing the hatred of the Rwandan genocide as indigenous, Mamdani sees it as a consequence of colonialism and the West. And the West does not look too civilized here.

The Silences of Whiteness

Whiteness silences itself by pretending that it has no meaning, no particular relation to a cultural privilege that is power-filled. The silence about whiteness presents it as though it were not a color; and colors everything else by doing so. If white is simply natural, then there is little or no history to it; no *before*. But before light skin had this whitened meaning – before the fifteenth century – white did not have the universalized power-filled meaning it has today. Just like there were no Indians, *per se*, until Columbus invented them; there were no Black slaves until they were constructed as not-Indian or not-white. These are relational and constructed meanings. Nothing is given here at the start. Color has no meaning in and of itself, which is not to say that it is meaningless, but rather to say its meaning is 'man'-made, and shifts, and can shift again.

George Fredrickson argues that Western white racism emerges in "prototypical form" in the fourteenth and fifteenth centuries, and he locates this historical trajectory with and of the West. Whiteness or its other – Blackness – had no particular significance for the Greeks, Romans, and early Christians. Slaves came in all colors. Not until the seventeenth century was slavery defined by Blackness. Racism then developed within the uniquely Western discourse of equality of the nineteenth century. Fredrickson locates this dynamic in the "dialectical interaction between a premise of equality and an intense prejudice". The doctrine of equality comes before racism. It sets in motion the exclusionary visions of who is thought worthy of this full humanity.[29]

Being white is an untruth for James Baldwin. "No one was white before s/he came to America. It took generations, and a vast amount of coercion, before this became a white country." Settlers denied the Black presence here and in the process of denial and subjugation "America became white".[30] W.E.B. DuBois argues in a similar vein that "we were not Black before we got here"; Africans were defined as Black by the slave trade. Today's whiteness was not firmly established until the nineteenth century.[31]

Color and race are more unstable and mixed than not. Delineations are always in part fabricated as though color and race were purer, more homogenous than they are. A majority of African-Americans have some European forebears; up to two-fifths may have American Indian blood. The gene structure is a mix of African, European, and American Indian. Five percent of white Americans may have African roots.[32] When color and race are named, the name is simply a fictional account. Colors have racial and sexual histories; *befores* that reveal complexity rather than simply marking bodies with partially fictional meanings. Bodies continue to parade with their colonized racialized and sexualized meanings long past their present realities because these markings remain.[33]

This kind of carryover, when labels mask really knowing and viewing, almost always disconnects the historical from the present, or misrepresents the history through an exclusive narrowed rendering. Most labels and identities obscure more than they reveal because they are singular rather than multiple. This was true of Marx's viewing of the proletariat. Yet his working class was much more diverse and plural before the industrial revolution. This has special importance for today's workers who are also defined through racial and sexual structures of exploitation that cannot be fully understood by the narrowed Eurocentric visor of the whitened and male proletariat.[34]

Naming is very often an abstraction of the real: singular labels stand in for a complex humanness. The reality of humanity is that it is sexed and colored in a variety of hues which are mostly not white. Meanwhile the dominant discourse of the West silently privileges whiteness and masculinism by normalizing each as the standard. This privilege is silenced by and through its absence. Yet the mistaken steps go backwards and forwards here. Subdivision and delineation by cultural colors do not work either. Instead Paul Gilroy imagines a "strategic universalism" which allows him to yearn for a "planetary humanism".[35]

White boys at Columbine High School bring guns to their suburban schools and shoot their classmates, and the nation is told that its children are in crisis. As such, white boys are seen as revealing a universal truth about the nation. But this construction should be in reverse: the silenced specific (white boys) parades as the universal (the nation's children) instead of showing this racialized specific as power-filled. The real truth is not stated: that white boy culture is deeply violent. There is a deafening silence about boys of color, or any girl in this universalized moment. White boys are the standard for the nation's children. All 'others' are excluded from the universal while the universal is truly not that at all.

At the same time, white boys with guns are viewed as an aberration, not as a statement of any generalized rule. Shortly before he turned his high-school into a battlefield, Eric Harris wrote in his diary that if he did not die in the school attack he would get a plane and ram it into a tall building in New York City.[36] It is too weird to not mention the connection here to September 11, 2001; Harris, a troubled teen in the US has the same fantasies as the Arab men who rammed their planes into the Twin Towers. But these men then became the universalized symbol for Islamic extremism. Violence by white boys does not transfer to whites in general because whiteness is not racialized by whites. I do not mean to equate all forms of 'terror'; yet whiteness as a site of racialized privilege occludes too much else. So, after the bombing of the Oklahoma federal building, it was said to be the worst tragedy and loss of life that the state had ever known. This was said even though 3,000 blacks died in the Tulsa race riots of 1921.

Differences, of any kind, are translatable because human differences are also connections. Only when the self is visioned as completely autonomous and individual do differences become totally distinct and separate. Humanity transcends and articulates polyversality simultaneously because no individual is ever completely different or totally the same as another. This is why I can know differences that are not my own; I can push through to a connection that allows me to see variety – even if in translated form through my own experience which is never identical with any other site.

Given the power-filled meanings of identity there is no escape from the language of race, gender, and class. And each of these labels already occludes and obfuscates the connection that exists between the multiple identities within, and through each. Constructions of difference and sameness permeate colonial and imperial thought. In these instances, difference is one and the same as 'othering'. So Muslims become identified with terrorism. Fundamentalism becomes the fanaticism of Islam, and not of Christianity. Modernity and rationality are identified with the West, backwardness and religiosity with Islam. There is no embrace of the rich human complexity within Islam, or the West.

The homogenizing of a person as different, both institutionalizes and hardens difference; it distances and dehumanizes the 'othered'. Those who are 'othered' become abstractly different, with almost no human content to who they are. At the same time sameness is constructed in relation to fictional characters, like Columbus. So democracy is constructed as treating everyone the same, when the notion of 'everyone' is already an exclusive category parading as the universal. And equality becomes derivative in this thought process as well; treating one the same as the fictionalized universal.

The opposition of difference and sameness through a process of silence and fiction constructs colonialism, imperialism, and global capitalism as one and the same with 'civilization', human rights, and democracy. This kind of closure, which is rooted in partial and exclusive viewings of places and people 'elsewhere', disallows an understanding of radical pluralism as being at the heart of democratic practices. It unforgiveably narrows the way that most of us are expected to live in this incredibly fascinating world.

Specifying Abstracted Gender

Difference, as othering, is written on bodies: in color, and in sex/gendered form. When born female, one becomes a woman. Each woman has a color and a sex and a class, and so forth. So one is a woman and also simultaneously much else. Feminism rejects patriarchy's fictional homogenization of women as though they are all the same, and also different from men in the same way. Difference 'others' women from the standard men. Men in this viewing are also privileged as white and not-working-class. Women of other colors than white are further 'othered' in complex form through race, along with other classes.

Women are uniquely diverse among themselves while also regulated within the same/different dichotomy of patriarchal global capital. It is hard to reclaim women's specificity given the power-filled words used to separate us. Women are oppressed by men and some women oppress other women. Women of other colors than white are positioned with less power than white women. And the naming here occludes the connections that also exist through these differences.

These complex layerings of power which disperse women do not completely prevent a shared sense of community, although it is one that must be carefully nurtured and sustained. The differences among women are sometimes said to overwhelm any notion of collectivity. Marxists, Muslims, liberals, conservatives, and postmodernists deny women a shared political gender identity. Women's activism across the globe resists this skepticism as feminists of all kinds struggle to humanize the world.

My personal moorings matter here. As a child and teenager I was punished as a race traitor. As the daughter of communists I was a traitor to my country as well. But I came to feminist activism later, more on my own, as a young woman in the US women's movement while in graduate school. Being female singled me out as different as I began my graduate career. I was often lonely. I had no women professors. Most of the other students were white men who were also much older than I was. I was not just female, but a feminist activist and writing a dissertation in feminist theory. My support came from women who were active with me in the movement. I spent a lot of time at school alone but loved the intellectual space I was forging for myself. Few of the men who taught or sat in my classes had any consciousness of their exclusionary language, or focus, or privilege.

I was female and not the kind of woman that most of the faculty felt comfortable with. As a feminist who was also antiracist and socialist I did not blend in easily. Political science, even today, is more conservative and more populated with white men than most other disciplines. It is the discipline that provides the disciples for the Bush administration's neoconservative Straussian policy makers like Paul Wolfowitz. I was outspoken. I did not dress in the professional uniform. I was not enough like the homogenized standard of what a woman is supposed to be. So, I was 'othered' as different: as not a man, and not enough like a woman.

This self-reflective wandering puts the fictional universalization of gender against my own individuality in the bold. My personalized knowing contrasts with the homogenization of gender generalization. My coming to consciousness was a process of seeing myself as an expression of the polyversal meaning of femaleness which connects to the wholeness of womankind without fictionalizing the parameters. My particular experience was unique, and hardly so at all.

My seeing is specifically local and intimate. Back then in graduate school, I had thought I would have an easy time finding a job when I finished writing the dissertation. I was sure that my passionate intelligence would be recognized and embraced for all it was. Even though I was a feminist, and 'knew' that women are not treated as 'equal', I believed it would be different for me. I started interviewing and looking for a job with a lot of the excitement of youth. I thought I was just too good for these male academics to pass me up. And I was unaware of the disconnect between my knowing, and my believing.

It was 1972. Affirmative action hiring was at its height. I went on more than twenty interviews. They were brutal. At the University of Washington, in Seattle, after presenting an excerpt from my dissertation, "Marx's Theory of Alienation and Its Import for Feminist Theory", I was asked by the chair of the search committee if I thought the birth control pill was a form of alienation. I hadn't mentioned the pill or pregnancy in my talk. I could not believe that after all the controversial points I had made, this was the question I was supposed to answer. I felt rage but theorized the query to address the issue of alienated choices and the body. My answer purposely ignored the humiliation that was intended. The questioner came back at me: "No, I mean what do you think personally about the pill?" The room was completely silent. Not one person tried to intervene. I finally got it. This was not a serious interview at all. It did not matter what I knew or how good I was. They – a room filled with men, only one woman among them – had no intention of hiring me. I was totally radicalized that day.

Most of the other departments I visited were similar in their lack of interest, although not all were as cruel. I was simply a woman to be checked off on their affirmative action report. Most of the time no one engaged me in discussion after my presentation; sometimes I was asked a question that had nothing to do with the topic I was discussing; other times I was asked whether I had thought about having a family; a few times well-known professors fell asleep while I spoke. Sometimes I looked out at the group before me and realized that I was not really there to them; that they were seeing someone that I did not know. I remember sometimes feeling like I could almost not breathe. Other times I opened my eyes as wide as I could so that the tears would not fall out. It all felt beyond unfair. I had worked so hard and had so much to offer.

In this process I was 'othered' as a female. My female body spoke of me in ways that were not me. No one saw me for who I was. I was simply whatever they thought I was: too radical, too feminist, too different. I hated being 'othered'. I hated having my true self not matter; to be made simply invisible. The oppressive visors of 'othering' have profoundly affected me. So, I take my childhood and moments in the academy to places 'elsewhere' in Cuba, Egypt, India, and Afghanistan to help me see, and know more.

Polyversal Humanity

Starting close to the self one can then push to inhabit the polyglot of global mixing. The notion of the global must be reclaimed – taken from capitalist hegemony – for a radically inclusive humanity. The notion of inclusivity recognizes a unity among peoples that is hard to fathom and must be achieved while safeguarding what Sri Aurobindo calls the race's "roots of vitality", which are "richly diverse in its [humanity's] oneness".[38] Diversity and not uniformity underlies life's "complex oneness". India's polyglot self is impossible to know fully in each of its meanings, although hybrid writers like Salman Rushdie can help move us in this direction.[39]

The self must be present if an earnest commitment to community is embraced. The love of humanity – as an inclusive polyversal – must therefore start close to home, and our home is the body. The Iranian filmmaker Moshen Makhmalbaf reminds us of the line by the Persian poet Sa'adi which rests above the portal of the United Nations: "All people are limbs of one body". He asked us to remember the humanity of the Afghans while the US makes war against them, reminding us that the first casualty of war is a "sense of genuine universal humanity".[40] He instructs people in the West that many in the Taliban are simply hungry Pashtoon orphans who attended the religious schools because they were hungry, and would be fed. These boys were hungry, rather than terrorist extremists. Makhmalbaf urges the West to take action against this hunger and impending death of at least one million Afghans from famine. Instead of Bush's "war on terrorism", Makhmalbaf reorients the rest of the world to look for the intercultural mixing of all of our humanity. He pleads for people outside of Afghanistan to try to see the real individuals who live the daily tragedy of death that has engulfed the country for the last twenty years. Each year "125,000 or about 340 people a day, or 14 people every hour, or 1 in about every five minutes" have been killed or die due to these wars. He wishes for an human outcry against war in Afghanistan, like there was for preserving the Buddhist statues from Taliban destruction.[41]

Ella Shoat speaks of a "polycentric multiculturalism" which can animate what she terms a 'plurilogue' of discussion. She writes out of her own experience of Jews and Arabs and Latinos being white and Black and Brown and Mestizo. This racial variety expresses a "chromatic spectrum" which demands new ways of naming what we see.[42] Such a notion of wholeness does not make us choose between false claims of pure identity; or purist notions of knowing. People of color walk around dreaming about this possibility of wholeness all the time. Henry Louis Gates wishes that his color was not the most important thing about him; and it is. "I want to be black, to know black, to luxuriate in whatever I might be calling blackness at any particular time – but to do so in order to come out the other side, to experience a humanity that is neither colorless nor reducible to color."[43] There is the desire to be more than our flesh; a desire to flourish with but beyond our bodily contours.

When Alexis de Tocqueville went on his fifteen-day excursion into the American wilderness he saw how the natives – who he calls Indians – had been wronged by the European settlers. He writes of how the Indians scorn the European 'servitude' to "useless riches"; and he finds them peaceful and creative. Still, for Tocqueville, the Indian is savage, and the European civilized. "It was pitiful to see how these unhappy people were being treated by their civilized European brothers."[44] It is not recognized often enough that the English came from a nation of monarchs, not democrats, and that Native Americans, especially the Iroquois, were egalitarian in social structure. North America became a unique blend of European *and* 'native'.[45] This sense of before is more lost than it is found.

Savagery and slavery – already in part a language about the 'other' – denies human will, human choice, self-knowledge, and the right to guide oneself. The constructed meaning of each erases the individuals who are described, which is an erasure of the human complexity of enslavement and 'othering', which is already encoded on our 'seeing'. It is therefore nearly impossible to know what slavery really is; or the totality of humanness itself. Wole Soyinka asks: "but what is slave?"; "what humanity is it?" Although there is a condition called slavery it is 'irrefrangible', impossible to refute, "though plagued with ten to a thousand varieties".[46] So slavery both falsely homogenizes the varieties of peoples within and does violence to those who persisted and resisted from inside. When I write of slavery I unwillingly recreate this violence.

Gandhi believed that one must have a "proper picture of what we want before we can have something approaching it".[47] Picturing what we, the resistant 'we' want demands a vision beyond the oppressiveness of the times we inhabit. It demands that we wonder why we should be alive, to what purpose it all drives, for what we are willing to die. Arundhati Roy tells us that the only dream worth living is the "dream that you will live while you're alive and die only when you're dead". We should live to create ferment; to create discomfort, to not be silent, to not merely whisper. We must live to make a difference that matters to those who suffer the "war on terrorism". There is no other choice, for Roy, when nuclear weaponry makes us fear life more than death; and when multiple millions of people have no safe drinking water, or basic sanitation in the world's biggest democracy.[48] The resistant 'we' must make a difference because too many are suffering in prisons, in refugee camps, in global factories, and in lonely fear.

Starting Again, Now

The stories of history are too partial; there is too much that those of us in the West don't see. We, the human "we", all are descendants of Africa at the chromosomal level; the genetic archive tells us (in a hereditary script) that we are all Africans through the Y chromosome. According to Luigi Luca Cavalli-Sforza, all humans share a common origin; human evolution began between 50,000 and 100,000 years ago in Africa, where many groups became differentiated over a long period of time. The first major expansion took place from East Africa to Asia, probably via Suez and the Red Sea. Genetically speaking, peoples are mixed through the diasporas of genetic geography and their adaptations. This model of human migrations and expansions from Africa assumes that genetic and therefore racial differences between people from different continents are superficial.[49] The Human Genome Project finds that human beings "share a virtually identical genome: 99.9 percent of their DNA is identical".[50] So there is little if any genetic/'scientific' basis to race; yet racism exists and flourishes.

New pictures of what Christ supposedly – really? – looked like are disseminated in March 2001, in *Newsweek* and other popular journals; the pictures show a Semitic and 'swarthy' face with kinky hair. Not much is written alongside the pictures. The pictures are simply revealed, and white Christians are left to fantasize whatever they choose.

Martin Bernal's *Black Athena* demands a rereading and reorienting of history towards Black Africa, away from Greece; a rethinking of the singularity of race itself which visions Jews from Ethiopia in Black skin; and a rescoping of origins of the beginnings of civilization. He argues that the deeper/closer you get to the true Hellenic roots of Greece, the closer you get to Egypt. Bernal reveals these Egyptian and Semitic traces in the Middle and Late Bronze age, while constructing how the Aryan model is established in the first half of the nineteenth century.[51]

The Aryan model, which still remains the dominant voice, claims racial purity rather than the mixing and traveling of its roots/routes. Black Egyptians and Semites are pushed to the periphery, and the Afroasiatic roots of Greece are fabricated as European or Aryan. According to Bernal, after the rise of Black slavery, European thinkers wanted to keep Black Africans distinct from European civilization.[52] This cultural arrogance and fictionalized presentation then became accepted as official history.

The overlapping mixes inherent in colonialism and imperialism can be traced through people's bodies, a kind of bio-imperialism. According to Alfred Crosby, in the early sixteenth century and for the next four centuries smallpox played an essential role in the spread of white imperialism. Europeans brought disease and destruction to the Aztecs, and Incas, and the Aborigines in Australia. Disease has operated as an overwhelming advantage to European invaders; and a devastating disaster to indigenous peoples. The traveling and mixing of populations clearly defines much of the *befores*. But Europeans also brought whiteness to the continents which they expanded. Just before World War One, thirty percent of the Argentine population was 'foreign' born white. Since World War Two, Australia has received more immigrants in proportion to its population size than any nation other than Israel.[53]

Multiraciality is internal both to the concept of race, and to the construction of any geographic place. And yet 'othering' and differentiating people on the basis of clear racial divides continues. The fictionalized accounts of the discovery of America, or the origins of Greek civilization, are embraced and affirmed in order to contain and pacify the 'newly' formed Eurocentric millennial multiracial/ethnic discourse of global capital.

Before a creative polycultural understanding of democracy can be embraced, US Eurocentrism must be fully displaced. Eric Wolf can assist here. For him, before AD 1000, the center of the world was not Europe but societies made by "peoples without history". Before 1400, Islam was the center of cosmopolitanism, given the trade routes of the time. He makes clear that European expansionism met with existing complex societies and cultures; that expansionism met with formidable cultural encounters. Wolf unsettles the usual distinction between center and periphery and shows instead that European capitalism has always had "peripheries within its very core". Heterogeneity defines each location. Although non-European countries became subordinate and dependent, this was not their early lot in life. Initially there was equality and even preference. The history of the non-West officially is historyless.[54]

Remixing It, Again, Now

The slave is created as slave; the "orient is made Oriental".[55] Racial singularity is a fantasy because mulattoes and mestizos already have European affiliations and mixed ancestry. Life expresses transcultural character and dialogic engagement rather than purity.[56] Today's mixings are not simply like before but they reflect new forms of hegemony with complex so-called democratic presentations. So "white boys want to be Black", and dress Black, until the police show up.[57] And Tiger Woods identifies as Cablinasian (a mix of Caucasian, Black, Asian, and Indian) but will know that he's not, the "first time the police pull him over because he's black".[58]

The 2000 US census form listed fifty racial combinations that one could choose from. One in twenty Blacks selected more than one racial category. Some who chose the singular identity of 'Black' said that "for all intents and purposes, you're either black or white in Mississippi"; or, "most blacks here see themselves as black and not something else";[59] or, "more black folks feel this is a prideful thing, and don't want to dilute themselves with all those notions we're part this and part that, although we all know we're part something else". Anthony Appiah, when interviewed about the census, said that he only chose Black to identify himself, even though he is a son of a white English mother, and Black West African father. He said that he privately identifies as biracial but that publicly he identifies as Black so that patterns of discrimination can be followed and addressed.[60] For others, identifying solely as Black means that they do not want to be seen as wanting to be more white; or less Black. Racial categories are oversimplified and overly homogenized, and hence not accurate; but accuracy has never been their purpose.[61]

Black people are not necessarily of African ancestry or a people from any specific place or time. Black is often white people's attitude toward people they designate Black. It is a "projection onto certain peoples who are deemed to be 'Black', as the 'other'". Under British rule, Indians were 'othered' as niggers. And today this means for Vijay Prashad that South Asians are defined by "banal exoticism", and a New Age orientalism which objectifies South Asian Americans as exotic and spiritual.[62] It is primarily structural racism that reproduces 'races' and their racialized meanings.

The US has more foreign-born workers than ever before. By 2050, whites will make up a slim majority of 53 percent of the population.[63] From this place, which is both old and new, I look to turn the global capitalist discourse of diversity towards an uncompromising polyversal subversive notion of humanity. I use Edward Said to help me here. He lived with the homelessness of being Palestinian, lived between cultures, felt permanently out of place and permanently different. But his lifelong desire and commitment was to use this personal knowledge to live bravely with and among these tensions, to build polyversal unities of humanity.[64]

Notes

1. K.N. Chaudhuri, *Asia Before Europe* (New York: Cambridge University Press, 1990), p. 180.
2. See Rosalind Pollack Petchesky, "The Body as Property: A Feminist Re-Vision", in Faye Ginsburg and Rayna Rapp, eds., *Conceiving the New World Order* (Berkeley: University of California Press, 1995), pp. 387–406 for a fabulously interesting discussion of the plural meanings of 'owning' the body.
3. "Harriet Jacobs", in Mary Young, ed., *All My Trials, Lord: Selections from Women's Slave Narratives* (New York: Franklin Watts, 1995), p. 64. Also see: Mary Lyons,

Letters from a Slave Girl: The Story of Harriet Jacobs (New York: Charles Scribner's Sons, 1992).

4. Gilles Deleuze and Felix Guattari, *What is Philosophy?* translated by Hugh Tomlinson and Graham Burchell (New York: Columbia University Press, 1994), p. 97.
5. Gilles Deleuze, *Difference and Repetition*, translated by Paul Patton (New York: Columbia University Press, 1994), pp. xix, 3, 30, 35.
6. K. Anthony Appiah, "Race, Culture, Identity: Misunderstood Connections", in Appiah and Amy Gutmann, *Color Conscious* (Princeton: Princeton University Press, 1996), p. 105.
7. Patricia J. Williams, *The Alchemy of Race and Rights* (Cambridge, MA: Harvard University Press, 1991), p. 125.
8. Paul Gilroy, *Against Race* (Cambridge, MA: Harvard University Press, 2000), pp. 181, 218.
9. "Introduction", in Chandra Talpade Mohanty and Satya Mohanty, eds., *The Slate of Life: More Contemporary Stories by Women of India* (New York: Feminist Press, 1994), p. 23.
10. K.N. Chaudhuri, *Asia Before Europe*, pp. 150, 152, 165, 180.
11. Amartya Sen, "Draper Lecture", New York University, Graduate School of Arts and Sciences, October 30, 3001.
12. Amartya Sen, *Our Culture, Their Culture* (Calcutta: West Bengal Film Centre, 1996), pp. 1, 2, 24, 46.
13. Lisa Yun, "Linking Africa and Asian in Passing and Passage", *Souls*, vol. 3, no. 3 (Summer 2001), pp. 5, 52, 54.
14. Manning Marable, "Transforming Ethnic Studies", *Souls*, vol. 3, no. 3 (Summer 2001), p. 15.
15. Gary Okihiro, *Margins and Mainstreams: Asians in American History and Culture* (Seattle: University of Washington Press, 1994), pp. xii, 41, 43.
16. Manning Marable, "Transforming Ethnic Studies", p. 15.
17. "The Lands Within Me: Expressions by Canadian Artists of Arab Origin", *Canadian Museum of Civilization*, October 19, 2001 to March 9, 2003. Curators Aida Kaouk and Constance Webel.
18. Kwame Anthony Appiah, "Cosmopolitan Patriots", in Pheng Cheah and Bruce Robbins, eds., *Cosmopolitics* (Minneapolis: University of Minnesota Press, 1998), p. 94.
19. Bruce Robbins, "Actually Existing Cosmopolitanism", in Cheah and Robbins, eds., *Cosmopolitics*, pp. 5–6. Also see Meyda Yegenoglu, *Colonial Fantasies: Towards A Feminist Reading of Orientalism* (Cambridge: Cambridge University Press, 1998), p. 38.
20. Deleuze and Guattari, *What is Philosophy?* p. 7.
21. Dennis Dalton, *Mahatma Gandhi* (New York: Columbia University Press, 1993), pp. 3–5. Also see: M. K. Gandhi, *The Collected Works of Mahatma Gandhi*, vols. 29 and 51 (Ahmedabad: Navajivan, 1972); and M.K. Gandhi, *Communal Unity* (Ahmedabad: Navajivan, 1949).

22. Wole Soyinka, *The Burden of Memory, The Muse of Forgiveness* (New York: Oxford University Press, 1999), pp. 13, 23, 26–7, 38.
23. Paul Robeson, *Here I Stand* (Boston: Beacon Press, 1958), pp. 48, 99.
24. Malcolm X, with the assistance of Alex Haley, *The Autobiography of Malcolm X* (New York: Ballantine, 1973), p. 366.
25. George Breitman, ed., *Malcolm X Speaks: Selected Speeches and Statements* (New York: Grove Weidenfeld, 1965), p. 175.
26. Farah Stockman, "The People's Court", *Transition*, Issue 84, vol. 9, no. 4 (Fall 2000), p. 40.
27. Mahmood Mamdani, *When Victims Become Killers* (New Jersey: Princeton University Press, 2001), pp. 10, 13, 14, 16, 25.
28. Ann Ducille, "The Shirley Temple of My Familiar", *Transition*, Issue 73, vol. 7, no. 1 (Spring 1998), p. 13.
29. George Fredrickson, *Racism: A Short History* (Princeton: Princeton University Press, 2002), pp. 6, 11, 12, 17, 47.
30. James Baldwin, "On Being 'White' ... and Other Lies", in David Roediger, ed., *Black On White* (New York: Schocken Books, 1998), p. 178.
31. W.E.B. DuBois, "The Souls of White Folk", in Roediger, ed., *Black On White*, p. 184.
32. Appiah, "Race, Culture, Identity", in *Color Conscious*, p. 70.
33. Radhika Mohanram, *Black Body: Women, Colonialism, and Space* (Minneapolis: University of Minnesota Press, 1999), p. xiv.
34. See Michael Hardt and Antonio Negri, *Empire* (Cambridge, MA: Harvard University Press, 2000) for a discussion of the proletariat as the multitude of people working for capital. However, they do not theorize the gendered decentering necessary towards understanding the totality of the multitude.
35. Paul Gilroy, *Against Race*, pp. 2, 96.
36. As quoted from the journal of Eric Harris which was released to the public December, 1999. This excerpt is found in Jean Baudrillard's, "L'Esprit du terrorisme", *Harper's Magazine*, February 2002, p. 13.
37. James Atlas, "Leo-Cons, A Classicist's Legacy: New Empire Builders", *New York Times*, May 4, 2003, p. wk2.
38. Sri Aurobindo, *The Human Cycle: The Ideal of Human Unity, War and Self-Determination* (Pondicherry: Sri Aurobindo Ashram, 1962), p. 409.
39. Sumana Raychandhuri, "Behind Mount Rushdie", *The Nation*, vol. 272, no. 3 (January 22, 2001), pp. 31–5.
40. Moshen Makhmalbaf, "Limbs of No Body: The World's Indifference to the Afghan Tragedy", *Monthly Review Press*, vol. 53, no. 6 (November 2001), pp. 29, 30.
41. Ibid., pp. 30, 31.
42. Ella Shoat, ed., *Talking Visions* (New York: MIT Press, 1998), pp. 2, 7:
43. Henry Louis Gates, Jr, *Colored People* (New York: Alfred Knopf, 1994), p. xv.
44. Alexis de Tocqueville, "Fortnight in the Wilderness", in George Wilson Pierson, ed., *Tocqueville in America* (Baltimore: Johns Hopkins University Press, 1938, 96),

pp. 255, 275.

45. Jack Weatherford, *Indian Givers* (New York: Fawcett Columbine, 1988), pp. 129, 135.
46. Soyinka, *The Burden of Memory*, pp. 69, 70.
47. Gandhi, *The Collected Works*, vol. 85, p. 33.
48. Arundhati Roy, *The Cost of Living* (New York: Modern Library, 1999), pp. 14, 19, 104.
49. Luigi Luca Cavalli-Sforza, *Genes, Peoples, and Languages* (New York: North Point Press, 2000), pp. xii, 39, 55, 91, 161.
50. Sandra Soo-Jin Lee, "The Genetics of Difference", *Color Lines*, vol. 6, Issue 2 (Summer 2003), p. 25.
51. Martin Bernal, *Black Athena*, vol. 1 (New Brunswick: Rutgers University Press, 1987). See especially the Introduction, and chapters 2, 3, and 4.
52. Ibid., pp. 1, 29, 30.
53. Alfred Crosby, *Ecological Imperialism* (New York: Cambridge University Press, 1986), pp. 207, 215–16, 302.
54. Eric Wolf, *Europe and the People Without History* (Berkeley: University of California Press, 1982, 1997), pp. 194, 196, 296.
55. Meyda Yegenoglu, *Colonial Fantasies*, p. 17.
56. Mary Louise Pratt, *Imperial Eyes* (New York: Routledge, 1992), pp. 101, 102.
57. Stated by rapper D.L. Hughly on MTV, March 3, 2001.
58. As stated in Ward Connerly "A Conversation on Race", *New York Times*, July 2, 2000, p.11.
59. As quoted in Eric Schmitt, "Blacks Split on Disclosing Multiracial Roots", *New York Times*, March 31, 2001, p. A1, A12.
60. As stated on NPR Morning News, March 13, 2001, "Race and the 2000 Census".
61. Adrian Piper, "Passing for White, Passing for Black", in Ella Shoat, ed., *Talking Visions*, p. 110.
62. Vijay Prashad, *The Karma of Brown Folk* (Minneapolis: University of Minneapolis Press, 2000), pp. 48, 68. 159.
63. Arian Campo-Flores, et al., "Redefining Race in America", *Newsweek*, vol. cxxxvi, no. 12 (Sept. 18, 2000), p. 39.
64. Edward Said, *Out of Place* (New York: Alfred Knopf, 1999).

4 Fictions of the West: Their De-racing and De-sexing

The West – as a state of mind, a set of privileged cultural values – identifies a singular location of power across various geographic sites. These sites are sometimes located in colonial spaces and sometimes in colonized spaces; sometimes in imperialist and sometimes in imperial locations. Most difficult is that the West is simultaneously a sliding symbol that misrepresents itself, changes meaning in order to obscure its homogenizing power, and promises what all humans want: freedom, equality and justice.[1]

When the West usurps the word 'democracy' for its own purposes, competing and contradictory conceptions of individuality, freedom, and equality are de-authorized. The democracy of the West was founded on slavery.[2] It is therefore unconscionable to describe Western Enlightenment theory as democratic given the practices of Caribbean slavery, slave rape and the dehumanizing horrors of the slave trade itself. By opening the West to its historical *befores*, we relocate eighteenth-century democratic theory to its exclusionary white privilege, its exploitative capitalist class relations, and its unforgiving patriarchal masculinism. If democracy exists here at all, it exists as a promissory at the sites of resistance.

Official history silences brutality through the regimes of its own power. Plunder, murder, and domination only survive as unrecorded whisperings. Fictionalized histories make sense of the American Revolution, the Declaration of Independence, and the Civil War without giving much recognition to the silenced players. Rights discourse may have been colonized by the West; but humanity is transnational and transcorporeal. Western individualism has coordinate 'elsewheres', with coordinate differences. In sum: democracy is spread across the globe in polyversal human forms from before and 'elsewheres'. These practices are silenced by the very democratic discourses that these struggles embrace.

Fictionalizing Civilization and Modernity

Civilization is characterized by a universalist notion of reason. Rationality as such, as a universalized construction, "veils its capacity to dominate, to repress, and to exclude". Supposedly all individuals can be rational and therefore civilized, but in actuality rationality is positioned against savagery (natives), emotionality (women), and sexuality (racialized others). These exclusionary moves are never stated as such. Instead silence prevails in the form of an inclusionary discourse while everyone but the white propertied male is made invisible. Through these moves of exclusion, rationality becomes a racialized/sexualized privileged location. David Goldberg says that eighteenth and nineteenth century liberal democratic thought "plays a foundational part in normalizing and naturalizing racist exclusions".[3]

A racialized discriminatory practice is internalized in the Western canon along with the erasure of its sexed/gendered history while a Westernized masculinist whiteness becomes the standard of reason. Civilization is marked by a silenced denial and negation of the plurality of peoples and the power domains they occupy. Their lives are not seen as contributory to history because they are simply ignored. Identity is delineated by power-filled racialized and sex/gendered discourses.

Civilized behavior is positioned against the uncivil savage, with primitive and inferior traditions. And this process assumes a layering of fantasy and desire which also becomes a part of the colonial relation. For Meyda Yegenoglu, the Orient, in eighteenth and nineteenth century fashion, is a "fantasy built upon sexual difference". Orientalism becomes powerfully mapped with a phallocentrism which makes the Oriental woman the veiled interior of a Western identity. Cultural and sexual difference collapse on each other.[4]

The myth of European superiority is naturalized right along with a Western-defined masculinity. Mary Louise Pratt identifies this imperial gaze with the establishment of northern European surveillance and appropriation of much else. In this viewing, there is a tendency to "see

European culture emanating out to the colonial periphery from a self-generating center". This obscures "the constant movement of people and ideas in the other direction". The flows are two-way, so clear divides do not hold in neat fashion. Center and periphery share dialogue as well as contestation, so the division between West and non-West is as distorting as it is real. The division itself establishes the West as the standard. Yet Europe is already influenced from 'elsewhere' and from before.[5]

Ashis Nandy and Partha Chatterjee write that India is neither Western nor "the antithesis of Western man". Pursuing the critique, Chatterjee notes that anti-colonialists are still dominated by European post-Enlightenment rationalist discourse. Yet if the origin of rationalist discourse was not confined to the West – because the West has always had fluid borders given imperialism and taken what it wants – then there is no complete opposition or negation to begin with. The West may be everywhere, but then so is the East, although not power-filled. The East and West are not 'ruptured', but are interconnected "in a seamless continuum in the neocolonial world".[6] Chatterjee says that nationalist thought is both imitative and hostile, but I wonder how he knows who exactly is imitating who.[7]

The African-American author Richard Wright described himself as having a split identity. "I'm black. I'm a man of the West ... I see and understand the non- or anti-Western point of view." He wrote of his double vision as a product of being Negro in a white Christian Western society. Though Western, in his writing he he is critical of the West because white men of the West colonized "colored humanity" in Asia and Africa.[8] He is in constant dialogue with the West, from the West and against the West. And this is not one and the same as saying that his origins are of the West. The West becomes invisible and hypervisible by erasing alternate dialogues. Such universalization smothers alternative memories and possibilities.

Amartya Sen asks us to review plural notions of freedom and tolerance 'elsewhere', like in Confucianism and Buddhism. "The valuing of freedom is not confined to one culture only, and the Western traditions are not the only ones that prepare us for a freedom-based approach to social understanding."[9] There are cross-cultural influences to be understood beyond the opposition West/non-West. The phrasing East/-non-East shifts the standard, but not the oppositional bordering of these locations. Language needs to recognize the mobility of democratic ideas from 'elsewheres' and back; and to the West and back again.

Patriarchal Colonialism and Its 'Others'

Historical liberal democratic theory sidelined all women and all slaves through officiated silences. The racialized system of patriarchal privilege was constructed, by its absence, into the bourgeois theory of the times. The episteme of racialized patriarchy was articulated in racialized voids. Black women, given their slave status, were excluded as the 'other'; without rights. White women were not explicitly excluded from bourgeois rights, but were implicitly erased within the abstract construct of propertied and masculinist individualism.

Gender inequality was natural, and therefore normalized in this form of democratic theory. So was the slaves' right not to marry. The right to property had no status for the propertyless slave. Individuals – fictionalized and imagined as white propertied males – were free to choose who they would become: free to achieve their dreams. The fact that white women were ascribed their female status as mothers and wives; and Black women were ascribed their female slave status as breeders in forced-sex relations, had no bearing on bourgeois democratic rights. This visible invisibility is the epistemic of racialized patriarchy.[10]

Patriarchy reproduces a racist masculinity which denies Black women a status like white women, as mothers. As breeders, their children were sometimes taken from them and sold, other times, beaten and raped. They had none of the protection that white women expected, even if the protection was part myth. Patriarchy and racism – the racializing of sex and gender – intertwine in the non-class status of Black slave women and men. Democracy at this time naturalized racialized patriarchy thereby normalizing a white and masculinist system of power. White middle-class women were shunted from view to non-public spaces and Blacks were both oppressed and repressed in the master/slave relation.

The more naturalized the hierarchies of color/race and sex/gender seem, the less they need defense. The normalized hierarchies of the white patriarchal and Black slave family establish the naturalized category of "free white men". Then civilization, rationality, and citizenship are written from this stance; some people are just written out of history.

Neither the 'aristocracy' of sex nor the 'aristocracy' of race are challenged; independence, opportunity, and individualism are normalized as exclusionary. The non-inclusivity of liberal democracy becomes self-perpetuating and embedded in anti-democratic facts. This closure leaves most of the people of the world 'othered' and outside. It is this dispossessed status that resists imperial empire. It is why so much of the world said no to the US making war on Iraq.

In late seventeenth century, John Locke was forced to challenge the prevailing patriarchal thought of his time, as a liberal democrat, in order to displace the dependent father-son relation with the independent free-choosing individual. Bourgeois democracy demanded this shift, but only for the market, not the family. Locke did not extend his liberal/bourgeois view of self-determination to white women or to slaves. Locke also did not extend rights to the white poor, but supposedly they had chosen their own lot.

Thomas Hobbes and John Locke sanctioned human bondage of slaves despite their defense of the liberal democratic 'rights of man'. Hobbes accepted slavery as an inevitable part of power. Locke thought slavery vile and miserable yet saw Negroes as chattels and brutes. He did not protest the enslavement of Black Africans and accepted the slave expeditions of the Royal Africa Company.[11] He assisted in the formulation of colonial policies and even wrote the constitution for the state of South Carolina.

The African slave trade and West Indian plantations enjoyed their golden years during the so-called Age of Enlightenment.[12] This "monstrous inconsistency" has still not fully dislodged the fictional origins of democratic theory.[13] According to Susan Buck-Morss, the slavery of non-Europeans underwrote the economy of the West, "facilitating the global spread of Enlightenment ideas" which were in full contradiction with such practices. Slavery made possible the economy that promised freedom to all; the "discourse of freedom and the practice of slavery" lived side by side. J. J. Rousseau condemned the institution of slavery while ignoring "the millions of really existing, European-owned slaves"; and embraced the French revolution as freeing people from the "'slavery' of feudal inequities".[14] Despite Rousseau's inattention to the practices of slavery, he is described as a radical egalitarian and democrat. This is a mere prelude to his deepest wishes that all (white) men should be free citizens and all (white) women good wives and mothers. Slavery and the enslaved woman are once again silenced and repressed from view.

Buck-Morss challenges the dominant readings of Hegel that say his master/slave dialectic was simply a metaphor to describe the human condition. She instead argues that his master/slave dialectic was based in fact, in learning from real slavery; that he knew about real slaves revolting against real masters; that eighteenth century Europeans were thinking about the Haitian revolution.[15] But Hegel does not write in critique of Black slavery. When he writes of world history he assumes that non-Europeans – American Indians, Africans, and Asians – are less human than Europeans. He assumes that the "temperate zone" provides the climatic conditions for human freedom and the world's history. He justifies colonialism and imperialism on the basis of European "civilization".[16]

I read Hegel from the places 'elsewhere' that he was looking towards. He saw a universal desire for freedom from these locations. Haiti, as a site, dialogically re-routes Enlightenment theory. Sites of human resistance pluralize the meaning of universal. Polyversal understandings of freedom were nurtured from multiple places although the domination of 'indebtedness' narrows the viewing. A polyversal viewing "rescues the idea of universal human history from a narrative of white domination."[17]

Many feminisms have developed out of the tension that promises individuals their freedom of choice and limits women to their non-choices as female. Some of these feminisms are built from a recognition that individual women are defined as part of a sexual class, which is also racialized, which demands more than liberal individualism to remedy the circumstance. And there are also "other-than-Western" formulations of these feminisms. Neither global capitalism with its racialized patriarchal underside, nor the Bush administration with its war talk, make these multiple forms of feminisms easy to see, or appreciate.

North America and Slavery

Tocqueville wrote of America as a frontier of European civilization. Indians were savages but also 'good'. A frontiersman is quoted as telling Tocqueville that he is not afraid of the Indians, that "they are worth more than we, if we have not brutalized them by our liquors, poor creatures". And Tocqueville also notes that this frontiersman prefers "the Indians to their compatriots, without however acknowledging them as equals".[18] Tocqueville never quite does so either.

Savagery was used as an "ideological justification for colonial appropriation of non-European territories, particularly in the Americas".[19] The Native Americans had to be denied their rightful place in order for colonialism to go forward. This was done despite the facts. Columbus noted in his journal the "open nature and goodness" of these people. He writes: "Of anything they have, if you ask them for it, they never say no; rather they invite the person to share it, and show as much love as if they were giving their hearts ..." In a letter written after the loss of the *Santa Maria*, he describes the Arawaks as a "loving people without covetousness". This did nothing to keep the natives safe from harm or exploitation. Less than one third survived the Spaniards and Columbus.[20]

Meanwhile Native Americans were becoming Indians, a "distinct people" and homogenized as such. Shortly before the American Revolution, Native Americans were entering the category "people of color" as they became connected by the colonists with slavery. Colonial law "turned native tribal citizens into Indians, people of color, and sometimes Negroes". According to Scott Malcomson these categories acquired stable meanings as synonyms for slave.[21] This process of racializing expresses the complexly contradictory politics of the American revolutionary period. White colonists demanded independence and self-determination for themselves during the peak period of the African slave trade into North America. Black slaves entered North America full force after the American Revolution. The anticolonialist revolutionary period parallels this increase of slaves into the colonies. The colonies obtained their independence while using slave labor.[22]

There are contradictory voices to hear during this period. Governor Dunmore of Virginia offered freedom to the "bondmen of his enemies", and this was read by slaves as a promise of freedom even though Dunmore withheld signing a bill against the slave trade. Negroes flocked to Dunmore for "the same love of liberty for which the colonists avowedly broke with the mother country". Yet Negroes – boys and old men who could not bear arms – were excluded. Each of the states had their individual policies on freed Blacks and slaves entering the military. In 1776 George Washington suggested that free Negroes who had already served in the army be re-enlisted, but no other colored volunteers should be accepted. Massachusetts passed an act, also in 1776, to exclude "Negroes, Indians, and mulattoes" from further serving in the military. John Adams worried that there were already too many Negroes in the Massachusetts militia. Benjamin Harrison and Ben Franklin decided to "reject all Negroes, bond or free". "Lunatics, idiots and Negroes" were exempted from pledging to "oppose British hostilities with arms".[23]

Slaves were feared by whites, and also seen as the property of someone else. The federal army became more selective along these racialized lines than local militias. Virginia left a door slightly open to the free Negro; otherwise the Negro-populated South was like the North in making military service white. As time progressed, the continental Congress took steps against the foreign slave trade. In Massachusetts, agitation against the slave trade began ten years before the Revolutionary War. In part this was due to the discourse of 'freedom' defining this period, and in part to the fact that there was a surplus of slaves in North American markets.

Although the earliest draft of the Declaration of Independence had a statement condemning the Crown for the slave trade – this was dropped to ease the concerns of slaveowners. Nevertheless, the universal claim, of "liberty and freedom for all" was taken to heart by slaves and abolitionists. Thomas Jefferson believed that the Negro was mentally inferior to the white man.[24] He thought this inferiority was "fixed in nature".[25] He argued that "to free Negroes was like abandoning children".[26] Being against the slave trade was not one and the same with being antiracist. Many who were critical of slavery still did not think that Blacks were equal with whites. Being an abolitionist was not equivalent to believing in racial equality.

At that point in time, most Blacks were slaves but some were free. Many were in the army, a few acted as spies, some did labor necessary to the war by felling trees, blowing up bridges, and making munitions. After the war many loyalists wanted their slaves back. Negroes who went with the British were shipped to the West Indies, Canada, and England. Those owned by loyalists or British subjects remained slaves.[27]

At the start, the American Revolution was not an all-white affair. Five men died at the Boston Massacre, and, according to John Adams, the first killed was a runaway slave – "a Negro with Indian blood". But the story of a Negro slave who stood against British power and opened the hostilities between Britain and the colonies is not one often told. Furthermore, within ten months after Lexington and Concord, most Negroes were excluded from further military service, and not heard of again.[28]

Tom Paine's was one of a few white voices that spoke openly against British colonialism and slavery. He wrote against England as an evil monarchy established in hereditary rule; he argued that America must separate and find independence from the mother country's selfishness, that "we need to go abroad for nothing" and should not be "cheated into slavery" as a British subject. For Paine, independence requires hostility to colonial dependency; and reconciliation is therefore impossible. Slavery does not remain a metaphor for colonialism but is specifically named as an unnatural and "uncivilized savage practice".[29] Slavery contradicts "justice and humanity". "Slave traders are devils; only the slave is the proper owner of his freedom."[30] Paine embraces the natural rights of all mankind; that rights are not simply local, but universal.[31] In the end, America turned its back on Paine and his more inclusive notion of democracy.

Science Fictions and Racialized Slavery

The slave trade was already in process when scientific claims of racial inferiority were called upon to justify it. Racial prejudice was thereby neutralized as factual: as though the central issues of race are 'empirical' anatomically, physiologically, and zoogeographically.[32] In *The System of Nature*, written in 1735, Carl von Linné (Carolus Linnaeus) articulates the hierarchical order of nature that he claims structures race. White supremacy simply exists because it is in the original ordering of men. The "constant and uniform difference of white supremacy" is justified by this very reading. This solipsistic thinking is created through accounts like: "Negroes are born white apart from their genitals and a ring around the navel, which are black." Then color supposedly spreads throughout the body according to climate.[33]

Immanuel Kant and David Hume both authorize the racialized standpoint of their day that Negroes were naturally inferior to whites. Hume states that there never was "a civilized nation of any other complexion than white". Kant believed that geography played a key role in deciphering racial meaning. In *Physical Geography* Kant writes that "humanity is at its greatest perfection in the race of the whites"; and the Negroes are far below them.[34] The Negro, found in dry hot locations, was well suited to this climate and grew strong, fleshy, "lazy, soft and dawdling". Physio-geography pretends to know what it knows. Racism is neutralized through science fiction.

Whites say that nature shows that Blacks are inferior, lesser than whites. This natural inferiority is used to justify the use of Black slaves and their labor. Blacks get written out of humanity by whites and their pretend science which seems to reappear in conservative moments. Biology is destiny. Geography is biology. Humanity is biologically determined. Humanity is white.

Imperial Democracy and the Slave Trade

The Portuguese, Dutch, French, British, and Spanish brought enslaved Africans from West Africa to the new world from the sixteenth through to the nineteenth century. It is hard to know how many people's lives were devastated by slavery in this period. After all, no one was counting. Some historians believe at least 15 million people were enslaved during this time. Sometimes, it is guessed that approximately 530,000 slaves were imported in the pre-Revolutionary period in America, while other historians think this slave trade affected 1,500,000.[35] Slavery remained a universal practice in the West Indies through the American Revolution.[36] There was no antislavery literature in France prior to the eighteenth century. Neither Montesquieu nor Voltaire challenged the practice.[37] Although the bestial practices of slave life were evident for anyone who chose to see them, colonialism as a discourse and a practice normalized slave life.

The history of different slaveries tells a disconnected story of human sorrow. The French West Indies supplied a huge market for slaves both inside and outside Europe.[38] The French Revolution and slave emancipation in Haiti are two very different-colored sides of a similar process. In Cuba, slave codes sanctioned flogging, stocks, shackles, and chains. By the mid- to late-eighteenth century Cuba had become a sugar economy dependent on its slave labor and plantation system, despite keen pressure on Spain, Portugal, and Britain to end the slave trade.[39] In the mid-seventeenth century the British captured Jamaica for the sole purpose of sugar production. By this time the Spaniards had already wiped out the indigenous people, and Jamaica became what Orlando Patterson calls "a monstrous distortion of human society". By the early eighteenth century, Jamaica was dependent on a largely mono-crop sugar-based system. But by 1822, when the price of sugar dropped, the abolition movement took hold. By 1834 the official end of slavery was sealed, but the system had already collapsed.[40]

The racially constructed imagery of African 'savagery' was used to defend the slave practices of colonialism and imperialism. Slavery was justified as a civilizing practice towards 'savages'. The civilized West would free Africa with its knowledgeable practices. Yet slaveholders knew better, as many of them in the colonies feared black rage if slavery were to end. These same colonists fought against the abolition of slavery because they thought it would lead to a bloodbath. Such fear is often a part of imperial rule. Exclusionary principles established in the eighteenth century continue at the core of US imperial democracy today. Racialized exclusions are modernized and updated to new racial 'others', without fully displacing the site of enslaved Blacks. And the US continues to parade as the civilizing force against evil.

The African slave trade came to an end over a protracted period of time because its institutionalized function was diminishing due to economic changes. The economic and legal demise of slavery as a practice, however, was no clear-cut linear process. Nor did all local areas respond similarly to antislavery rhetoric, or new law. Slavery was abolished in the French empire in 1794 and then reinstated, for twenty more years, by Napoleon. French policies were responsible for much of the racist depiction of Africans in European culture through this period.[41] By the 1660s, slavery had become the dominant form of labor; French wealth in the Caribbean camouflaged this wickedness. Enslaved peoples were treated as though they were subhuman, or nonhuman, and were written out of the human imaginings for freedom and equality.[42]

It is not fully possible to 'really' see or know slavery, as it was. Too little is documented and documentation is too removed from slavery's despicable practices. Slavery, as a normalized colonial practice, still 'others' Africa. Western slavery demands an individuated truth-telling. This telling can then be used to rewrite the pain and humiliation of the enslaved to find the humanity and democratic possibilities silenced.

Orlando Patterson sees the need for truth-telling somewhat similarly. He writes that it is the domination inherent in slavery that gives rise to the concept of freedom itself. "Before slavery people simply could not have conceived of the thing we call freedom."[43] Slaves put an ultimate value on freedom and would jump from a ship into "shark-filled waters" rather than live without it. Although Patterson believes that some people deny others their freedom, "no one dares deny its virtue". Yet Patterson appears to identify freedom as a peculiarly Western idea; although some notion of freedom exists elsewhere, he says, it remains unarticulated as such.[44]

The Sexualizing of Enslaved Women

Specifying slavery means seeing that the enslaved were both male and female. And although both shared an horrific and sometimes "deformed equality" of exploitation and oppression, this equality does not mean sameness or identity.[45] The sexual relations of slavery bespeak complicated interracial moments because sex was very often extorted as a key pattern of enslavement. Sexuality is already racialized so slavery operates within this webbed structuring of power. Ronald Hyam writes in *Empire and Sexuality* that sex is at the heart of racism; that white men's fear of black men's access to white women is at the core of white supremacy. Both copulation and concubinage express white men's obsession with the "super penis of black men".[46] We see the "white children of slavery"as a documentation of the sexual side of slavery.[47] This defines the practice of slavery as both racialized and sexual brutality, with incredible consequences for enslaved black women, and for their relations with free white women.

Sexual exploitation is at the heart of colonialism, imperialism, and global capitalism. Each economic system has its particular historically specified sexualized economic mode. Rape has long been a part of nationalist and colonialist capture. Rape of Black enslaved women was a usual and ordinary practice for white slavemasters. It continues to function as symbolic of conquest and nation building. During World War Two the Japanese military provided their troops with Korean, Chinese, Taiwanese, Filipino, and Vietnamese sexual slaves as part of its doctrine of military control.[48] Serb rape camps were established during the Bosnian war as part of the nationalist policy of misogynist ethnic cleansing.[49] Today's globalization offers sex trafficking as central to tourism.

Hortens Spillers sees the captive, enslaved body as living with "crimes against the flesh". Slavery is an "hieroglyphics of the flesh". She unveils a silenced history of the sexual violations of captive females and their rage against their oppressors. For Spillers, enslaved women are "unprotected female flesh"; their female bodies are "ungendered" as such; unprotected unlike the white woman's. Black women's femininity has no sacredness in slavery. Instead there is an "open exchange of female bodies in the raw". The enslaved woman is dispossessed; she stands outside the established symbolics of (white) female gender.[50]

Despite slave women's horrid treatment they fought back with whatever means they had. They used natural abortion methods when they could, against nonconsensual sex. Slaves like Harriet Jacobs ran away and hid under floorboards for years to avoid sexual abuse. Kimberly Springer notes that slave women resisted gender oppression and gendered violence whenever possible; Springer sees these early acts of defiance as an unrecorded 'first wave' of feminism. Black women's activism, along with anti-slavery and anti-lynching campaigns, spotty and disorganized as it might have been, predates the usually recognized beginnings of US (white) feminism.[51]

The sexual dynamics of slavery encode the racialized system of bondage with a particular heritage of violence. This heritage uncovers a different notion of gender than that which is expressed in the protectionist masculinist fantasies of white men towards white women. Black enslaved women were the vehicle of sexual freedom for white men which allowed white men free sexual rein towards them. This freedom openly contrasts with, but also simultaneously silences, white men's notions of white woman's chasteness. This history is a story of white men's desire for and violence towards Black slave women. A Black slave woman had no legal standing and as such she could not be 'officially' raped. She could be violated with no recourse available to her because neither her body nor her soul had legal status.

Adrienne Davis calls this forced sexual labor of enslaved women the "sexual economy of slavery". For her, only enslaved women were forced to labor continually across established gender boundaries of field hand and concubine. They were caught in a ferocious system of "brutal gender subordination", without any of the rights of white women. And they gave birth to enslaved children because the fathers of this forced sex were unknown to law.[52]

Davis names slavery as a racialized sexual economy, "a racial economics of sexual relationships". Yet, there is no 'official' recognition of these sexual relationships in slavery. Marriage itself was an exclusionary institution, which for almost two centuries did not allow slaves to marry. Marriage, in this instance, is racialized as white, as it is gendered in favor of the husband. Davis finds the compelling story of interracial sex in slavery in the legal attempts of white men to transfer their wealth to formerly enslaved Black women and their children. These property transfers raise issues of affection between the races that cannot be entirely grasped by the exploitation/rape model. These types of sexual families reflect the complex interracial realities of slavery – from rape to consent – and pose the difficult query of whether true affection can exist between a slavemaster and an enslaved woman.[53] But to limit the sexual economy of slavery to rape silences the subversive possibility of genuine interracial desire.[54]

For Davis, the sexual regulation of the Black woman/white man dyad creates access for the white man; the white woman/Black man dyad restricts and separates. Apartheid is the dynamic to keep Black men from white women; and access is the dynamic that makes Black women available to white men. Sexual exploitation is the end of the latter, while segregation is the concern of the former. Davis asks us to examine how when you "switch the gender" you "switch the reading" of miscegenation law. Slavery is then a system of sexual exploitation within a system of engendered racism.

Davis writes of the court case *State v. Celia*, which involved a woman called Celia who, bought as a slave at the age of fourteen, killed her master after five years of living with almost daily rape. Celia said that she killed Newsom as he was trying to rape her. Missouri law allowed for the use of deadly force if a woman was defending herself from sexual assault. But Davis makes clear that Celia was not granted status as a woman, only a slave. Although her sexual abuse was well-documented by others as well as herself, she was not allowed to charge her master for his crimes because at the time in Missouri, Blacks could not testify against whites in a court of law. Celia was his property; she was Black, he was white; he had access, she had no voice. This system of sexual racism allowed Celia to be found guilty, and hanged.[55]

W.E.B. DuBois writes of the "sexual chaos" that was always a possibility in slavery. He indicts the polygamy that resulted from the concubinage of Black women to white men, and the polyandry among Black women and selected Black men on plantations for breeding. Dubois speaks of the mixed blood that travels through enslaved peoples and the fact that masters sold their own children. There was no protection for the slave from "cruelty, lust, and neglect" or the intermingling of Black and white blood.[56]

Nell Irwin Painter describes the female rivalries that accrued between white and Black women through their relation to white men. Women of different races and classes became co-mothers and co-wives. The slave woman becomes a victim here in ways that the slave-owning woman did not. Yet white and Black women, and Black men, all shared deep resentment towards white men's access to Black women. White women, from their place, saw Black women as sexual competitors with a kind of equality, while Black men and women saw an extreme form of exploitation and oppression.[57]

Female slaves were used for their labor and for sex. And some of this sex was homosexual. Nell Irwin Painter writes that masters wanted and abused their enslaved men and boys, and mistresses their female slaves.[58] The submission and obedience demanded of slavery crossed all boundaries. Raping enslaved people was the ordinary outcome of the subhuman status of slave women and men. Because of that status, slavery must be seen as a spiritual agony and "soul murder" of those confined within it. The "family secrets of slave-owning households" was a part of the pattern of neglect, abuse, and horrific brutality.[59] The betrayal that many white women felt is positioned here against the exploitation and degradation of all slaves. So the simple exploitation model – focused on the color of labor – is too evasive and silencing of the fact that slavery was a sexed and raced abomination.

The sexual side of slavery spills everywhere – to punishment and beatings; to nudity on the auction block which was often read to mean promiscuity by the buyers. According to Deborah Gray White, one master was said to "rather paddle a female than eat when he was hungry".[60] Mothers were beaten in front of their children, and their children were beaten in front of their mothers, for the pleasure of masters and mistresses.

One can only wonder and try to imagine the psychic life of enslaved women. I know that their deep pain is not entirely approachable. These women were not considered to be a part of the weaker sex; nor did they do lesser work than male slaves. They were considered the equal of male laborers, and more so when they were pregnant. They did the labor of the plantation, and built incredible bonds between themselves and their families while doing so. They saw their children sold off to another plantation owner and sent away, not knowing what would become of them.

I wonder if their grief differentiated between their children. Did they grieve similarly knowing that some of these children were born from the unspeakable brutality of their own rape? There are too many questions not even asked given the multiple stories and complex narratives of this period. And even the stories told are spoken with compromise. Mary Prince, an ex-slave, writes as an abolitionist but knows she cannot make her sexual exploitation by her white master too stark for her readers. She is forced to speak in whispers.

Prince writes of floggings and whippings of naked bodies; sleeping in narrow stalls made more for cattle than humans; the horrible goodbyes that marked each slave's life; the savagery of her mistress. Yet her wrath is saved especially for her master. He would strip himself naked and order her to wash him in a tub of water. "This was worse to me that all the licks." He was 'indecent', with "no shame for his servants, no shame for his own flesh". Prince laments, sometimes opaquely, that no element of decency or modesty was shown to the slave: "men, women and children are exposed alike".[61]

The histories of slavery are most often cleansed of their sexual underside. Eugenia Jones Bacon, a writer from a prominent slave-owning family, writes a slave love story, but with no sex. Her main character is Lyddy, a beautiful young Black slave, who remains virtuous throughout, as if she "were a white woman". The fictional plot tells of a series of romantic trials and depicts slave life through the romance of Lyddy and Marlborough. It is a humanizing effort at seeing slavery, but completely impossible as a true story. Lyddy would never have been allowed protection of her female slave body; such virtue was not a choice for enslaved women.[62]

The story of interracial enforced sex reappears over again wherever gender and racial borders are being carved anew. This distorted history continues to misrepresent the relations of sex across the color line. Ida B. Wells thought this was very much the case at the height of Black men's lynching. So often Black men would be lynched for "rape of a white woman" when the accusation was simply an excuse to "get rid of Negroes who were gaining wealth and property". Lynching was a system of terrorization to keep Black men in their place, and to keep them from adultery with willing white women. Black men were not assaulting white women; rather, "illicit associations" between them were "bleaching a large percentage of the Negro race". Wells believed that Southerners had not gotten over their resentment that the Negro was no longer their plaything. Lynching was part of this anger, directed especially towards the illicit interracial sex of the time.[63]

Nell Painter asks us to revisit the feminist icon Sojourner Truth from inside these thoughts. Painter argues that Sojourner has become more symbol than real, more cleansed than messy; a Black woman that white feminists could more easily embrace. Painter argues that Sojourner was a northern slave, even though she is so often assumed to be from the South. That she did not have thirteen children as assumed. That she was more a reformist than a radical like Frances Harper, who most white women of the time were less ready to acknowledge. Painter also argues that Truth did not make the "Ar'n't I A Woman?" speech so often attributed to her by white feminists. Instead, Painter says that Sojourner has been turned into a hero, rather than an authentic Black woman. The symbolic imagery of Truth has displaced the complicated historical person. Given this, it should be expected that many silences surround the real Sojourner Truth. According to Painter, she hated her mistress Sally Dumont, and Painter asks us to consider whether this was not the case because Dumont sexually abused Sojourner. Truth directly says little because it is so 'unaccountable' and 'unnatural' that the 'uninitiated' would not believe her.[64] Once again there are whisperings to try and hear.

Bell hooks writes of the way that African-American women still today feel themselves standing on the auction block, with exposed bodies for sale to be exploited. Their history of shame and exposure and nakedness has given Black women a complicated dread of their own female flesh. She writes of this "inherited body image", of bondage, stripped, naked – for others. And hooks traces nineteenth-century Black female obsessions with bodily cleanliness, modesty, and the repression of the erotic … to the auction block.[65]

The sexual roots of slavery unsettle the borders of racialized identity. Interracial unions challenge the neatly constructed racial boundaries of colonial rule. Men of one race and class desiring women of another; and women of one race wanting women of another, destabilizes the racial exclusivity internal to racism as well as colonialism. Colonialism depends on clear designations between the colonial subject and metropolitan citizen. Interracial unions challenge the physiological fixity of race and with it the cleanly marked divides necessary to imperial control.[66] When white German men married women of color in their colonies before World War One, such marriages were looked upon with disfavor. German men were not allowed to pass on citizenship to these wives and children. There were marriage bans on mixed marriage and race mixing given the need for clear racial divides between colonizer and colonized.[67]

Slavery puts in view a site of resistance alongside exploitation as enslaved people fought for their freedom despite barbarism. No Black slave totally existed inside slavery because their own humanity pulled them outside, and stood against their debasement and defilement. The contented slave is a myth, one that attempts to salve the conscience of masters, colonizers, and imperialists. Enslaved women were raped by masters, were raped in front of their children, watched as their children were raped, watched as their lovers were raped, and yet also had consensual sex with other slaves as well as with masters. Out of this horrid sexual vulnerability they fought for themselves and their children. They knew their enslavement was wrong because their bodies were theirs to own and control. Their own human yearnings told them this was so.

The silences of slavery have written an inhuman history of humanity itself. Black slavery must be remembered to remind the West that a liberatory democratic theory is possible, and it is one which disallows the racializing and sexualizing of humanity.

Notes

1. David Theo Goldberg, *Racist Culture* (Cambridge, MA: Blackwell, 1993), p. 165.
2. David Brion Davis, *The Problem of Slavery in Western Culture* (Ithaca: Cornell University Press, 1966), pp. 30, 31.
3. David Theo Goldberg, *Racist Culture.*, pp. 1, 119.

4. Meyda Yegenoglu, *Colonial Fantasies* (New York: Cambridge University Press, 1998), p. 11.
5. Mary Louise Pratt, *Imperial Eyes* (New York: Routledge, 1992), pp. 91, 138.
6. Radhika Mohanram, *Black Body: Women, Colonialism, and Space* (Minneapolis: University of Minnesota Press, 1999), pp. 187, 191.
7. Partha Chatterjee, *Nationalist Thought and the Colonial World* (Minneapolis: University of Minnesota Press, 1986), pp. 1, 2. Also see Ashis Nandy, *The Intimate Enemy* (New York: Oxford University Press, 1983).
8. Richard Wright, *White Man, Listen* (New York: Anchor Books, 1957), pp. 1, 47.
9. Amartya Sen, *Development as Freedom* (New York: Anchor Books, 1999), pp. 235, 243.
10. See Zillah Eisenstein, *The Radical Future of Liberal Feminism* (New York: Longman, 1981); and Zillah Eisenstein, *Hatreds: Racialized and Sexualized Conflicts in the 21st Century* (New York: Routledge, 1996) for fuller discussion of these points.
11. David Goldberg, *Racist Culture*, pp. 27, 28. Also see Susan Buck-Morss, "Hegel and Haiti", *Critical Inquiry*, Summer, 2000, p. 826; and John Locke, *Two Treatises of Government*, Book 1, Chapter 1 (London: Cambridge University Press, 1960).
12. David Brion Davis, *The Problem of Slavery in Western Culture*, p. 391.
13. Winthrop Jordan, *White Over Black* (New York: W.W. Norton, 1968), p. 289.
14. Susan Buck-Morss, "Hegel and Haiti", pp. 820, 822, 830, 836.
15. Ibid., p. 845.
16. Emmanuel Chukwudi Eze, *Race and the Enlightenment* (Oxford: Blackwell, 1997), pp. 112, 149. Also see: *Hegel's Philosophy of Right* (New York: Oxford University Press, 1952).
17. Susan Buck-Morss, "Hegel and Haiti", pp. 843, 865.
18. Alexis de Tocqueville, "Fortnight in the Wilderness", in George Wilson Pierson, *Tocqueville in America* (Baltimore: Johns Hopkins Press, 1996), pp. 255, 256.
19. Peter Hulme, "The Spontaneous Hand of Nature: Savagery, Colonialism and the Enlightenment", in Peter Hulme and Ludmilla Jordanova, eds., *The Enlightenment and its Shadows* (New York: Routledge, 1990), p. 17.
20. S. Lyman Tyler, *Two Worlds: The Indian Encounter with the European, 1492–1509* (Salt Lake City: University of Utah Press, 1988), pp. 54, 84, 180.
21. Scott L. Malcomson, *One Drop of Blood: The American Misadventure of Race* (New York: Farrar Straus Giroux, 2000), p. 38.
22. David Brion Davis, *The Problem of Slavery in Western Culture*, pp. ix, 8, 256.
23. Benjamin Quarles, *The Negro in the American Revolution* (Chapel Hill: University of North Carolina Press, 1961), pp. 15, 16, 17, 32.
24. Ibid., pp. 18, 40, 42, 187.
25. Emmanuel Eze, *Race and the Enlightenment*, p. 95. As quoted from Thomas

Jefferson, "Notes on the State of Virginia", 1787.

26. David Brion Davis, *The Problem of Slavery in the Age of Revolution, 1770–1823* (Ithaca: Cornell University Press, 2002), p. 179.
27. Benjamin Quarles, *The Negro in the American Revolution*, pp. 67, 200.
28. Ibid., p. 13.
29. Thomas Paine, "Common Sense", in Michael Foot and Isaac Kramnick, eds., *Thomas Paine Reader* (New York: Penguin, 1987), pp. 74, 103, 105–6.
30. Thomas Paine, "African Slavery in America", in Foot and Kramnick, eds., *Thomas Paine Reader*, pp. 52, 53.
31. Thomas Paine, "Common Sense", in Foot and Kramnick, eds., *Thomas Paine Reader*, p. 66.
32. Phillip Sloan, "The Idea of Racial Degeneracy in Buffon's "Histoire Naturelle", in Harold Pagliaro, ed., *Racism in the Eighteenth Century*, vol. 3 (Cleveland: Case Western Reserve University, 1973), p. 310.
33. Emmanuel Eze, *Race and the Enlightenment*, pp. 11, 24, 60.
34. Ibid., pp. 33, 63, 49. Also see: Immanuel Kant, *Observations on the Feeling of the Beautiful and Sublime* (Berkeley: University of California Press, 1960).
35. Philip Curtin, *The Atlantic Slave Trade* (Madison: University of Wisconsin Press, 1969), p. 5.
36. David Lowenthal, "Free Colored West Indians: A Racial Dilemma", in Harold Pagliaro, *Racism in the Eighteenth Century*, p. 335.
37. William B. Cohen, *The French Encounter with Africans* (Bloomington: Indiana University Press, 1980), pp. 35, 131, 134.
38. C. L. R. James, *The Black Jacobins* (New York: Vintage Books, 1963), pp. 12, 174, 360.
39. Franklin W. Knight, *Slave Society in Cuba during the Nineteenth Century* (Madison: University of Wisconsin Press, 1970), pp. 48, 50, 58, 76. Also see Eric Williams, *From Columbus to Castro: The History of the Caribbean 1492–1969* (New York: Harper and Row, 1970).
40. Orlando Patterson, *The Sociology of Slavery* (Teaneck: Fairleigh Dickinson University Press, 1969), pp. 9, 29.
41. William Cohen, *The French Encounter With Africans*, pp. 180–95, 207, 280–82.
42. Sterling Stuckey, *Slave Culture* (New York: Oxford University Press, 1987), p. 285.
43. Orlando Patterson, *Slavery and Social Death* (Cambridge: Harvard University Press, 1982), p. 340.
44. Orlando Patterson, *Freedom in the Making of Western Culture* (New York: Basic Books, 1991), pp. ix, 1, 42.
45. Angela Davis, "Reflections on the Black Woman's Role in the Community of Slaves", *Black Scholar*, vol. 3, no. 4 (December 1979); and her *Women, Race, and Class* (New York: Random House, 1981).
46. Ronald Hyam, *Empire and Sexuality* (New York: Manchester University Press, 1990), pp. 203, 204.

47. Nell Irvin Painter, "Of Lily, Linda Brent, and Freud", in Catherine Clinton, ed., *Half Sisters of History* (Durham: Duke University Press, 1994), pp. 97, 101.
48. Yoshimi Yoshiaki, *Comfort Women* (New York: Columbia University Press, 2000).
49. Zillah Eisenstein, *Hatreds: Racialized and Sexualized Conflicts in the 21st Century*, especially chapters 2 and 3.
50. Hortens Spillers, "Mama's Baby, Papa's Maybe: An American Grammar Book", *Diacritics*, vol. 17, no. 2 (Summer 1987), pp. 67, 68, 73, 75, 80.
51. Kimberly Springer, "Third Wave Black Feminism?", *Signs*, vol. 27, no. 41 (Summer 2002), pp. 1061, 1062.
52. Adrienne Davis, "'Don't let nobody bother yo' principle': The 'Sexual Economy' of American Slavery", in Sharon Harley, ed., *Sister Circle: Black Women Represent Work* (New York: Rutgers University Press, forthcoming), pp. 2, 6, 8, 19, 23. Also see Sharon Harley and the Black Women and Work Collective, ed., *Sister Circle: Black Women and Work* (New Jersey: Rutgers University Press, 2002).
53. Adrienne Davis, "The Private Law of Race and Sex: An Antebellum Perspective", *Stanford Law Review*, vol. 51, no. 2 (January, 1999), pp. 229, 237, 246, 247.
54. Tina Andrews, *Sally Hemings: An American Scandal* (New York: Malibu Press, 2001), pp. 3, 38.
55. Adrienne D. Davis, "Loving Against the Law: The History and Jurisprudence of Interracial Sex", unpublished paper, presented at the Cornell History Colloquium, March 2001, p. 8.
56. W.E.B. DuBois, *Black Reconstruction in America* (New York: Russell and Russell, 1935, 1963), pp. 11, 35, 44.
57. Nell Irvin Painter, "Of Lily, Linda Brent, and Freud", pp. 100, 103.
58. Ibid., p. 96.
59. Nell Irvin Painter, "Soul Murder and Slavery: Toward A Fully Loaded Cost Accounting", in Linda K. Kerber, Alice Kessler-Harris, and Kathryn Kish Sklar, eds. *US History as Women's History* (Chapel Hill: The University of North Carolina Press, 1995), pp. 129-30, 134, 146.
60. Deborah Gray White, *Ar'n't I a Woman?* (New York: W.W. Norton, 1999), pp. 9, 32, 33, 36, 51, 120.
61. Mary Prince, *The History of Mary Prince* (New York: Penguin, 1831), pp. 11, 16, 19, 11, 24, 25, 37.
62. Eugenia Jones Bacon, *Lyddy: A Tale of the Old South* (Athens: University of Georgia Press, 1998).
63. Ida B. Wells, *Crusade for Justice, The Autobiography of Ida B. Wells* (Chicago: University of Chicago Press, 1970), pp. 64, 69, 70, 137.
64. Nell Painter, *Sojourner Truth: A Life, A Symbol* (New York: Norton, 1996), pp. 14, 16, 164, 287.
65. bell hooks, "Naked Without Shame: A Counter-Hegemonic Body Politic", in

Ella Shoat, ed., *Talking Visions* (New York: MIT Press, 1998), pp. 65–7, 69.

66. Ann Laura Stoler, "Sexual Affronts and Racial Frontiers", in Frederick Cooper and Ann Laura Stoler, eds., *Tensions of Empire* (Berkeley: University of California Press, 1997), pp. 198, 208, 225.
67. Lora Wildenthal, "Race, Gender, and Citizenship in the German Colonial Empire", in Cooper and Stoler, eds., *Tensions of Empire*, pp. 263, 267–8.

5 Colonialism and Difference: The 'Othering' of Alternative Democracies

India is described as the most populated democracy despite the caste system and the incredible poverty of millions. This democratic status is bestowed on India because of its colonial history with British rule. But there is another, more silenced story of Indian democracy to be told here: that of an anticolonial critique of the materialism and imperialism of the West. This critique, articulated by Mahatma Gandhi as well as by Bengali theorists, locates anticolonial struggles as an alternate site of democratic theory. The understanding of democracy of Gandhi, Tagore and others is written from below; from the underside of imperial power. This positioning means that they see and know differences/diversity as part of the very meaning of humanity.

The US today is awash in diversity language, but in a non-progressive, non-egalitarian form. Multiculturalism has become a manipulated discourse to enable global capitalism and neoliberalism. Corporatist needs span across nations, and this multiplies the numbers of people of color that are put in view. When the entire globe is the corporate site, whites become a minority. Imperial leaders like Bush and Cheney are poised to retain and protect white dominance, despite dissident voices from 'elsewhere'. They re-racialize the formulations of democracy through the US wars of/on 'terror'.

At this juncture, democracy has been downsized at home and abroad and designed in privatized form. This neoliberal model extends from the US, to Russia, to Egypt and on, and on. The neoliberals have succeeded in equating individual freedom with self-sufficiency and success. Diversity is marketed while protecting the core structures of white privilege with its classed and gendered structural divides.

Today multiple thousands of Indians live in the US, creating a great variety of different communities. Mumbai and Calcutta exist in Queens. Bharati Mukherjee writes that "we're a billion people, but divided into so many thousands or millions of classifications that we have trouble behaving as a monolith".[1] The population of the world has always been diverse. It is not as though new kinds of people in new colors have sprouted, but the visibility of this multiplicity in sites of power is new. The fictional accountings of US history and Enlightenment discourse never made sense to those who were dispossessed in these official renderings.

Bengali theorists celebrated their 'difference' from within colonial rule. And England elided and constructed racial homogeneity, from this difference, to create its empire. Akbar (1542–1605), the third-generation Mogul emperor of India, was known for his religious tolerance and his embrace of difference, especially to non-Muslims. He issued prohibitory edicts against *sati* (the forced burning of a widow alongside her dead husband) and the marriage of pre-pubescent girls, condemned slavery and the slave trade, and he promoted social reform.[2] Neglect, however, led to the loss and destruction of Akbar's writing and records so that it is hard to document much of this *before*.[3]

The shifts and changes from before to now involve 'more' of everything. There is more transnational exploitation, more people moving from one border to another, more wealth for a few, more poverty for the many, more variety of people living in any one locale. But the 'more' of everything does not make things more creatively diverse, or more inclusively viewable, because power is more concentrated and narrowed. Neoliberals argue that power is available everywhere so that it exists nowhere in oppressive form. Yet individuals have power so the structural limitations of power are made invisible. And if structural power is invisible there is supposedly no limit to one's opportunities. There is no racism; then there are only individuals, each to be blamed for themselves.

If differences are simply individual and not structurally enforced, then diversity is easily attained without a restructuring of power. But racial diversity remains unequal because of the silenced inequalities of before and now. The democratic promissory is limited by historical inequalities embedded in the present; the privileged white center remains in place. Transnational globalization remains a gendered and racialized structure of power which disallows equality. Globalization is twenty-first century imperialism. Diversity, as a power-filled discourse, silences the problem of inequality and modernizes colonialist discourse. Multiracial talk enhances the new fictions and distortions of global capitalism and its rhetoric of democracy. But there are other counter-stories of democratic diversity that help to indict this neoliberal opportunist embrace.

There are newly uncovered visors for people living in the US since 9/11, if they wish to use them, to see the discontent of peoples 'elsewheres'. US hegemonic foreign policy with its thuggery is not good for democracy anywhere. Embedded in these voices of resistance is a more plural and encompassing vision of democracy, than the West acknowledges. Similar voices have existed before in the anticolonialist viewpoints of Gandhi and Bengali theorists. Let us look here to see a direct contestation and complex dialogue with and against Western democratic promissories. Colonialism of the West is indicted for its exclusivity of difference and its undelivered promises to the masses of humanity.

Polyversal Universals

It is theorists and activists in India, not England, who pondered a notion of democracy which stretched to encompass the notion of human totality: a vision of unity in diversity, rather than sameness. Multiples, not singularities, define much of Indian life and thought. Devi, one of the most revered Indian goddesses, is represented in a myriad of forms. She is diverse and one at the same time. She remains one and many, and one in the many, and many in all the parts of the one.[4] A divine absolute exists but in plural forms; so likewise does the spiritual freedom of the individual as he or she finds universal connection. Individuality is not in opposition to one's universal meaning. Singularity and plurality are not positioned against each other.

For B.C. Pal, the individual is a synonym for the universal. For Mahatma Gandhi and Sri Aurobindo, human unity is a struggle of the self but the self is always connected to the nation, or its universal meaning.[5] They criticize both capitalism for its competitiveness and socialism for its enforced social harmony. Neither gives room for a self that is both free and in harmony with others. The self reveals the tension between individuality and community, between freedom and equality. This self as supreme and noncompetitive and as connected and not derivative of the totality expresses a key tension for an other-than-simply Westernized democracy.

Eighteenth- and nineteenth-century writings of the Indian renaissance are anticolonialist; the nation is problematized as othering the self. Rabindranath Tagore wrote that any special culture that is disconnected from the universal is not true at all. He writes: "I am not against one nation in particular, but against the general idea of all nations." For him, India must create a "unity in diversity".[6] He prefers an "other-than-Western" universalism to an anti-Western nationalism. There is a spirituality in this thought – much like Gandhi's concern for the soul. But this is not a simple religiosity that can be appreciated in Western guise.

The notion of an "other-than-Western" universalism bespeaks a notion of individuality that premises the individual as a member of several wholes. This rich pluralism is made up not of parts and wholes, but of wholes in the whole.[7] And these writings are preoccupied with freedom, because freedom and self-rule were denied in the colonial relation. One's freedom is defined by self-realization and social unity. These denials were structured by a colonialism that narrated a discourse of civilized rule, and democratic homilies. Gandhi, Tagore and Aurobindo's democratic imaginings are responses to colonial rule, and yet are not simply bounded by these constraints. Their democratic theoretical embrace of diversity required a different notion of individuality and unity which presumed fluidity and openness. They also articulate a notion of spirituality that is not easily decipherable in noncontinuous parts.

Western thought is often characterized as 'realist' and nonspiritual while Eastern thought is depicted as the opposite. The Western thought of Plato and Descartes is described as rational while Indian thought is said to be static. But Bengali theorists view the self as a mix of spirit and reason. The self is connected to the 'divine' in them. This sense of a larger spiritual life is a process of evolution and change.[8] Spirituality, which must be translated culturally, recognizes the connectedness of people's souls.

Spiritual thought, as a method of seeing, can provide representations that are falsely homogenizing. Bengali theorists do not explicitly exclude women from their democratic visionings, but they are too often silenced in these discourses. Women form the silenced backdrop against which identity is formulated for men. As such, women symbolically represent the community rather than the individual selves within the community. Women wear the sari and with it represent the nation. They are asked to be self-sacrificing loyal and faithful wives.[9] They are left to the loneliness and isolation of seclusion.[10] Boys and men are privileged while the realm of the sacred is woman-filled. Kali, the great goddess of primal energy, is considered "the 'forceful' form of the great goddess Durga". She destroys evil. Signifying a vision of the whole, Kali becomes Supreme and all powerful. She is one in herself, belonging to no man and representing divine feminine spirituality: the sacred as woman.[11]

Kali has endless knowable forms, although she is One. Her many manifestations and expressions are of one consciousness, and one meaning. Singularity and plurality are not separate coordinates, because one elucidates the other. Spiritually, women are one with life; they express a dynamic potency, as the cosmic womb. The woman's body both is a unity and embraces a diverse wholeness.[12] In contrast to Kali's spiritual power, 'real' women are expected to obey their husbands, and worship them before all else. The ideal woman is the ideal wife, and not Kali.[13] Diversity is expressed in the divine realm of Goddesses; not by women in everyday practice.

The Hindu patriarchal storyline is culturally specific and also utterly translatable. Woman is divine and pure *and* also treated as the 'other'. The silences of 'real' women's lives – their labor, their sexuality, their oppression – are uncovered and articulated by feminists in India.[14] The use of women as the symbol of nationhood, and as the protector of family virtue demands a structural critique of the patriarchal colonialism that reproduces gender differentiation and privilege. Feminisms in India develop this critique of masculinism in diverse cultural ways. This diversely unified critique of patriarchal privilege begins to express important anticolonial feminist dialogues.

The well-known Indian filmmaker Deepa Mehta defies the simplistic overarching language used to decipher women's lives. Her films seek to open and create multiple choices that individuate women while revealing the constraints of their experience. In her film *Fire* she carefully exposes the deadening disciplining of desire in women as well as in men. She exposes the fantasized family as a location of pain and loneliness and asks that women be free to choose whatever it is that they come to desire. This desire tells the story of lesbian lovers. Patriarchal oppression, though located in familialism in India in this instance, is translatable to other sites. It is a polyversal story that Mehta tells and one with rich local roots/routes. It is not surprising that her film *Earth*, which tells the story of India's partition, in antinationalist form, finds herself "missing home but not knowing where home is anymore".[15] She is a filmmaker who narrates stories of democracy – by opening choice while trying to ignore existing constraints – and has been called a traitor from all sides, inside and out of India, for doing so.

Gandhi's Democratic Visionings

For Gandhi the spirit of truth was all pervading and universal. He was committed to finding and living the truth and he came to believe in the process of militant nonviolence as a form of discovery.[16] This belief in *satyagraha* (nonviolence) was compelled by his focus on inner freedom; as a way towards finding national freedom, harmony, and social equality. Gandhi's struggle for self-awareness is wrapped up in the larger political struggles of his day. He believed that individuals must free themselves from the passivity of colonial domination. Gandhi therefore believed that individual liberation from fear was essential to national liberation as well.[17] The process of throwing off the domination of colonial subjugation is individually politicized and politically individualized because the individual identity of the colonized self has been so long denied.

Gandhi's formative years were spent in London and South Africa. where he experienced color prejudice rooted in Indians' slave labor.[18] Gandhi's ideas blended his different experiences and did not defer to geopolitical boundaries. He argued that there were no impassable barriers between East and West; that there was no such thing as Western or European civilization; that there was only modern civilization, which was purely material. For Gandhi, modern civilization was the problem, not Britain *per se*. "India's salvation consists in unlearning what she has learnt during the past fifty years."[19] However, Gandhi was more accepting of European 'civilization' in his youth. He passed the bar exam in England in 1891, and knew English law, but nothing of Indian jurisprudence. At this earlier point in his life he thought British rule had been beneficial to India.[20] Later, Gandhi shed his British suit and tie for the homespun cloth of India.

The individual and national struggles for freedom were tightly interwoven for Gandhi. A nation cannot be free before the individuals constituting it are themselves free. Personal self-rule and self-realization is attained through the examination and control of the self. Gandhi believed that he must be one of the "poorest of the poor" to truly gain this self-knowledge. Self-knowing can emanate from one's 'body-labor' – the manual labor necessary for earning one's livelihood.[21] This individual labor becomes a foundation for national liberation and independence. India's freedom struggle starts from within each person allowing for social reform and self-purification. This public and private process begins the journey towards freedom, towards *swaraj*.[22]

Gandhi's life was defined through the independence struggle of India as well as the internal strife between Muslims and Hindus, and caste and non-caste Indians. He was staunchly opposed to the partition which would demarcate India and Pakistan as separate nations, and he worked tirelessly against hateful exclusionary practices. Starting always with the self, he made his body a part of his political practice and often used fasting as an extraordinary attempt at bringing emotional attention to the bloodshed of his day. Fasting was his nonviolent weapon. Often when he fasted others found that they could not eat easily, or stay removed, knowing that he was "bearing responsibility for us all".[23] Through his body he brought extraordinary attention to the intimate politics of the self. Gandhi's body was a "body politic" because the self was *already* in dialogue with the nation.

It was Gandhi's common practice to touch physically anyone with whom he spoke in order to acknowledge his connection with them. Gandhi's siting of the body as his most visible and communal political instrument remained a powerful aspect of his anticolonialist stance. He was in a constant struggle to control his body and deny its bodily needs. He used his frail body as a symbolic weapon for peaceful dialogue. He cleansed his body through enemas, through fasts, through sexual denial. His private flesh stood as a public indictment against the imperial suited bodies of the men who ruled India.

Gandhi's politics embraces the body as the starting place for building a politics of truth. His truth could be discovered by freeing the mind and body; by purifying himself from the excesses of sexual desire and material wealth. After assisting in his wife Kasturbai's delivery of their fourth child Gandhi decided that he must free himself of his lust, and thereby free her from childbirth.[24] In 1906 Gandhi took a vow of abstinence, although without discussing this decision with Kasturbai.[25] He thought material simplicity and sexual denial would allow him to experience the "wholeness of humanity". For Gandhi, sexual repression curtails chaos and particularism. Repressed sexuality was a necessary element for revealing the process of nonviolence and inclusiveness. Gandhi's realization of a common humanness required an inclusive notion of identity which rejected violence and partiality.[26]

Gandhi had married at thirteen. According to his own admission, he lusted uncontrollably, at first, for his wife. He was horribly jealous and was "unbearably unjust" to her.[27] He was completely overbearing and controlling. He felt dominated by this lust and lack of control and knew he had to become "fairly free" of "the carnal appetite". But whilst Gandhi freed himself from desire, he also denied women their own sexual selves. He was against the use of contraceptives because sex, if not tied to reproduction, should be avoided. He viewed women not as sexual beings with their own desires, but as mothers, and as above sex, as such. He thought women should not have to meet men's sexual appetites; that they should have a right to deny men's pleasure; and that contraceptives made women too available to men's demands.[28] In Gandhi's rendering, women are pure and have no sexual desires of their own. No one can suffer more purely and nobly than a woman. Woman is the incarnation of *ahimsa*, meaning that she has infinite love and capacity for suffering. Women's lack of desire allows for a limitless power of truth.[29]

Gandhi's desexed woman is an equal partner to man. Woman has the same soul and potential as man. Man and woman are of equal rank but not identical: they supplement each other, while home life remains entirely the sphere of woman.[30] But this difference does not disable women as political activists. Gandhi depended on women, often more than men, to be the political actors in the struggle against colonialism. Most of his disciples in the ashrams were women. He depended on women to manufacture contraband salt and to picket foreign cloth and liquor shops. And he orchestrated the making of khadi – handspun home-loomed cotton cloth – by women. He named a woman to succeed him as head of the Indian National Congress.[31]

Gandhi's search for self-discovery and his deep belief in human freedom are articulated through his own struggle with his bodily needs and desires. This bodily start gives him a visor through which to glimpse inclusivity; what he calls a communal unity. The body is used to formulate a fuller embrace of the multiple challenges that define humanity. Originary aspects of political theory are expressed through the body as a visor for humanity's democratic desires. He stands against modern civilization's materialism; he stands against exclusionary identities of Muslim and Hindu; he desires a united India and a diverse universalism. His democracy is not simply Eastern spiritualism, nor is it simply anti-Western nationalism. He expresses differing and original fragments which dialogue with, and critique the officially pre-established *befores*.

Gandhi's body, although problematically desexed, is his powerful political site for inclusivity and truth. He rejects a notion of modernity that demands the exploitation of people. He chooses a notion of individuality that rejects crass materialism and human dependence. As such he provides a decisive vision of an anti-materialist "other-than-Western" democracy. But this vision must be rewritten to encompass the desire for sexual freedom and women's liberation alongside it.

Totality and Alternative Universalisms

In oppositional form, European thought is said to be about rights; Hindu thought is about evolution and evolving, about *dharma. Dharma* is concerned with reconciliation, rights with resistance; *dharma* demands self-abnegation, rights demand self-assertion; *dharma* focuses on collectivism, rights on individualism; *dharma* embraces synthesis, and rights antithesis. Given these readings, Bipin Chandra Pal argued that India must interpret itself for itself.

B.C. Pal wrote that the universal is expressed through 'the whole' and the whole is viewed as "a concrete Reality, or as an abstract Idea of Principle". One needs to view the parts to the whole as one and the same with the "whole in its parts"; or, one sees the whole in its parts. Finding the whole through and in its parts allows for a harmony of the concrete with the abstract. So the individual can only fulfill himself in and through society. The individual and society are interdependent, dependent on one another for self-fulfillment. This relationship of the self to the social whole is an organic one.[33]

B.C. Pal did not support an independent India. Instead he wanted a federated empire of equals; a loyal partnership of freedom and justice. He feared the color divide and pan-Islamism and thought a cooperative India and England stood a better chance of addressing the divisive issues of the day. He believed in a combination of isolation and association, freedom and federation for building an independent India.

B.C. Pal thought a "representative imagination" was necessary for others to understand India and her needs. This understanding means "killing the conceit of the self" as something apart and thus "seizing the universal everywhere". The self is not annihilated, or denied, but rather is seen in all things; it is not a self cut separate, apart, and isolated. Pal thought that one must be willing to lose oneself in another's image in order really to see beyond one's own parameters. "No one can correctly interpret anything without himself becoming that thing."[34]

For B.C. Pal, collectivism is the real philosophy of democracy, and the conception of the whole is not one of unity but of totality. Totality is a living whole committed to a universal humanity. And yet, the totality does not destroy or subsume duality or differentiation.[35] Although Pal was highly critical of the caste system and the idolatry of the Hindus he also believed in his own kind of gods and goddesses. The plural Gods and Goddesses represent the "eternally self-differentiated Being of the Absolute". The Hindu's God becomes the God of all.[36] And the mother of the nation is also the mother of us all because she is the mother of humanity for Pal. The nation becomes the universe because nationality becomes universalized through the cult of the mother as the source of humanity.

Eastern India, home of Bengali theory, was greatly mobilized by the ideals of freedom and equality of eighteenth century Enlightenment thought. Criticism of caste hierarchies was a rich location from which further to devise a dialogue with democracy in its multiple forms. Bengali reformers knew the plurality of their own existence as well as the enforced homogeneity of their colonizers. B.C. Pal sees his own pluralism as an expression of totality which breeds disdain for the enforced oneness of the British. This becomes the locale for his writing alternatives to established Enlightenment theory.

The colonial subject position allows for a more inclusive viewpoint given the differentials of power. Their subject viewing requires a plural stance as a matter of sheer survival. Democratic abstracted universals and their silenced exclusions are the stuff made by colonialists who are blinded by the very invisibility of their own privilege. The identity of the self, smothered in the demands of colonialism, still remains within view from this imperial site. Abstraction denies the multiple realities and locations of power relations, so that differing 'unities' are viewed from above and from below.

Diversity in Democratic Unity

Bengali anticolonialist theory demands that democracy be written from below, from inside the relations of domination to an outside that encompasses the totality of the entirety of oppression. Accordingly, the colonized are written into and not out of history. Differences are neither made up, nor silenced, but celebrated as part of the nation as a whole. The fake universalism of imperial democracy is uncovered for its suffocating and disciplining of difference.

As part of the Indian renaissance that began in the 1850s, Rabindranath Tagore critiqued the nationalism of religious exclusivity to find a more inclusive notion of nation. He also wrote of the need for "unity with diversity" from the site of the colonized. He argued for the need to recognize a totality which is derivative of differences and multiplicity. Differences express the richness of his culture, the dignity of individuals and the value of their freedom. This "unity in diversity" denies that unity means uniformity or a homogenized oneness.[37]

For Tagore, imperialist nations deny difference and term this denial 'unity'. Instead, he recognizes an individuality that achieves "real unity in matters in which they are one". Real unity is founded on real freedom. Diversity applauded by the powerless rejects a notion of homogeneity as unifying. Tagore writes of a nonuniform unity because "only those who are different can unite".[38] He celebrates the democratic capabilities of nonuniformity rather than the neoliberal antidemocratic realignment of difference today.

"Diversity in unity" means that individuals are allowed their uniqueness but not their selfishness. For Tagore, a lone individual is a fragmented being; the self always has the capacity for union.[39] Speaking in China in the early 1920s Tagore states: "Let all human races keep their own personalities, and yet come together not in a uniformity that is dead, but in a unity that is living." He criticizes the West for its "untruths and hypnotic phrases" which breed "an arrogant exclusiveness against all other races". He dislikes the mimicry and affectation of the materialist West, even though the West awarded him a Nobel prize.[40] Asia and Africa have been sacrificed merely to provide the West with "fastidious fashion" and "an endless train of respectable rubbish". He sees the West as filled with greed, and Western democracy as like "an elephant whose purpose is to give joy rides to the clever and the rich".

Tagore demands that there be freedom for all differences; and that law must allow the free expression of difference. And he challenges anticolonialists to think for themselves, outside the parameters of the colonizer. Tagore says that terms like 'extremism', and 'moderation', are words invented for 'us', by those with power over us, but not by us. He agrees with Gandhi that the national question must start with the individual's own personal struggle to free themselves from domination. This personal struggle, for Tagore also, starts with the inner spirit in order to rid the self of its slave mentality. There must be inner hope. "A man's homeland has to be a projection, as well as mirror of his inmost life."[42] And this process of moving toward self-realization – of one's obligations and responsibilities – is painful and challenging. People must demand authority over themselves and not acquiesce; they must believe that they will make things better.

Tagore writes about a fish who swims continuously in a glass jar, repeatedly hitting its head. When the fish is set free it continues to swim around in a small circle. "Glass is not water, nor water glass," so people must seek their freedom and not live in constrained circumstances. He knows that mistakes will be made as people demand the right to decide their own fate, but there is no alternative if national subjugation is to be overthrown. "We believe in virtue and we shall risk our lives to pursue it."[43]

National subjugation, for Tagore, is imbricated in the use of English as a foreign language. He believed that it is hard to think and be critical in a tongue that is foreign and displacing. If there is to be an "irrigation of learning", it can't be done through a false linguistic uniformity. The use of English inevitably turns our minds towards the West. There is an inertness of "borrowed acquisition". When there is endless tedium over the learning of grammar and ridiculous spelling, good "ideas come late". This enforcement of the English language colonized Indian education and detached the learning process from people's affective associations in their lives. Tagore insisted that India must accept the difficulty of multiple languages. "Linguistic uniformity is not necessary for intellectual unity." Through the differences of language a "true unity", rather than enforced unity, will emerge. This unity need not be divorced from English influence but cannot be dominated by it. Tagore uses the metaphor of a river being fed by waters that exist outside the country to explain his model of education. He says Indians can allow "a channel from the West, but not a flood".[44]

Complex Oneness and One More Bengali

Sri Aurobindo (Ghose) (1872–1950) was sent to England, at age seven, to be educated. Like Gandhi, he also came to challenge these initial moorings. He, too, wrote from the body, using yoga to realize the soul of a spiritual India. His aim was to discover self-understanding and self-recognition in order to translate justice and altruism, and activism and quietism into a "rich humanity". For him, reason and spirituality were not hostile to one another but intertwined and mingled. Spirituality necessitates finding one's deepest potentialities through self-searching and self-controlled expansion. This process of discovery is intimately both individual and communal, like the self. Spirituality recognizes the "freedom of the human soul".[45]

Sri Aurobindo recognized that the unity of mankind is hard to grasp and therefore must be achieved while safeguarding the race's "roots of vitality". This conception of unity requires that it must be "richly diverse in its oneness". In this sense, oneness is encompassed with diversity; not in spite of it. Unity, then, involves the movement "from a simple to a complex oneness". Liberty is the condition of "vigorous variation" and "self-finding".[46] The "unity in diversity" demands that cohesion be soundly formed out of a multiplicity of identities.

Unity is embraced with the oneness of connectivity as well as uniqueness. Difference is not problematized but rather becomes the vehicle by which a full notion of community is expressed. Those who have suffered the constraints of fictionalized homogeneity have no interest in silencing the differences that reside within themselves. Their imagined democratic communities move beyond their own silenced narrative of exclusion. Their belief in their humanity and humanness demands a nonhomogenized recognition of humanity's particularities. In this visioning, individuals are communal; and communities are contained in the individuals within them.

For Sri Aurobindo, yoga is the activity of finding the Divinization of the whole of mankind. Yoga expresses the Divine in humanity. It transforms the whole being: spiritual and mental and physical combine to form the salvation of humanity.[47] As such, the individual is not isolated; but expresses a particular domain of Divine transcendence. And the meaning of transcendence remains open to new discovery. Sri Aurobindo has no patience with "enforced dogma, cults, and moral codes". One's spiritual evolution develops as one finds oneself "more and more united with the collectivity and the All".[48] This is a fluid religiosity which encompasses a complex understanding of the self within its larger spiritual domains.

Sri Aurobindo rejects the dichotomous split between the self and the collective. Spirituality allows a recognition of the infinite: the power of a vast spiritual universality. 'Gnosis', the coming together of "the universal self and its spirit, allows for the highest dynamics of spiritual existence." And this amounts to knowing, or having consciousness, of the "supreme world mother".[49] Only through this route can a unified non-colonialist nation be built. "Only through the call of our Mother and the voice of all her sons and not by any other unreal means" can the bondage of India be swept away.[50] The mother, once again, stands as purifier and unifier of the whole. Real women, however, are left to the very old patriarchal silences from before that continue to dominate their life choices.

For Sri Aurobindo, "association is the mightiest thing in humanity; [association] is the instrument by which humanity moves", and it is how humanity grows. For India, it must "unite, be free, be one, be great!" He asks for loyalty to the nation. The nation is more than soil, it is a living thing, "the mother in whom you move and have your being". By default the nation is made up of 'brothers', and their universality is encompassed in the iconography of the "mother nation". We are all 'brothers', and meet in a common place, our "common Mother".[51]

Sri Aurobindo depends on the colonialist homogenization of gender difference to build his nation. He supports nonviolence, rather than violence, as a political strategy. But when he writes of noncompliance, he warns that the resistance must be "masculine and bold". Only a resistance that is masculine in nature can build a strong nation. He fears "a nation of women who know only how to suffer and not how to strike". Gandhi responds that he wants the "feminine nature of non-violence" instead of the male aggression of the British raj.[52] However, both Gandhi and Sri Aurobindo deny the diversity of sex and gender in their constructions of democracy. Each ascribes homogenized viewings to women which fly in the face of the richly diverse and inclusive notion of individuality that they say they believe in. As such, patriarchal silences continue to define their alternate theories of anticolonialist democracy.

Bengali theorists imagine a democracy that does not fully celebrate the uniqueness of individual women. This engendering of the nation occludes the very individuality and diversity that they claim is necessary for a total inclusive oneness. The vision of the nation as "mother of us all", is not one of diversity in unity. The unity of "mother of the nation" smashes women's variety and re-colonizes women for nation building once again. The diversity and realness of the nation is defined by and for men, as brothers coming to self-actualization. Woman, as mother, becomes an abstraction of the whole without becoming an active force in the unity. Spirituality, in this sense, can become dangerously similar to abstracted notions of Western rationality which also exclude women's full selves. Given the silences of history which articulate male privilege in normalized form, the specificity of humanity always must locate itself simultaneously as male and female. Otherwise patriarchal privilege will continue to traverse geopolitical borders and maintain systems of domination.

The notion of individuality – although circumscribed in masculinist form – and its connectedness to diversity *and* unity forms the heart of Bengali democratic theory. The individual is not selfish, or competitive, but rather simultaneously unique and part of a bigger whole. This is a vision that speaks with a promise of inclusivity and challenges Western colonialism by doing so. It is an alternate, an-other view of what noncolonialist democracy can potentially portend. As such it indicts bourgeois formulations of individualism as culturally supremacist and undemocratic even though women and girls still remain colonized.

Gandhi and the Bengali theorists deepen and thicken democratic theory in "other-than-Western" form by connecting the individual to its other parts. They therefore cannot think of unity without its multiplicities, or of people without their connectivity, or of individuals without their bodies. But they remain dominated by masculinist imperial views that continue to create silences and oppression of women. They have yet fully to decolonize women, and therefore themselves.

Notes

1. Bharati Mukherjee, *Desirable Daughters* (New York: Hyperion, 2002), p. 199.
2. M. Athar Ali, "The Perception of India in Akbar and Abu'l Fazl", in Irfan Habib, *Akbar and His India* (Delhi: Oxford University Press, 1997), p. 220. Also see: R. Krishnamurti, *Akbar: The Religious Aspect* (Baroda, India: Baroda Press, 1961).
3. Vincent Smith, *Akbar: The Great Mogul, 1542–1605* (Oxford: Clarendon Press, 1917).
4. Vidya Dhejia, ed., *Devi: The Great Goddess* (Washington, DC: Arthur Sackler Gallery, Smithsonian Institution, 1999), p. 205.
5. Dennis Dalton, *Indian Idea of Freedom* (Haryana, India: Academic Press, 1982), pp. 70–6, 100.
6. Rabindranath Tagore, *Towards Universal Man* (London: Asia Publishing House, 1961), pp. 7, 17, 26.
7. V.R. Mehta, *Foundations of Indian Political Thought* (New Delhi: Manohar Publishers, 1992), p. 264.
8. S.K. Maitra, *The Meeting of the East and the West in Sri Aurobindo's Philosophy* (Pondicherry: Sri Aurobindo Ashram, 1956), pp. 2, 8–10, 31, 47.
9. Prabhati Mukherjee, *Hindu Women* (New Delhi: Orient Longman, 1978), pp. 42–4.
10. Rama Mehta, *Inside the Haveli* (New York: Penguin, 1977). Also see Vrinda Nabar, *Caste As Woman* (New Delhi: Penguin Books, 1995); and Malladi Subbomma, *Hinduism and Women* (Delhi: Ajanta Books, 1992).
11. Ajit Mookerjee, *Kali, The Feminine Force* (Rochester, Vermont: Destiny Books, 1988), pp. 11, 25, 61, 69.
12. Ibid., pp. 30, 35, 97.
13. Prabhati Mukherjee, *Hindu Women*, pp. 13–17.
14. Anees Jung, *Unveiling India* (New Delhi: Penguin, 1987); and Madhu Kishwar and Ruth Vanita, *In Search of Answers: Indian Women's Voices from Manushi* (London: Zed Books, 1984).
15. Deepa Mehta, "Why I Make Films", panel discussion at Ithaca College, Park School of Communications, October 2000.
16. Mahatma Gandhi, *Gandhi, An Autobiography: The Story of My Experiments with Truth* (Boston: Beacon Press, 1993), p. 504.
17. Dennis Dalton, *Mahatma Gandhi* (New York: Columbia University Press, 1993),

pp. 25, 56, 169.

18. Benudhar Pradhan, *The Socialist Thought of Mahatma Gandhi*, vol. 1 (Delhi: G.D.K. Publishers, 1980), p. 16.
19. Ibid., pp. 6, 7.
20. Mahatma Gandhi, *Gandhi, An Autobiography*, p. 172.
21. Pradhan, *The Socialist Thought of Mahatma Gandhi*, vol. 1, pp. 5, 180.
22. Dennis Dalton, *Mahatma Gandhi*, p. 6.
23. Ibid., pp. 146, 162, 163.
24. Eleanor Morton, *The Women in Gandhi's Life* (New York: Dodd, Mead & Co., 1953), pp. 66, 67.
25. Mahatma Gandhi, *Gandhi, An Autobiography*, p. 208.
26. Gandhi, "Letter to H.S.L. Polak", in K. Swaminathan and C.N. Patel, eds., *A Gandhi Reader* (Hyderabad, India: Orient Longman, l988), p. 6.
27. Morton, *The Women in Gandhi's Life*, p. 22.
28. Mahatma Gandhi, *Gandhi, An Autobiography*, pp. 13, 14, 297.
29. Pushpa Joshi, *Gandhi on Women* (Ahmedabad: Navajivan Publishing House, 1988), pp. 78, 259, 316.
30. S.R. Bakshi, *Gandhi and the Status of Women* (New Delhi: Criterion Publishers, 1987), p.61.
31. Morton, *The Women in Gandhi's Life*, p. 232.
32. Bipin Chandra Pal, *Memories of My Life and Times*, vol. 1 (Calcutta: Bipinchandra Pal Institute, 1973), pp. 29, 32, 38, 68.
33. Ibid., p. xii.
34. Bipin Chandra Pal, *The Soul of India* (Calcutta: Choudhury and Choudhury, 1911), pp. vi, vii, 39, 42.
35. B.C. Pal, *The Soul of India*, p. 12, 92.
36. Ibid., pp. 185, 186, 194, 273.
37. Rabindranath Tagore, *Towards Universal Man*, p. 22.
38. Ibid., pp. 246, 247.
39. Ibid., p. 323.
40. Shakti Das Gupta, *Tagore's Asian Outlook* (Calcutta: Rupashree Press, 1961), pp. 6, 7, 58, 59.
41. Rabindranath Tagore, *Towards Universal Man*, p. 311.
42. Ibid., pp. 102, 103, 109, 120, 256.
43. Ibid., pp. 177, 186, 197.
44. Saumyendranath Tagore, *Rabindranath Tagore and Universal Humanism* (Bombay: Asian Printers, 1961), pp. 212, 216, 222, 224.
45. Sri Aurobindo, *Reason and Beyond Reason* (Chowpatty: Bharan's Book University, 1963), pp. 22, 47, 59, 60, 62.
46. Sri Aurobindo, *The Human Cycle and the Ideal of Human Unity* (Pondicherry: Sri Aurobindo Ashram, l962), pp. 266, 490.
47. S. K. Maitra, *The Meeting of the East and West in Sri Aurobindo's Philosophy*, pp. 55, 56, 58.

48. Sri Aurobindo, *The Future Evolution of Man* (Pondicherry: Sri Aurobindo Ashram Press, 1956), pp. 13, 50, 112.
49. Ibid., p. 111.
50. Sri Aurobindo, *Speeches* (Pondicherry: Sri Aurobindo Ashram Press, 1922), p. 38.
51. Ibid., pp. 93, 115.
52. Dennis Dalton, *Mahatma Gandhi*, p. 40. Also see Sri Aurobindo, *The Doctrine of Passive Resistance* (Pondicherry: Sri Aurobindo Ashram Press, 1952), p. 36.

6 Nonwestern Westerners: The Difference Color Makes

The global economy dates from at least the slave trade and demands a viewing that includes the colored majority of the world. It should be no surprise, then, that it is African-Americans who reveal the colonization of and human debt that is owed Africa in their re-visionings of democracy. Blacks in the West write a more inclusive and non-racist democratic theory. They write in order to put the racialized exclusions and invisibilities created by imperial power in the bold. Slavery and Africa are the sites from which their democratic imaginings are uncovered. They live in the West with "other-than-Western" eyes.

The voices of W.E.B. DuBois, Ida B. Wells, Paul Robeson, Malcolm X, and Martin Luther King put the painful life of racialized color in view so that a more inclusive picture of humanity can be envisioned. They identify their own problematized color and look 'elsewhere' to see people like themselves in Asia and Africa. They look at the slave trade to see the connections between Black and Brown people in the US and Ghana, Nigeria, Sudan, and so on. Their site of racialized bodies spans the globe.

DuBois, Wells, Robeson, Malcolm, and King see more of the *befores* than most whites see. They do not falsely universalize the notion of individuality, nor silently assume its whiteness, nor feel included by abstracted notions of rights. Living with their bodies they know that they are the 'other' and are differentiated from the standard of 'whiteness'. Living with their skin means knowing the connection between the self and larger communities of people of color. Given the power-filled meanings of color, they know they are *not* white. And they turn this knowledge towards critique, and the possibility of a polyversal democracy.

I am no racial or gender essentialist although color and ovaries are never insignificant to social construction. People's racialized and gendered bodies matter enormously in their writing of democracy. The more the individual's multiple identities are recognized and not silenced as unitary, the greater the vision of inclusiveness. As Bengali theory suggests, unity is discovered within its parts, which are never simply partial. In order to move toward an earnest polyversality it is necessary to particularize the diverse needs that constitute the whole of humanity. Aimé Césaire reminds us to not lose ourselves in a segregation of the particular, or in a dilution of the universal.[1]

Bringing the globe into fuller sight means seeing Blackness differently. Femi Kuti, a popular Nigerian singer, demands "Blackman Know Yourself". In this well-known song he urges: "Blackman know yourself, Be confident, Our ancestors civilized this world – know yourself, don't forget your part".[2] Black people must reclaim their lost history from before so that the memories can inform the future for us all. But instead, today's capitalists sanitize the global relations of capitalism which have long been critiqued by pan-Africanists. This newly articulated 'globalization' images a global village that continues to exclude Africa and where the exploitative relations of colonialism and imperialism remain, but in multiracial guise.

Slavery, Racism and Globalism

Seeing an encompassing unity in humanity means viewing and understanding the slave-trade as part of the before that defines the present. Once one traces slavery and its routes, Africa necessarily becomes an integral part of the globe. The history of slavery is neither simply ours or theirs because the progeny of slaves and slaveowners are forever linked. Beds and lives have been shared.[3] Slavery is a specific type of apartheid but miscegenation denies this separateness.

If races are cross-breedings over time, genetic blends cut across racial boundaries. Yet, the notion of race fuses with experience in static ways, so much so that Claude Lévi-Strauss says that we no longer have any idea what we are really talking about. Instead, what is cultural is assumed to be racial, yet much more is known about culture than about race.[4] And if biology itself is cultural, then identities are intimately fluid. If the meaning of race can be opened to its cultural constructions and genetic mixtures, then anything, even nature, can be opened to its contextual moment.

Through using sets of genes known as haplotypes as fossils, biologists have uncovered invisible races and their connections to each other. They are thinking that the Basques are aboriginal Europeans; and that Sephardic Jews resemble Arabs; and that an Igbo from Nigeria might be a part of the Lemba, a tribe of Israel lost in southern Africa.[5] Ethiopian Jews, sometimes called Falashas, are Black. Their tribal symbol is of a Star of David with an elephant inside.[6] They fled to the Sudan in the 1980s to escape persecution and date back to the second century BC.[7] Supposedly, the Falashas and Lembas derive from the same origin.

The mixing of African Black, native Caribbean, native American, and European white shades the color of race differently in varied cultural forms. DuBois, Robeson, and Malcolm X exposed the enforced rigidities of the color divide in the hopes of transcending it. Their writing remains as important as ever given the racialized politics of the US today. The racist commitments of men in the top echelons of US power is disgusting. President Bush nominates known segregationists to the federal bench with no apology. Attorney General John Ashcroft spoke at Bob Jones University, despite its ban on interracial dating. Ashcroft, when Attorney General in Missouri, was central in delaying compliance with a desegregation plan in St Louis, and as recently as 1999 he said that he would like to do more to defend the legacy of Jefferson Davis, a known segregationist. Trent Lott, then Majority Leader of the Senate, celebrated Strom Thurmond at his 100-year birthday party by stating that he wished that Thurmond had won the presidency in 1948 for the segregationist States Rights Party. With these remarks Lott opened up "racial wounds" and was forced first to apologize – he said he misspoke – and then to resign. But he did not misspeak; his record for years was one supportive of segregation.[8] These men bespeak the contemporary status of an awful racist history.

Although the African slave trade is long passed, and silenced, discussions of slavery still seep into political conversations. It was a revelatory moment when, on the eve of the US war on Iraq, well-known singer and activist Harry Belafonte criticized Colin Powell for doing the "slavemaster's work". Belafonte accused Powell of occupying a place in the "master's house" and forgetting about the people of color who would die in this war. Belafonte, standing behind his anti-war statement on CNN's *Larry King Live*, reiterated the importance of knowing and connecting to the history of slavery, both its horrors and its rich culture of song and hope.

Belafonte spoke out against Colin Powell and the Iraq War because he was deeply troubled that men and women of color were being asked to wage a war that was not in their interest. He wants Blacks to reject the values that have been set by their slavemasters, to remember how to protest and dissent and reject the values of materialism that trap them in greed. Belafonte fears that people of color are losing their connection to their diasporic heritage. He wishes that Colin Powell, and other people of color, would stand against all war, and resist the destructive forces of militarism. Belafonte believes it is people of color who must stand on behalf of the soul of this nation.[9]

DuBois and the Color Line from Africa

In the mid twentieth-century, W.E.B. DuBois wrote of a universal humanitarianism filled with diverse tongues and a variety of skin colors. He strove to conceptualize a more inclusive notion of humanity. He saw an early and frequent contact and connection between Europe and Africa, that there was Negro blood in Asia Minor as far as the Black Sea. He put the US debt to Africa in view. "America was built on Africa"; "America became through African labor" the center of the sugar and cotton empire.[10] Black slavery "took ten million human beings from their mother continent … to hell".[11] This bondage lasted for four centuries and created a blood debt.

Africa forms the heart of 'civilization' for DuBois. Colonialism was the disastrous destruction of the culture and richness of so-called 'primitive' peoples. DuBois both grieved for and celebrated the innovative capacities of those thought of as 'uncivilized' in their struggles against 'civilization'. He indicts self-proclaimed democracies as undemocratic given their dependency on the exploitation of other peoples' labor.[12]

DuBois recenters Egypt as both African and advanced in its development and civilization. He writes of fourteenth century Black African culture as equal to Europe's; that Negroid influences in Egypt were key to its civilization. This primacy is reversed during the slave trade of the eighteenth and nineteenth centuries. Africa is 'othered' and rewritten in world history to rationalize Negro slavery. DuBois refocuses history in order to recognize the role of the Negro in making the world. Human civilization was carried north from Black Africa. The trade in human beings between Africa and America is the source of the "collapse of humanity" and the end of "European civilization". The earliest moments of modern democracy reside in the slave revolts in Cuba, Jamaica, Haiti, Mexico, and Brazil. DuBois decries the process by which "all that was human in Africa was deemed European or Asiatic".[13] For DuBois, 'whiteness' prevails because it owns the earth.[14]

By default, Black slavery became sanitized by making the slave less than human. Slaves were written out of humanity, but DuBois writes them back in. For DuBois, slavery was inhumane, and the slave human. The slave was forced to call another, master. The slave was helpless to defend herself. Slavery required absolute subjection. Slaves were degraded and defiled. No slave could testify in court, own anything, legally marry or have a family. Slavery's power was completely arbitrary and irresponsible. Yet America celebrates as though it were a democracy.

DuBois asked what the Fourth of July could mean to an American slave. He answers that it is a day "that reveals to him, more than all other days in the year, the gross injustice and cruelty to which he is the constant victim". DuBois mocks America's claim to "superior civilization" alongside the enslavement of millions. Full emancipation for DuBois meant the emancipation of labor, and this means freeing "the majority of workers who are yellow, brown, and black".[15]

DuBois was a radical democrat. He believed that racism was a fundamental flaw in the existing practices of liberal democracy. Manning Marable writes that for DuBois, "the greatest casualty of racism is democracy". Democracy must be built on peace, and freedom from poverty, ignorance and disease.[16] Capitalism only further degrades the Negroid peoples by means of the demands of the market, and this was especially true of the cotton plantation.[17]

DuBois, like Belafonte, thinks that the slave spiritual stands at the heart of a national cultural form which tells the "sorrow songs" of this spiritual heritage.[18] Africa and Asia are connected from prehistoric times through the Black race which existed on both continents. As such, it is doubtful to DuBois, whether one can ever know which continent is the point of origin. Writing in 1915, his main concern is to see the "strong brotherhood of Negro blood throughout the world", which he sees as a "common cause of the darker races" against the insults and injustices of Europeans.

DuBois's vision is one of a humanity inclusive of colored peoples. "Most men in this world are colored. A belief in humanity means a belief in colored men". He believed that a new unity was in the future, one made by colored races and working classes everywhere.[19] But he does not specify Black women unless he is trumpeting their rights against white men's exploitation. Otherwise he speaks of Blacks as a 'brotherhood', and does not put a 'sisterhood' in clear view.

DuBois sees the whole colored world alongside socialism and communism. He condemns the US as hostile to democracy, as "the last center of white supremacy and colonial imperialism". He rejects white privilege as a given. Skin color was a mild curiosity in the Middle Ages. Whiteness did not become a resource of power until the eighteenth, nineteenth and twentieth centuries. Before the eighteenth century there was an acceptance of humanity as diversely multicolored. Whiteness, as such, is a recent invention and discovery.[20]

The color line, as a racial divider, developed as a result of the wealth created by slave labor, greed, and worldwide trade. More specifically, DuBois, writes of the historical formulation of the color line: "Labor was degraded, humanity was despised, and the theory of 'race' arose." The nineteenth century established that the white people of Europe have a "right to live upon the labor and property of the colored peoples of the world".[21]

DuBois specifies the complex illegality of the slave trade's history. By 1700 the trading of humans was integral to the life of the colonies. They could not subsist without slave labor. Slaves became the "strength of the Western world". DuBois estimates that about 25,000 slaves were brought to America each year between 1698 and 1707. All sorts of prohibitory state laws were passed from 1789 to 1803 and yet slavery continued, the slave trade thrived, with starts and slumps alongside the attempts to suppress it.[22] Even though it became illegal in 1807, US slavery continued until 1865.

Through the first half of the nineteenth century there is much economic change and industrial development. The demands of the cotton industry enhanced the importance of slave labor and the price at which slaves sold. A slave cost $325 in 1840 and $500 in 1860. Whites feared their own dependence on this labor, as well as the freed slave. DuBois writes with anguish: "Of all that most Americans wanted, this freeing of slaves was the last. Everything black was hideous. Everything Negroes did was wrong. If they fought for freedom, they were beasts; if they did not fight, they were born slaves. If they cowered on the plantations, they loved slavery; if they ran away, they were lazy loafers. … The bites and the blows of a nation fell on them." Color caste is supported by white labor which fears freed Blacks. The subordination of colored labor is used to make profit for whites the world over. For DuBois, the only place that democracy is to be found is "in the hearts of black folk".[23]

Within this system of colored caste, DuBois paints a picture of incredible variety. There was no one kind of slave, no one kind of slavery. Slavery varied from a mild serfdom in Pennsylvania and New Jersey to an aristocratic caste system in Maryland and Virginia. Massachusetts was always somewhat reticent about slavery, even while it was practiced. In 1776, committees on slavery were set up to resolve that selling and enslaving the human species is a violation of the natural rights of men, as well as in contradiction with the principles of liberty and equality upon which the nation was founded. But the resolution was not passed. In Rhode Island a law was passed in 1652 prohibiting lifelong slavery, but this was never enforced.[24] These varied deliberations can be read as a non-universal endorsement of the brutality of slavery, but with little consequence.

As early as 1638 there were demands to end the slave trade. By the mid-1660s through to 1760 antislavery sentiment grew, but still with little effect. Throughout the 1770s and 1780s there were many attempts to restrict, to prevent, and to abolish slavery. But there was no unified national antislavery movement before 1774. Then the First Continental Congress imposed restrictions on trade with England, demanding the non-importation of goods dependent on slavery, and making the importation of slaves illegal. It still took thirteen more years until trading in slaves was discontinued.

DuBois is careful to note that in 1860 only 7 percent of the total population of the south owned most of the 4 million slaves.[25] Nevertheless, in South Carolina a grand jury claimed that the slave trade, if reestablished, would be "a blessing to the American people, and a benefit to the African himself". There was much pressure to repeal legislation against the slave trade, and illegal importations into the South increased; only in 1861 did Lincoln begin enforcement of antislave trade regulations.

DuBois supported the revolutionary Toussaint L'Ouverture, leader of the Haitian slave revolts. He thought that Toussaint L'Ouverture's actions intensified the antislavery movement in the colonies and assisted the final 1807 prohibition of slavery. He also believed that the Haitian revolt led to Napoleon's willingness to sell Louisiana.[26] DuBois connected the struggles of Black people across the globe to give voice to an enlarged notion of human liberation. And he shows how Black people's struggle enlarged democracy for whites as well.

During US Reconstruction public schools opened opportunities as much for poor white children of which less than half were attending public school at the time, as Black children. The rights to vote and be a juror were given to thousands of whites with no land, along with Blacks. Barbarous forms of punishment such as stocks and whipping posts were abolished for both races. It was the Black man's struggle to end slavery, according to DuBois, that established the beginnings of democracy for poor whites and Blacks alike.[27] Despite these changes, DuBois was deeply disappointed in the aftermath of the abolition of slavery. The freed slave in 1863 was a long way from being a free 'man'. DuBois knew early on that the "problem of the twentieth century is the problem of the color line, the question as to how far differences of race, which show themselves chiefly in the color of the skin and the texture of the hair, will deny half the world their full capacities".[28]

DuBois joined the Communist Party in 1961. After visiting Russia he wrote: "… if what I have seen with my eyes and heard with my ears in Russia is Bolshevism, I am a Bolshevik." His belief that "the emancipation of man is the emancipation of labor and the emancipation of labor is the freeing of that basic majority of workers who are yellow, brown, and black" underpinned his thought. By freedom, DuBois meant full economic, political and social equality in thought, expression and action. With this freedom there is no discrimination based on race or color. His hope for civilization required the inclusion of all human elements with the exclusion of none.[29] Although DuBois supported and admired Gandhi he was unable to accept his notion of nonviolence. The minority status of African-Americans, and the violence used to suppress them, would not allow them this luxury.

DuBois encouraged Blacks to resist their oppression and stand firmly against discrimination. Resistance meant recognizing one's double consciousness, one's 'two-ness'; being an American and a Negro with two souls, two sets of strivings, one dark body with two warring ideals.[30] DuBois thought that Blacks needed to work autonomously from whites in order to build an integrity and solidarity with each other. Autonomy was different from discrimination, for DuBois, because the purpose was not to exclude or punish but to empower. Blacks needed to celebrate themselves in order to resist the negativity and oppressiveness of their ordinary lives. To engage each other in this way is to turn the abhorrence of Blackness into creativity. DuBois's articulation of this "strategic separateness" bespoke the power-filled meanings of race.

DuBois meant to open democracy to all people by thwarting, rather than neutralizing, the color line. Color becomes radically plural without white privilege. Color is de-raced and simply becomes a myriad of shades irrespective of power-filled meanings. Black and Brown and Yellow peoples are no longer expressive of racial 'difference' but rather acknowledge the plurality of humanity itself. Over and again DuBois threads connections between struggles for human liberation. For him, non-Europeans in South Africa "suffer a tyranny" similar to Nazism and therefore the defeat of German Nazism was only a step toward the ending of human tyranny.[31]

In "The Damnation of Women" DuBois expresses great contempt for the white man's use and abuse of Black women. As such, he recognizes the centrality of Black women's oppression to all the problems of the coming century. Although he is usually identified with naming the color line as the key problem of the twentieth century, he also believed that "the uplift of women is, next to the problem of the color line and the peace movement, our greatest modern cause".[32] His linkage of these realms – racism, the oppression of women and world peace – is important to his re-visionings of democracy. But he does not develop a view of Black women's distinct gendered oppression.

DuBois's personal life poses problems for a discussion of Black women's liberation. It is sometimes said that he spoke a public feminism while privately practicing adultery, as well as misusing his power and position as a sexual predator. He had what was understood at the time as a "publicly correct marriage", but an "adulterous private life" which was "tolerated by the talented tenth".[33] There is a nonunique story here of the contradictoriness of men's personal and political treatment of women similar to that of Thomas Jefferson, Martin Luther King, Bill Clinton, and Jesse Jackson. This contradictoriness expresses the complex relationship between the public and private domains of patriarchal gender.

DuBois reveals a patriarchal attitude towards marriage in letters to his daughter Yolande. After she married Countee Cullen, an accomplished poet, Yolande wrote to her father expressing her deep sadness and loneliness in the marriage. DuBois, who was a great fan of Cullen, implored her at first to "help a great poet become greater". He chastised her and told her to "get out of the center of the picture" and "stop thinking of yourself". Later, when Cullen revealed his homosexuality to Yolande, DuBois wrote to her once again asking her to keep trying to make the marriage work. But if she cannot, he says: "You have my love and trust and I shall always be your affectionate father."[34] How do I assess the letters? On the one hand these are personal letters written between a father and daughter, when the father thinks his daughter is selfish and immature. On the other hand these are letters written by W.E.B. DuBois who privileges men's needs in marriage while silencing homosexuality.

However, DuBois also wrote scathing critiques of white men's misuse and abuse of Black women. He specified the particular plight of Black women in slavery's system of exploitation. The cruel weight of slavery falls on Black women, with no "legal marriage, no legal family, no legal control over children".[35] He called white men's treatment of colored women a disgrace. He criticized the double standard of female chastity for white women and colored sex for white men. He wrote of the soul of Black womanhood needing freedom to thrive.[36] He also wrote critically of the British abuse of Indian women,[37] and had an exceptional voting record in support of women's rights in the US.

DuBois wrote with sensitivity about women's racial oppression and the contradictory injustices practiced towards them. "Immediately in Africa, a black back runs red with the blood of the lash, in India, a brown girl is raped; in China, a coolie starves; in Alabama, seven darkies are more than lynched; while in London the white limbs of a prostitute are hung with jewels and silk." Of the white Southerner he says: "Southerners who had suckled food from black breasts vied with each other in fornication with black women, and even in beastly incest. They took the name of their fathers in vain to seduce their own sisters.

Nothing – nothing that black folk did or said or thought or sang – was sacred."[38]

Despite these insights DuBois assumes that Black women's needs are derivative of claims made for the race as a whole. It is Black masculinity that is of key concern to DuBois, and this is the case even when he worries about the costs of defiling Black women.[39] DuBois writes that he dreams "of a world of infinite and invaluable variety"; and the human variety is of "color and skin, hair and nose and lip". This pluralism must know freedom "in all possible manner of difference, topped with freedom of soul to do and be, and freedom of thought to give to a world and build into it, all wealth of inborn individuality".[40] Anything less, for DuBois, is not democracy. Yet, there is no mention of gender apartheid here.

DuBois did not indict gender divisions as historical constructions, like he did the color divide. He did not condemn the way Black women are expected to exist for Black men, rather than for themselves. He writes that it is "mothers and mothers of mothers who count rather than fathers", and he leaves in place the masculinist privilege and injustice that this fantasmatic divide reproduces.[41] He wrote in critique of Black women's abuse by white men but not in critique of Black men's abuse of Black women. It has been left to feminists within Black communities, like bell hooks, Angela Davis, Barbara Smith, Toni Cade Bambara, Toni Morrison, and others, to give voice to these silences. Ida B. Wells began these whisperings early on.

DuBois left the US to live his last years in Ghana. While visiting his home and the DuBois Institute in Ghana, I remember thinking how sad it was that he thought he had to leave the US to find an inviting home. It is a tragedy that this incredible humanist felt more comfortable 'elsewhere'. It is even sadder to think that he would still choose Ghana today.

Sexual Silences and Black Lynching

Ida B. Wells (1862–1931) wrote with a passionate mind on behalf of Black people during a time of back-pedaling and intimidation. She was born a slave but later became a schoolteacher and journalist. At the age of twenty-two she was forcibly removed from a White's Only section of a train in Tennessee on her way to Memphis. She challenged the Jim

Crow laws in the courts and lost. Ida B. Wells witnessed the end of the progressive period of Reconstruction and the new wave of racial segregation especially in the South. As long as slavery existed, Black labor was the "backbone of the South" so it was rare for a slave to be killed because they were worth too much. But after Emancipation a new method of intimidation, lynching, came into fashion. Because Wells felt the "gates to freedom"closing she began a weekly newspaper, the *Free Speech*, to tell the world about the lynching of Blacks.[42]

Wells exposed this newest form of racial treachery for what it was: a racist act which white people justified by means of sexual lies. She wrote the silences surrounding Black men's and white women's sexuality to expose lynching for what it was. She was determined to reveal what she saw as the real 'truths' about white women's desires and white men's fears about interracial sex with Blacks. She refused to accept that if there is sex between a white woman and a Black man it means rape. Instead she saw rape as an excuse rather than as a reason for lynching. For Wells, racial hatred rather than sexual violence explained the lynching of Black men through the 1890s.[43] During the 1880s and 1890s as many as 100 people were lynched each year, the numbers reaching a peak in 1892.

Lynch law was despicable to Wells; it bespoke nineteenth century's barbarity rather than civilization. She exposed the cruel lie that "Negro men rape white women". She warned Southern white men to be careful when they charge Black men with rape because they will only call attention to and damage "the moral reputation of their women." She continued: "White men lynch the offending Afro-American, not because he is a despoiler of virtue but because he succumbs to the smiles of white women." Wells wrote of white women's sexuality and desire at a time when their sexual purity was at a premium. She called attention to white women as "willing partners" and tells the story of Sarah Clark, a white woman who loved a Black man and was indicted for miscegenation. In order to escape punishment she swore she was not a white woman, and then continued the relationship.[44]

Lynch law brands Black men as "rapists and desperadoes" in this "land of liberty".[45] Wells wanted an honest accounting of the dishonesty because interracial sex, when it happens, is usually voluntary. It is often "clandestine, and illicit", but not rape. The mixed-race children of white women tells a different story of consent than that of the mixed-race children of Black slave women. She therefore criticized the Woman's Christian Temperance Union for not speaking out against the "burning, hanging, and shooting of Negroes" for crimes they did not commit.[46]

Wells also wrote on behalf of Black women, who were also sometimes lynched, though less frequently. She despised the way that the "contemptuous defamation" of Black women is used to dispirit and "dishearten the Negro". She lamented the exclusion of herself and other Black women from the 'noble' and 'refined' notions of womanhood reserved for white mothers and maidens. Wells took credit for Black women's 'virtues' and appeared to subscribe to the Victorian model of chasteness, extending it to Black women, as well as white. She wrote of Black women's ability to 'uplift' the race, adding that it was up to women to show their purity, with a "stainless life".[47] It is these ordinary women, as daughters, sisters, wives, and mothers – not queens – she said, who make the world.

Ida B. Wells delivers an important indictment of white racist terror which paraded as a form of sexual protectionism. According to Joy James, Wells demystifies rape, and with it the rhetoric of lynching.[48] The racism practiced here is deeply sexualized in its silenced repressions. Black men are sexual predators towards white women, and this picture is drawn against the historical backdrop of Black women's sexual availability to white men. However, Wells does not develop the masculinist viewings which affect both white and Black women in that both are viewed in passive ways. In the first instance white women need to be protected from Black men. In the second instance Black women are accessible without choice to white men; and Black men are unable to protect them. Neither view allows women sexual desire or choice. This silencing remains because much of Wells's depiction of lynching unveils the sexual but not the engendered forms of racism. This precludes seeing women as offering resistance simultaneously to the white masculinist aspects of racism and the racist forms of patriarchal privilege.

African Polyversalism

I grew up listening to Paul Robeson records. I knew him as a communist song writer of Black liberation struggles. I can still hear his deep low voice in my head as I write. I had never read any of his speeches or essays until doing research for this book. I stumbled on his writings as I read about the slave trade and Africa.

Robeson's Negro identity etched his entire sense of self. And for him, "the origin of the Negro is African".[49] So he was always both Negro and African. The two identities were connected, and united Black and Brown people across the globe. His identity was never simply local and individualized; nor simply Black. His keen sense of racial identity did not narrow him but instead allowed him a sense of greater community. "And even as I grew to feel more Negro in spirit, or African as I put it then, I also came to feel a sense of oneness with the white working people whom I came to know and love."[50]

Robeson's music and essays put slavery continually in view. At the time he was born, former slaves and their children made up almost the entire Black population in America. It follows that he sings the sorrows and the strengths of slaves' lives. He acknowledges this part of history in order to demand a different future. His future imagines a worldwide humanity filled with freedom for each person's soul. Robeson fought white supremacy wherever he saw it: in the *befores* as well as the present, without regard to geographical boundaries. "Can we oppose White Supremacy in South Carolina and not oppose that same vicious system in South Africa?"[51]

Robeson's US passport was revoked in 1950. The State Department's brief charged him with political activities dedicated to "the independence of the colonial people of Africa". His transnational antiracist commitments were seen as unpatriotic and disloyal to the US. He wrote that his right to travel was deeply connected to his humanity, like the right not to travel was at the heart of chattel slavery. He wrote that it is those who "oppose independence for the colonial peoples of Africa who are the real un-Americans".[52] He believed that Africans and African-Americans share a history that must continue to challenge the abstracted universals that express racial privilege. Robeson sought to build a global movement of liberation, not the globalization of people of color's exploitation. Today's rhetoric of neoliberalism attempts to re-silence dissident global voices like Robeson's.

Robeson believed that Negroes would never be liberated in America, or 'elsewhere', unless they could find one voice to speak with, against oppression. "The one voice in which we should speak must be the expression of our entire people on the central issue which is all-important to every Negro – our right to be free and equal." On all other issues, he acknowledged, there are great differences that do not allow a single voice. Robeson opens his sense of Black identity to the entire globe with all the diversity this necessitates, but he also believes that a unified voice is possible when freedom and equality are at stake. He advocates a "unity based upon our common viewpoint as Negroes" that subordinates divisiveness. But this muting and compromise cannot exclude anyone, nor can one partisan view be allowed to dominate. The leadership must place "the interests of our people, and the struggle for those interests, above all else". Robeson calls for a leadership that encompasses "all walks of life", from "all parts of the country", from "every viewpoint", to develop a strategy of liberation.[53]

Robeson searches for a common ground to bring about racial liberation. This demands a give and take of clashing viewpoints that can subordinate partisan interests to "the Negro interest". He asks Negroes to come together and set aside all that divides them, "Negroes all".[54] Robeson works toward building a unified base for politics while rejecting enforced homogeneity. His unity requires the complex process of respecting conflict without being stymied by it. Such a notion of unification is important for the postmodern moment when the uniqueness of identities splinters the oppressed in so many directions that it is only the oppressors who are unified.

Today's globalization leaves Africa outside, so the *befores* of slavery and colonialism are also erased. Exploitation and oppression are normalized and naturalized as though they are one and the same with democracy and freedom. It has never been easier for the US to universalize and capture this language given the revolutions of 1989 and the lack of a visible alternative. The possibilities for an inclusive democracy have shrunk alongside the plunder of global capital and the militarism of the US. Robeson would not be pleased. Neither would Kwame Nkrumah.

Kwame Nkrumah, a leader of the Pan-African movement, shared many of Robeson's commitments but on the other side of the globe. Born in Ghana, educated in Britain and the US, he along with Jomo Kenyatta of Kenya and Julius Nyerere of Tanzania believed that Africa's economic independence was central to ending global imperialism. Nkrumah advocated the building of local industry and trade unionism and repudiated all forms of racism. He met with Nehru in the 1950s and had earlier supported the Indian struggle for independence. Throughout the 1950s there was a continuing Afro-Asian understanding of the shared plight of Third World countries.[55] There was a shared belief in alternatives to capitalist imperialism.

Nkrumah led the struggle for Ghanaian independence and was a keen advocate of political resistance. He organized boycotts, strikes and non-cooperation to break the hold of capitalism. Building political solidarity, he believed, was a key part of this process and was necessary to any struggle for economic emancipation and political freedom. Although very much influenced by Western notions of democracy advocated by socialists like Harold Laski, Nkrumah stood against the West and its systems of exploitation. He fought to take "positive action" using all "legitimate and constitutional means" to cripple the forces of imperialism in Ghana. His vision of a truly democratic Ghana was expressed through his dialogue with and against the colonialism and imperialism of the West in relation to Africa.[56]

But the dialogues between US Blacks and Africa, and between African nations themselves, to find connection and political viability have been largely silenced again. US militarism, along with imperial capitalism and neoliberal privatization, resilences issues of racism. I therefore must remember to remember DuBois, and Robeson, and Martin Luther King.

War, Globalization, and Humanity

Martin Luther King also targeted the exclusiveness of racism to demand a more inclusive viewing of democracy. He put Blacks in view to envision a more humane humanity which also spanned the globe. His notion of civil rights demanded a color-filled democracy. His commitments to freedom and equality guided his antiracist platform and agendas. Although King is most often revered as a racial integrationist and reformist, he purported a revolutionary humanism. His writings connecting racism, militarism, and imperialism are more poignant than ever. Although King is best known for his "I have a dream" speech, I choose to remember his Riverside Church address against the Vietnam War, "A time to break silence", in April 1967. In this speech he spoke of the webbed connections between racism and war and advised the Civil Rights Movement to speak out against the war in Vietnam. Using Gandhi's politics of nonviolence King indicted the violence of the US military-industrial complex.

I read "A Time to Break Silence" again as the US was preparing its "war on terrorism" in Afghanistan. King all too poignantly warned against US involvement in Vietnam while allowing racism at home. He condemned the disproportionate use of Black troops to fight a war for democracy when these same Blacks suffered racist indignities and inequalities in their home country. "We were taking the black men who had been crippled by our society and sending them eight thousand miles away to guarantee liberties in Southeast Asia which they had not found in southwest Georgia and East Harlem." King criticized the war's hypocrisy and manipulation of the poor and Blacks alike. He writes of the "cruel irony" of watching "Negro and white boys on t.v. screens as they kill and die together for a nation that has been unable to seat them together in the same schools".[57]

Given King's own commitments to non-violence, he was particularly critical of the repeated use of violence by the US government. He believed that there were "loyalties which are broader and deeper than nationalism … we are called to speak for the weak, the voiceless, for victims of our nation and for those it calls enemy, for no document from human hands can make these humans any less our brothers". According to King, the human family needs peace, not militarist interventions. He therefore did not view the US as liberators in Vietnam; the Vietnamese, he said, "must see Americans as strange liberators". Instead, the US had become the oppressors, smashing Vietnamese culture and country alike. King repeatedly spoke of how US policy created more, not less, hatred. "Each day the war goes on the hatred increases in the heart of the Vietnamese and in the hearts of those of humanitarian instinct. The Americans are forcing even their friends into becoming their enemies."[58]

The similarity between King's words and the words of dissident voices against the US "war on terrorism" in Afghanistan and Iraq bespeaks a frightening historical continuity of US empire building. King fought to end violence and militarism and to build democracy for all the peoples of the globe. He spoke as a "citizen of the world", arguing that the US must "disengage itself from a disgraceful commitment".[59] King asked the US government to "get on the right side of the world revolution" and conquer the "giant triplets of racism, materialism and militarism". He believed that the only hope for US democracy was to declare "eternal hostility to poverty, racism, and militarism". With extraordinary relevance to our present crisis, King implored the US that "we can no longer afford to worship the God of hate or bow before the altar of retaliation". King called for a "world-wide fellowship" of "non-violent coexistence"; otherwise, he predicted, we will all be consumed by "violent co-annihilation".[60]

If King were alive today he would once again "break silence" and demand an end to the wars that wreak havoc on the weak, and bomb innocent people. He would acknowledge, once again, how difficult it is to speak out against one's own government in time of war, but speak he would. He would once again say that we cannot afford a war that leaves our own poor homeless and that breeds new racism; he would once again say that we must speak on behalf of the weak in our nation and for those it calls our enemy. He would once again ask us not to see terrorism elsewhere while not recognizing it in its racist forms at home. And most of all, King would ask that US foreign policy show humility and love, not hate.

King was killed just at the point that he chose to connect the struggles against US racism with struggles against US imperialism, just at the point that he opened his picture of humanity to the globe. King firmly believed that the greatest defense against an enemy is to remove the enemy's reasons for hatred. Once again, this is not a time for silence.

Revisioning Separatism and Enlarging Humanity

As a teenager, I remember, I often saw Malcolm X on the news. This was the early-to-mid sixties. He was usually depicted as an angry man: a Black separatist who hated white people. My parents' lives had been too defined in and by the Civil Rights Movement to accept easily some of Malcolm's early, separatist stages. They were white and there was much less room for whites to navigate with Malcolm. I think this influenced some of my initial critical reaction to Malcolm X.

Malcolm X's separatism was positioned against the integration strategy of King. Malcolm was a dangerous revolutionary, Martin was a reasonable civil rights reformer. The first was hateful and violent, the latter was full of love and knew how to passively resist. By the time each was murdered, their struggles were more similar than different. Both had become global in their views, antimilitarist, and nonexclusionary in their vision of humanity.

After Malcolm's death in 1965, I read his writings from the last years of his life. In the latter part of his life he had become very critical of materialism; he had espoused what he termed 'anti-dollarism'.[61] This 'dollarism', as he saw it, was a worldwide problem and not simply located in the US. He was critical of "an international Western power structure" – consisting of American, French, English, and European interests. These interests were simultaneously registered on local, national and international levels.[62] Malcolm had become an internationalist, an antimaterialist, and a spokesperson for a radically inclusive democracy by the time he died.

Malcolm, like DuBois and Robeson, connected his Black identity to his African roots/routes. All of the Western hemisphere – North America, South America, Canada, the Caribbean, the French West Indies – he saw as part and parcel of an African heritage. The race problem was international, not simply national. Racism was a human problem and he wished to create a politics that spoke to this shared transnational oppression. "I believe in human rights for everyone, and that none of us is qualified to judge each other, and that none of us should therefore have that authority." He thought Blacks needed to fight against the "common enemy" and never each other, so he sought to downplay intra-racial conflict.[63] Sounding much like Robeson, he argued that all Black, Brown, Red and Yellow peoples must submerge their differences in the spirit of unity, in order to disarm the common oppressor.[64]

For the sake of unity, Malcolm's multiracial politics sidelined artificial differences. For Malcolm, Robeson, and Nkrumah, this unity expressed shared priorities without being ignorant of conflict. Malcolm states in the platform of the Organization of African American Unity (OAAU) that people need to submerge their artificial divisions and focus instead on freeing themselves from the essence of their oppression. This solidarity cannot be created without understanding that the problem of African-Americans is an international problem and that their fate is forever linked with the people of Africa.[65]

Malcolm X embraced Islam, as a religious philosophy that celebrates humanity, in his antiracist struggles. Millions of Muslims across the globe today also embrace the democratic promissory of Islam as a critique of the racism and materialism of US empire building. But Malcolm X finally left the Nation of Islam because he thought it defied its democratic promise. The more Malcolm believed in building multiple political alliances, the more inadequate the Nation of Islam became for him.

Malcolm's thoughts about Black separatism changed over his lifetime. He believed that Black–white unity was not possible until Blacks found their own sense of identity. Blacks cannot unite with others before they have united with themselves. Therefore, for Malcolm, separatism was a first step towards unity. He clarifies that separation means autonomy; integration means complete assimilation; and segregation means an enforced separation of Black from white. Separatism is simply a stage toward being treated as human beings. We are not fighting for separation, he insisted, but for "recognition as human beings ... for the right to live as free human beings in this society".[66] His separatist stage lasted for most of his life. Up until his visits to Africa near the end of his life, Malcolm spoke of integration as hypocrisy.

According to Malcolm, black people are in a mental prison in the US. They must push their minds to look beyond America, and to see that people of color are a majority of the globe.[67] Malcolm's struggle was not limited to civil rights in the US but rather embraced "human rights for the black man". He thought little of civil rights legislation because he thought it would not be enforced, and that it simply made America look as though it were sincere about Black people's rights. He thought "civil rights" was merely an "angelic image of dollarism".[68]

Malcolm argued that his separatism was never racist. He was not against someone because of their race, but only because of their actions.[69] White skin is not the enemy; rather the people who practice racism are the problem. He is not against people because they are white, but because they are racist. Moreover, the race problem is not a Negro or American problem but is a human problem, a problem for humanity."[70] By 1964, and his trip to Mecca, Malcolm develops his thoughts about whites more fully, after meeting whites in Africa who were deeply committed to the struggle against racism. "Travel broadens one's scope. Any time you do any travel, your scope will be broadened. It doesn't mean you change – you broaden." Leaving the US to travel to Africa and Asia allowed him to see differently and more broadly. The more he traveled the more he worked with people of all kinds. He came to accept the idea of intermarriage between the races because humanity is one family.[71] Significantly, his travel to Africa provoked him to question his earlier dismissal of all whites as racist. In Africa he writes: "I wish nothing but freedom, justice and equality: life, liberty and the pursuit of happiness – for all people."[72]

After visiting Africa and the Middle East he was also convinced that democratic countries must demand progress for women.[73] Although he does not develop a critique of the gendered aspects of racism he assumes that women will be a part of the human rights struggle. The specific road women must travel is left unstated, so there is little way to know whether if Malcolm had not been murdered he would have turned his eyes more fully in this direction.

Malcolm was committed to change by "any means possible"; he could not ascribe to nonviolence when defense of oneself was needed. He thought that Blacks can only be nonviolent with nonviolent people.[74] He saw the struggle against racism as necessitating fearlessness. Blacks' strength lay in letting those in power know that they were willing to do whatever was necessary to gain their rights. This would transfer fear to those in power. "You get freedom by letting the enemy know that you'll do anything to get it."[75]

As Malcolm focused more on the exploitation of nonwhites by the West he drew attention to people's class as well as their race. The exploitation by the imperial West focused him on Africa once again. He examined the effects of automation and the displacement of existing markets on Africa. He urged African-Americans to build bridges to Africa in an attempt to fight against the new racist forms of imperialism. By the last year of his life he recognized racism as a transnational structure of domination and that South Africa, Angola, Mozambique, and African-Americans in the US were part of one struggle. The colonization of Blacks in Africa is tied to the menial position of Black men in the US.[76] He extended this view to the Middle East and South America. The struggle for human rights must be taken out of the local domain of the US and into the international arena populated by Brown people. He wished to make the world see that "our problem is not a Negro problem" or an American problem but a human problem: a problem for humanity.[77]

Malcolm X enlarged and diversified the struggle for human liberation. "The oppressed masses of the world cry out for action against the common oppressor."[78] But today's embrace of the globe by the discourses of the powerful invert the gaze of DuBois and Malcolm. Instead of speaking on behalf of the colonized, global capital universalizes, once again, for the imperialists' interests. Africa, rather than being seen as a resource of democratic possibilities, remains a silenced repository of a throwaway economy.

Two weeks before Malcolm was shot dead he was detained at a Paris airport on his way to deliver a speech. He spoke from the airport instead. His message was directed to African-Americans and to the African community throughout the world. He told them that they must unite "wherever we are ... work towards unity and harmony for a positive program of mutual benefit". Malcolm wished to build a unified global movement to fight racism and 'dollarism'.[79] He took his Black skin as a site of specificity structured by racism and exposed it in order to build an enlarged picture of humanity. Although his initial viewings were exclusionary of whites he escapes this particularism and emboldened a polyversal humanity in the end.

Each of these "race democrats" – from DuBois to Malcolm – use their particularized racial viewing in order to see more diversely, and to see more thickly. Their process of specifying racial silences allows for a humane universalizing of people's rights. By naming the false homogeneity of whiteness they write a more inclusive, polyversal humanism.

The Silencing of Racialized Gender

It is telling that so little is said by DuBois, Robeson, Wells, King, and Malcolm about how patriarchal privilege negates the practice of democracy for Black women, or about how the particularity of Black women's lives need to be both de-raced and de-sexed. But, sexist is not the charge I mean to make here, even though DuBois and King were philanderers.

It is not unimportant that Martin Luther King sidelined women activists like Mary McLoud Bethune, Ella Baker, and Fannie Lou Hamer, or that Jesse Jackson lost his leadership role in Black communities because of an extramarital affair. It is not just accidental that almost all the racialized media events of the last decade – from Clarence Thomas, to Rodney King, and O.J. Simpson, and Abner Louima – have all had sexualized subtexts. Nor is it incidental that Bill Clinton, described as 'almost' Black by Toni Morrison, was derailed for his sexual escapades.

Simply put, race and sex always exist intermingled, and side by side. Miscegenation and mixed races are merely proof of this complex history. Yet, antiracist democratic theory silences both sexual desire and gender oppression. Desire is too chaotic to theorize politically. Black men will speak on behalf of Black women against white men's racism towards them. But Black men's misuse of Black women stands outside this racial dialogue and with the gender divide.

My point is that the re-visioning of democracy remains starkly incomplete without attention to the problem of gender oppression. An embrace of racial diversity across the globe remains hobbled by inattention to the particular variety of girls' and women's lives, structured by a sexual and gendered color line. The attempt to enlarge the consciousness of the colonized – as a majority site – is truncated by masculinist blinders.

Some feminists within Black communities name the system of racialized patriarchy in order to dismantle it. But more often than not, antiracist politics do not demand a place for women at the table. Instead deep silences remain about male privilege which normalizes and depoliticizes the construction of racialized gender privilege as natural. The agenda at the 2001 UN conference against racism and xenophobia revealed this pattern once again, despite the hopefulness of antiracist organizing for it.

The World Conference Against Racism

The third UN-sponsored World Conference Against Racism, Racial Discrimination, Xenophobia and Related Intolerance (WCAR) took place in Durban, South Africa, in August, 2001. The location of the conference was chosen to celebrate the end to apartheid rule in South Africa and to allow for a more plural and complex understanding of other types and forms of racism as they are practiced in the twenty-first century. The conference focused on issues of white supremacy but also on many other forms of racism. Conference participants represented Roma (gypsies), the Dalits and casteism affecting some 200 million untouchables in India, the Chinese of Tibet, Chechens, Kurds, Native Americans, Aboriginals of Australia, African Brazilians, Palestinians, and refugees and migrants from everywhere. Women's specific identity as female was collapsed into these other racial identities.

Many at the conference wished to focus these practices of racisms squarely in relation to global capitalism and its special use of peoples of color across the globe. Some wanted to make the relationship between globalization, the growth of poverty and discrimination, and suppression of human rights explicit. A few participants wished to call attention to the neoliberal policies of South Africa itself. Others focused on the huge numbers of refugees and migrants, a majority of whom are women and girls. A plethora of voices and concerns were initially expressed. All were united in the desire for an expansive discussion that would broaden the understanding and particularities of the myriad forms of racial and ethnic oppression presently suffered.

But sadly, this multiplex set of issues was quickly reduced by the US delegation to two highly controversial topics: Israeli racism and slave reparations. The enormously promising gathering of peoples from around the world was quickly rejected by the US delegation as partisan and narrow. The US delegation, led by Colin Powell, said it would have no part in a conference touting the highly contentious claim that Israel is an apartheid state practicing racism against the Palestinian people. Nor would the US entertain a proposal condemning slavery as a crime against humanity, and seeking reparations to families of slaves. The US delegation was so provoked by these two initiatives that on the first day it walked out on the conference and refused to participate.[80] This arrogant behavior was performed as an act of aggression on those seeking to end racist practices in their varied forms across the globe. Instead of engaging in dialogue with much of the rest of the world, the US turned its back on the conversation.

A majority of people in the US are ignorant of the fact that much of the world deeply believes that Israel's treatment of Palestinians, and the denial of a Palestinian state are apartheid practices that are fundamentally racist. And most of the world blames the US for the support and sustenance it gives Israel. Israel has transformed its earlier 'othered' status as a safe haven for homeless Jews into that of an oppressor state. And it uses the antiterrorist rhetoric of the US to justify the annihilation of Jenin and the occupation of Palestinian territories.

Nelson Mandela says of this: "Palestinians are not struggling for a state, but for freedom, liberation and equality, just like we were struggling for freedom in South Africa."[81] Hanan Ashrawi speaking against Israeli apartheid, asks for help so that Palestinians do not have to succumb to their own dehumanization. Instead, she says, Palestinians must "enhance the struggle for dignity, equality, freedom and justice as an act of collective affirmation on behalf of humanity as a whole".[82] The following statement to the conference of the Palestinian NGOs makes clear that the Palestinian struggle against racism must be connected to other antiracist struggles. "Palestinians acknowledge that they are not the only victims of racism in the world, and stand united in full solidarity and support of all other victims of racism, including those seeking reparations such as the Africans and African descendants and indigenous peoples, the Roma, the Tibetans, those combating caste discrimination including the Dalits, Bhuraku, Osu and Rodiya and all others seeking a platform and voice that is otherwise being denied to them."[83]

I have recently signed advertisements and petitions calling on Jews to speak against Sharon's Israeli policies. I have always rejected Zionism because of its singular and exclusionary sense of citizenship. Today I, along with many other Jews, wish to speak out openly against the militarism of Israel without allowing this to feed and sustain anti-Semitism.

The US government turned its back on the WCAR rather than participate in important global antiracist conversations. Official government discourse also refused to recognize the connection between slavery and current-day discrimination of African-Americans. Nor would the US grant that slavery was a "crime against humanity" and consider establishing reparations. The US refusal of dialogue sent a terrible message of disdain to the rest of the world. The hostile US posture towards reconciling with a past rooted in slavery reopens old wounds.[84]

The US pulled out of the Conference just days before September 11, 2001. Although dialoguing at the conference would not have averted the disaster of that day, US actions at the conference bespeak the larger issues of US racial arrogance. And US racism and Western imperialism look very much the same to the rest of the world. Sounding quite similar to Martin Luther King, Samir Amin writes that there "can be no united front against terrorism without a united front against international and social injustice".[85] This being the case, the US grows more rather than less vulnerable, despite its massive military power.

I do not want to deepen the silence surrounding the specificity of girls' and women's gendered oppression at the WCAR. The particular abuse of women and girls in sex trafficking, in the horrific degradation of the Bosnian rape camps, in the lives of Afro-Brazilian domestic workers, in the reality of migrant and refugee life, demands a women's agenda that is "based on inclusivity and a feminist anti-racist analysis". In women's groups across the UN conference, there was a call for recognition of the particular differences like religion, language, and race that define women's lives in shared ways. Although women are not a homogeneous group they share a unique form of sexual exploitation that needs a voice.[86]

The women's caucus at the WCAR stated that "we recognize the dehumanization of racialized women throughout the world who have suffered multiple forms of discrimination under colonialism, slavery, indentured labor, ethnic cleansing, foreign occupation, armed conflict, the caste system, socio-economic marginalization through globalization, homophobia, and trafficking in women".[87] The focus was on racially marginalized women and the intersections between gender and racism that bring both women's poverty and violence against women to the fore of the struggle against racism. These are important beginnings for locating a promissory site for seeing more inclusively and democratically.

Women of color seek to pluralize the viewings of humanity to the more inclusive site of their own experiences. Because this site has such radically democratic potential, it should be no surprise that it is women and their bodies that are central – whether silenced or in view – to the "war on terrorism", as I will shortly show. But first, a mention of possible hope for building resistance against US hegemony.

Building Resistance and Hope

I was quite excited to leave the US for the 2003 World Social Forum (WSF) in Porto Alegre, Brazil. The WSF is a global initiative based on the belief that there is a "universal planetary citizenry" which must articulate the belief that "another world is possible", one free of war, hunger, disease, and misery. The two earlier WSF meetings held in 2001 and 2002, rejected neoliberal/capitalist priorities and the excessive inequities being visited on most countries as part of these policies. The charters that resulted from these gatherings stated that "political action is the responsibility of each individual and the coalitions they form" and that the WSFs are a place for diverse agendas to be openly discussed. Our purpose in Porto Alegre was to "carry forward dreams and social projects, analysis and predictions, alternatives and strategies for the 'here and now'".[88]

Each WSF is a "big meeting of smaller meetings"; a "coalition of coalitions"; a "movement of movements", a "gathering of gatherings", that attempts to put forward alternative visions for the troubled political times in which we all live. It is an important attempt to "speak to power" – to have tens of thousands of people speaking out, making noise, standing against enormously powerful forces which selfishly grab too much for themselves.

One of my first thoughts upon arriving at the conference was that much like the globe itself, the WSF was big, maybe too big, and yet not big enough. People from everywhere were there and yet very few people from countries in Africa and the Middle East attended. As one might expect, Europe and the US were overrepresented because wealth and privilege allow that. And lots of people from countries in South America participated because it was easier and less expensive for them to get there. Huge numbers from Brazil attended. I expect that the election of President Luiz Inacio Lula da Silva, known as Lula, of the Workers' Party (PT), energized this large mobilization of peoples and delegations from Latin countries. There was enormous excitement in Porto Alegre about Lula's election. People there are extremely hopeful that he will create a real democracy for Brazilians. Already he has rejected multi-million-dollar plans to buy new fighter jets and has declared a war on hunger with this money instead.

It has been roughly estimated that 100,000 people were at the WSF. The conference proceedings took place at three sites; meetings, workshops, and plenaries were held at each. On the first day it was hard to know where to go because the programs had yet to be printed. It became quickly obvious that things were not going to be easy or simple: there was just too much to do and too many people for things to go smoothly. There were hundreds of workshops to attend and participate in. But the disorganization did not prevent important discussions from happening; nor did it dampen people's excitement. It did, however, reduce attendance at many meetings that never got publicized, and it limited exposure of the issues they raised.

I assume that few of us who attended the WSF had the same experience. Like the globe, you cannot experience the whole of it from any one particular site. As it should, the WSF hosted spokespersons for a wide swathe of concerns, but without some of the necessary organization to initiate cross-dialogue and coalition building. I attended the WSF as a delegate of the Women's Economic Development Organization (WEDO). Throughout the five days I was in Porto Alegre, I met with women activists, and a wide array of women's NGOs, and feminists of all kinds of identities. However, the focus of many of these discussions – on the particular effects on women and girls of globalization and its militarist vision – was not a dominant theme at the WSF. The sessions I attended attempted to better specify the particular realities of women refugees, and girl/women sweatshop workers; the specific plight of women as rape victims in war; and the growing numbers of women and girls affected by HIV and AIDS. Before the WSF was over, it was clear that many of us were already hoping that the next year's WSF would better expose these issues as central to an anti-globalization stance for the world community.

Because globalization and resistance to it were defined in the more traditional leftist/progressive venues of the WSF, overlaps between its multiple systems of power were insufficiently elucidated. Noam Chomsky and other luminaries critiqued capitalism and neoliberal policies, but did not address the specific uses of patriarchy and racism by global capital. Many of the women delegates I shared my time with thought that insufficent attention was paid to the reality that the new working class of global capital is disproportionately girls and women of color.

Despite this, there were whisperings of a women's/feminist voice at the WSF. Women from across the globe, representing a variety of feminisms, attempted to articulate new strategies to resist the growing militarization of the world. There was open resistance to the increasing marketization/privatization of everything public: be it health, or welfare, or education. Most of the feminists from South American countries united around what they termed an anti-fundamentalisms politics. The campaign, which was called "Against Fundamentalisms, People Are Fundamental", seeks to develop radically democratic politics to resist the growing excesses of extremism, be they religious, anti-woman, capitalist, etcetera. Coalition building was a continual theme, especially among and between women's activists from each of the NGOs represented. Alliance building among women's activists, through and across differences, was keenly embraced at all these meetings.

Joanna Kerr, director of the Association for Women's Rights in Development (AWID), wrote upon returning from Porto Alegre that the WSF "brought together global social movements including the women's movements ... but there is still limited cross-fertilization or alliance building across these movements". She went on to state that feminist and women's activists need to address their marginalization within the broader anti-globalization movement.[89]

Despite these limits, at the WSF serious attention was paid to US policy towards Iraq, to Palestine, and to the "war on terrorism". It was made repeatedly clear that much of the world detests the US government and its militarist and antidemocratic policies. I kept feeling, keenly, that as a citizen of the US I have a newly added responsibility to try and make another world possible. In many of the meetings I attended, people were eager to know more about antiwar activities in the US and also about women's activism related to women's struggles in Afghanistan, Rwanda, and India.

There were also earnest attempts at widening and deepening debates and connections, even if incomplete. This was very true of the international AIDS meeting where the concern was to build concrete policy options to address the disease both locally and globally. The beginnings of a common agenda for the transnational level were agreed between ACT Up, the Women's Network, and Oxfam. The AIDS theme was named "One World, One Fight" and "Globalize Human Health".

Shortly before leaving for home I attended a small workshop about the recent murderous riots in Gujarat, India. The filmmaker Deepa Dhanraj spoke about the film she hoped to make in order to document the recent atrocities visited on Muslims by Hindus. She especially wanted to uncover and expose the particular abuse Muslim women faced in the rioting. She shared with us her concern that in all the coverage of the Gujarat riots in India, that there had been virtually complete silence about the sexual abuse, rape and murder of Muslim women during them. But she wanted her film to do more than record the violation of Muslim women. She wanted it to show how Muslim women are organizing against this kind of violence and how Hindu feminists join them in these struggles to create a better world, free of violence towards women. She intended her film to show the complexity of local patriarchies within the larger system of globalization. It is in such specific and particular ways that the WSF created new spaces for people to begin to envision alternate political locations for resistance and the nurturing of new imaginations.

I left for home thinking how incredible it was that all these people had come to continue their work to change lives for the better, with their eyes on justice for us all. In all my conversations at the WSF, both privately and in meetings, I found that everyone was determined to extend the promise of a truly democratic and just life to the entire people of the planet. People embraced each other for the best of what humanity can imagine and create. I also remember thinking at the conference that people in the US do not understand well enough the havoc that our country creates for others across the globe.

On my trip home, the Lula button I wore on my jacket was greeted with nods of approval from many people of all types in the Porto Alegre and San Paulo airports. The airports in Brazil were so much friendlier and more relaxed than at home. It was sad to realize, upon setting down at JFK airport, that I was re-entering the home country of the "wars on terrorism". There were the wands and the screeners waiting for me in full force, again. This is not the kind of life I want for any of us.

Notes

1. Aimé Césaire, *Discourse on Colonialism* (New York: Monthly Review Press, 1972), p. 25.
2. As quoted in Keleba Sannah, "Here Comes the Son", *Transition*, Issue 85, vol. 10, no. 1, p. 139.
3. Edward Ball, *Slaves in the Family* (New York: Ballantine Books, 1998), p. 1.
4. Claude Lévi-Strauss, *The View From Afar* (New York: Basic Books, 1985), pp. 4, 5, 6.
5. Seth Sanders, "Invisible Races", *Transition*, Issue 85, vol. 10, no. 1, pp. 79, 96, 97.
6. Tudor Parfitt, *Travels Among the Lost Tribes of Israel* (London: Weidenfeld & Nicolson, 1987), p. 152.
7. Tudor Parfitt, *Operation Moses: The Untold Story of the Secret Exodus of the Falasha Jews from Ethiopia* (New York: Stein & Day, 1985), p. 64.
8. Frank Rich, "Bonfire of the Vanities", *New York Times*, December 21, 2002, p. A21; and Paul Krugman, "The Other Face", *New York Times*, December 13, 2002, p. A39.
9. "A Conversation with Harry Belafonte: 'Remains of the Day-O'", *Transition*, Issue 92, vol. 12, no. 2, pp. 131, 133, 137.
10. W.E.B. DuBois, *The World and Africa* (New York: International Publishers, 1965), pp. 123, 130, 227.

11. W.E.B. DuBois, *Black Reconstruction in America: An Essay Toward A History of the Part Which Black Folk Played in the Attempt to Reconstruct Democracy in America, 1860–1880* (New York: Russell and Russell, 1935, 1963), p. 727.
12. W.E.B. DuBois, *Color and Democracy: Colonies and Peace* (New York: Harcourt, Brace and Co., 1945), pp. 43, 76.
13. DuBois, *The World and Africa*, pp. 52, vii, 43.
14. W.E.B. DuBois, *Darkwater: Voices From Within the Veil* (New York: Schocken Books, 1920), p. 30.
15. W.E.B. DuBois, *Black Reconstruction in America*, pp. 10, 14, 16.
16. Manning Marable. *W.E.B. DuBois, Black Radical Democrat* (Boston: Twayne, 1986), p.1.
17. Sterling Stuckey, *Slave Culture* (New York: Oxford University Press, 1987), p. 278.
18. Hazel Carby, *Race Men* (Cambridge, MA: Harvard University Press, 1998), p. 109.
19. W.E.B. DuBois, "The Negro Problem" and "The World and Africa", in David Levering Lewis, ed., *W.E.B. DuBois, A Reader* (New York: Henry Holt & Co., 1995), pp. 52, 53, 220.
20. W.E.B. DuBois, "What is the Meaning of All Deliberate Speed?", and "The Souls of White Folk", in Levering Lewis, ed., *W.E.B. DuBois, A Reader*, pp. 423, 453.
21. W.E.B. DuBois, *The World and Africa*, p. 19.
22. Nathan Huggins, ed., *W. E. B. DuBois Writings: The Suppression of the African Slave Trade to the U. S. of America, 1638–1870* (New York: Library of America, 1986), pp. 12, 13, 88, 96.
23. DuBois, *Black Reconstruction in America*, pp. 125, 130.
24. Huggins, ed., *W.E.B. DuBois Writings*, pp. 14, 39, 40, 169.
25. DuBois, *Black Reconstruction in America*, p. 32.
26. Huggins, ed., *W.E.B. DuBois Writings,* pp. 50, 169, 172, 174, 179.
27. DuBois, *Black Reconstruction in America,* pp. 637, 669, 713.
28. W.E.B. DuBois, "Negroes and the Crisis of Capitalism in the US." and "To the Nations of the World", in Levering Lewis, ed., *W.E.B. DuBois, A Reader*, pp. 622, 639.
29. W.E.B. DuBois, "Russia, 1926", and "The Black Worker", in ibid, pp. 582, 606, 614, 616.
30. Marable, *W.E.B. DuBois*, p. 37.
31. DuBois, *Africa and the World*, p. 40.
32. DuBois, "The Damnation of Women", in *Darkwater*, p. 181
33. Brent Hayes Edwards, "One More Time", *Transition*, Issue 89, vol. 11, no. 1 (2001), p. 102. Also see: David Levering Lewis, *W.E.B. DuBois* (New York: Henry Holt, 2000), pp. 186, 225–8, 274.
34. Mason Stokes, "Strange Fruits", *Transition*, Issue 92, vol. 12, no. 2, pp. 65, 66.
35. DuBois, *Darkwater*, p. 169.
36. W.E.B. DuBois, "Woman Suffrage", David Levering Lewis, ed., *W.E.B. DuBois A Reader*, p. 298.

37. DuBois, *Africa and the World*, p. 25.
38. DuBois, *Black Reconstruction in America*, pp. 125, 728.
39. Carby, *Race Men*, pp. 25, 33.
40. DuBois, *Africa and the World,* p. 261.
41. "Damnation of Women", in *Darkwater*, pp. 163, 164, 168.
42. Ida B. Wells, *The Memphis Diary,* edited by Miriam De Costa-Willis (Boston: Beacon Press, 1995), pp. 5, 191.
43. Paula Giddings, "Missing in Action: Ida B. Wells, the NAACP and the Historical Record", *Meridians*, vol. 1, no. 2 (Spring 2001), p. 6.
44. Ida B. Wells, "Southern Horrors", in her *On Lynching* (New York: Arno Press, 1969), pp. 4, 8, 10, 42, 54.
45. Ibid., p. 14.
46. Ida B. Wells, "A Red Record", in *On Lynching*, pp. 81, 86.
47. Wells, *The Memphis Diary*, pp. 181, 185, 188.
48. Joy James, *Shadowboxing: Representations of Black Feminist Politics* (New York: St Martin's Press, 1999), pp. 46, 132.
49. Paul Robeson, "I Want to be African", in Eric Foner, ed., *Paul Robeson Speaks: Writings, Speeches, Interviews* (Secaucus, NJ: Citadel Press, 1978), p. 88.
50. Paul Robeson, *Here I Stand* (Boston: Beacon Press, 1958), p. 48.
51. Ibid., pp. 11, 64.
52. Ibid., pp. 64, 67.
53. Ibid., p. 99.
54. Ibid., p. 108.
55. Kwame Nkrumah, *I Speak of Freedom* (London: Heinemann, 1961), pp. 67, 169. Also see Kwame Nkrumah, *The Autobiography of Kwame Nkrumah* (New York: Thomas Nelson and Sons, 1957), and his *Consciencism* (London: Heinemann, 1964); and Opoku Agyeman, *Nkrumah's Ghana and East Africa* (London: Associated University Press, 1992).
56. G. K. Osei, ed., *Twelve Key Speeches of Kwame Nkrumah* (London: African Publication Society, 1972), pp. 3, 12.
57. Martin Luther King, "A Time To Break Silence", in James Washington, ed., *A Testament of Hope, The Essential Writings of Martin Luther King, Jr* (New York: Harper Collins, 1986), p. 233.
58. Ibid., pp. 234, 235, 238.
59. Ibid., p. 238.
60. Ibid., pp. 240–2.
61. Malcolm X, "A Meeting in Paris", in George Breitman, ed., *By Any Means Necessary: Speeches, Interviews and A Letter by Malcolm X* (New York: Pathfinder Press, 1970), p. 114.
62. Malcolm X, *The Final Speeches*, February, 1965 (New York: Pathfinder, 1992), p. 144.
63. Malcolm X, "Letter from Cairo", in Breitman, ed., *By Any Means Necessary*, p. 111.
64. Malcolm X, "Twenty Million Black People in a Political, Economic, and Mental Prison", in Bruce Perry, ed., *Malcolm X: The Last Speeches* (New York: Pathfinder

Press, 1989), p. 51.
65. Malcolm X, *The Final Speeches*, pp. 257, 258, 267.
66. George Breitman, *The Last Year of Malcolm X: The Evolution of a Revolutionary* (New York: Pathfinder Press, 1967), pp. 57, 65.
67. Malcolm X, "Twenty Million Black People", in Perry, ed., *The Last Speeches*, p. 45.
68. Malcolm X, *The Final Speeches*, p. 43.
69. George Breitman, ed., *Malcolm X Speaks: Selected Speeches and Statements* (New York: Grove Weidenfeld, 1965), p. 96.
70. "Introduction", in Bruce Perry, ed., *The Last Speeches*, pp. 14, 15.
71. David Gallen, *Malcolm X As They Knew Him* (New York: Carroll and Graf, 1992), p. 208.
72. Malcolm X, "Letters from Abroad", in Breitman, ed., *Malcolm X Speaks*, p. 59.
73. Malcolm X, "Short Statements", in Breitman, ed., *By Any Means Necessary*, p. 179.
74. Malcolm X, "The 'Young Socialist' Interview", in Breitman, ed., *By Any Means Necessary*, p. 162.
75. Malcolm X, "To the Mississippi Youth", in Breitman, ed., *Malcolm X Speaks*, p. 145.
76. Malcolm X, "Answers to the Questions at the Militant Labor Forum" and "The 'Young Socialist' Interview", in Breitman, ed., *By Any Means Necessary*, pp. 21, 161.
77. Malcolm X, "An Appeal to African Heads of State", in Breitman, ed., *Malcolm X Speaks*, p. 75.
78. Malcom X, *The Final Speeches*, p. 58.
79. Malcolm X, "On Being Barred From France", in Breitman, ed., *By Any Means Necessary*, p. 174.
80. Michael Lerner, "The Danger of Walking Out at Durban", *New York Times*, September 5, 2001, p. A19; Jane Perlez, "How Powell Decided to Shun Conference", *New York Times*, September 5, 2001, p. A8; Serge Schmemann, "US Walkout: Was It Repudiated or Justified by the Conference's Accord", *New York Times*, September 9, 2001, p. A16; and Rachel Swarns, "US And Israelis Quit Racism Talks Over Denunciation", *New York Times*, September 4, 2001, p. A1.
81. Nelson Mandela, "Mandela on Israel", available at El-Akhbar Newspaper, afandem@ access.com.eg Also see "After Durban – A Symposium", in *Poverty and Race*, vol. 11, no. 1 (January/February 2002).
82. Hanan Ashrawi, "World Should Intervene to end the Israeli Apartheid", an address in Durban, South Africa, August 28, 2001. Available at: http://rezeq.com
83. Statement of the Palestinian NGOs to Government Delegates at the World Conference Against Racism, Durban, South Africa, September 6, 2001. Available at http://www.batshalom.org
84. Manning Marable, "Along the Color Line", November 2001, available at www.manningmarable.net
85. Samir Amin, "World Conference Against Racism: A People's Victory", *Monthly Review*, vol. 53, no. 7 (December, 2001), p. 23.

86. See the reports by WICEJ members on the UN World Conference Against Racism. Available at: www.wicej.addr.com
87. See the "Women Standing at the Intersection of Race and Gender", Women's Caucus Statement to the World Conference Against Racism, Durban, South Africa, September 4, 2001, pp. 1, 3.
88. Visit www.forumsocialmundial.org.br/home.asp for statements and documents pertaining to the 2003 WSF.
89. Available at: jkerr@awid.org

7 Feminisms and Afghan Women: Before and After September 11

Feminisms, differently defined, have been around for as long as women have existed. They take different forms and shapes, and can have cacophonous-sounding names. Much like democracy itself, feminism is often wrongly equated with the West, or rather Western women. Now in the aftermaths of September 11, 2001 it is more urgent than ever to recognize the polyvocal articulations of feminisms so that they may be threaded back to their earlier histories and pushed forward towards their more immediate understandings of freedom and equality.

At this historical moment I look to find more richly inclusive and expansive understandings of the complexity of feminisms by looking at: the aftermaths of terrorism in the US; women in Afghanistan, now and before; and the role of Bush administration women in marketing the Afghan war. The varied faces of women and their feminisms are my present site for imagining through and beyond the anti-democratic US war of/on 'terror'. The context of this moment defines the contours of feminist possibility.

The possibility of liberatory feminisms emerging at this time is fraught with difficulty. At first it appeared as though US mainstream feminism had successfully called world attention to the Taliban's horrific treatment of Afghan women. But this attention was quickly captured by First Lady Laura Bush along with the rest of President Bush's women helpmates. They took the post-September 11 moment and appropriated the language of women's rights for a right-wing and neoliberal imperial agenda. Yet, at this same time, there are anti-imperialist feminists in the US along with women activists elsewhere – some of whom are self-proclaimed feminists, others not – who seek to democratize the globe for women and the rest of humanity. This is a moment of extreme tension between US imperial feminism and all the other feminisms of the globe which search for liberatory democracy.

I locate my exploration at the intersection between women's rights as a complicated discourse, and the burqa – the all-encompassing blue body wrap – as a complex symbolic. This is the site from which to understand the complex power struggle embodied in the US war against Afghanistan. But first a note of context is necessary to clear some space for thinking – openly, critically, historically – in terms of a before and after, September 11, 2001.

September 11, 2001 has not changed everything, as so many in the US say. It has just made clear how much context, perspective, and location matter. Suffering and fear have just not been at center view for too many in the US until now. Remember that the people of Chile mourn a different September 11 and came to know a constant trauma and grief living under the US supported terror-filled dictatorship of Augusto Pinochet. Remember that the US bombed Iraq with tons of 'smart' bombs in 1991. Think across and beyond to the children of Afghanistan and Iraq who still, this minute, suffer unbearable poverty. Or, look to the majority of Palestinians and Israelis who live with daily crises, surrounded by fear and uncertainty given US support of a minority of fanatics led by Sharon in Israel. All the while, the language of freedom and democracy is used as justification and cover.

It is also vital to remember other things: the US economy was in trouble before September 11, 2001; Boeing was angling for its defense contract before September 11; the airlines were in financial trouble before September 11. Also remember, the three thousand people who were murdered on September 11 came from over sixty different countries. Remember, also, the horrible bombings in Nigeria and Sudan; the students in high school then, like my daughter, who were expected to wear flag pins and would not; the millions of workers who have lost their jobs since September 11; the incredible profits being made by the military-industrial complex from the wars of 'terror'; that Planned Parenthood has faced anthrax threats for years; that college campuses are being targeted as sites of antipatriotism. Remembering at this moment is subversive and stands against the erasure of political history.

So, one needs to try and see what is not easily visible. Rethink invisibility; rethink as overt the covert realms of power that are not being named. Do not give into the falseness of the 'terror'-filled moment even though this is a time of insecurity and fear. Do not pretend that having to use a plastic spoon to spread cream cheese on your bagel in the airport – instead of a plastic knife – makes you safe. Don't allow yourself the luxury of thinking that more police, more surveillance, more war, make any of us safer. None of humanity will be safe until the world understands that present antiterrorism rhetoric is an assault on democracy for us all.

Nor will women in the US know the truths of women 'elsewhere' if they do not recognize that women in colonized countries have struggled for their rights for centuries. Margot Badran and Miriam Cooke have long recognized the feminists in Egypt, Algeria, Iraq, Iran, and so on. The notion of a 'sisterhood' spread across the globe dates back, at least, to the early nineteenth century. One should just not assume that global means oneness, or homogeneity here, but rather that awareness and contact between women, across nations, has a history in the *before*. Early flows, between the East and West born out of the slave trade and colonialism bespeak an historical dialogue between feminisms.

Global flows are not new. Kumari Jayawadena poignantly documents the role of some Western women as anticolonialist. British colonialism in South Asia spoke a "domination by European males of colonized women". And some colonial women did not accede to this process. They instead were sometimes attracted to "concepts of woman's power (shakti) in Hinduism, androgynous deities, female goddesses like Kali and the high status of women in ancient Hindu and Buddhist societies". In this instance, this historical flow is from East to West.[1]

On Global Misogyny

A masculinist-militarist mentality dominates on both sides of the ill-named East/West divide. The opposition implied by this divide is not simple or complete. Flows between these locations have always existed, and they occur today more than ever. Furthermore, the two sides of the divide share foundational relations, even if differently expressed, especially in terms of male privilege. Neither side embraces women's full economic and political equality or sexual freedom. In this sense fluidity has always existed between the two in the arena of women's rights and obligations. The Taliban's insistence on the burqa and the US military's deployment of women fighter pilots are used to overdraw and misrepresent the oppositional stance.

Although some women on both sides of the divide live with daily terror of physical violence it is unusual to focus attention here: on the transnational, or global aspects of male violence, be it in militarist or more privatized and individualized form. Catherine MacKinnon asks when the daily terrorizing of women will be recognized by the rhetoricians of antiterrorism; when men will critique this daily violence alongside the condemnation of violence towards women outside their own borders.[2] I wish to extend this antiviolence frame to allow us to see the complex narrative of violence towards men as well as women within the global context.

At present, economic flows of the global economy simply lessen the East/West divide further. The bin Laden family itself represents this form of globalism. The family's money is tied to multiple Western investments such as General Electric, Goldman-Sachs, Merrill Lynch, Microsoft, and Boeing.[3] One can easily assume that bin Laden's fury is directed as much at his family as at the West, which is a deadly combination. The quick and easy East/ West divide is also not helpful politically, as the United States champions democracy while banding together with military dictators and kings.

It is crucial to locate and name the privileging of post-September 11 masculinist power with all its destructiveness. The silencing of women's unique voices, but most especially the voices of Afghan women and feminists – who criticized the early US support of the Taliban – needs to be exposed. Women have fought and resisted the Taliban as well as other forms of Islamic extremist misogyny for decades. Fundamentalist misogyny has no one singular site or home. Women across the globe continue to resist gender apartheid and sexual terrorism in the diverse war sites where they continually reappear: Bosnia, Chechnya, Rwanda, Algeria, Nigeria, and Palestine. Activist groups like Women against Fundamentalism, Women Living under Muslim Laws (WLUML), and Women in Black give transnational voice to women struggling against the oppressiveness of misogynist law. They also indict the United States for supporting regimes that practice atrocities toward women.[4]

Yet instead of seeing and hearing from these women activists, CNN presented Afghan women as burqa-covered creatures in need of saviors. After the Taliban retreat from Kabul, the world was shown uncovered women's faces smiling as the air hit their skin, despite the fact that most women, especially in rural areas, continued to wear the burqa. In all this, we need to be reminded that Afghan women have another activist history to be recounted; that in Algeria it has been women, since the revolution in that country, who have fought tirelessly for democratic rule; that it was the women's vote in Iran that allowed the more moderate Mohammed Khatami to be elected twice.

If people in the US saw and heard more about these kinds of involvements by women, many more people would be wondering about how gender apartheid and sexual terrorism are crucial aspects of these political times: how the patriarchal aspects of the global economy today feed the fires of hatred toward women everywhere, and how ending this hatred/fear of women is central to creating a democratic globe. Different forms of sexual terrorism affect women across the globe in similar and different ways. All the women I know have learned to live productive lives alongside the terror/fear of rape: we do not walk alone at night if we can help it, we do not put ourselves at risk if we can figure out what this means, we fear for our daughters' safety when they are among men we do not know.

I do not agree with the columnists who attributed September 11 solely to the anger of bin Laden and his followers toward the excessive greed and irresponsibility of global capitalism and its white supremacist ways. Nor did September 11 happen simply because the global economy is displacing men from their earlier livelihoods. These explanations are valid, but September 11 must also be viewed in relation to the way that male patriarchal privilege orchestrates its hierarchical system of domination. The age-old fear and hatred of women's sexuality and their forced domestication into womanly and wifely roles informs all economies. Global capitalism unsettles the pre-existing sexual hierarchical order and tries to mold women's lives to its newest needs across the East/West divide. Differing factions within the Taliban are fully aware of the stakes involved here, which is in part why they root their war strategy in the active subordination of women.

When women in Afghanistan or Algeria are driven out of school and not allowed to hold jobs, we should remember that they continue to work as mothers and caretakers in desperate situations of famine and displacement and grotesque killing. Many of these women, who are sick of the war, are not obedient slaves. You do not bother oppressing those who are already docile and powerless. You only veil and stone and murder people you fear for the power they have. Women in countries throughout the Muslim world have been sorting out their own democratic conception of Islam for decades. Their effect has not gone unnoticed by radical fundamentalist misogynists of all sorts. So the Taliban is not simply traditionalist and patriarchal: it is part of this modern struggle to sort out Islamic practices.

The Taliban read and interpret Islamic practice as patriarchal men, with their masculinist and vested interests as such. Members of Al Qaeda seek to rescope their understanding of their male privilege in particularly anti-US fashion for this very contemporary global capitalist moment. And they use their religious beliefs, as they selectively interpret them, to do so. And although I am no friend of misogynist fundamentalism, wherever it thrives, demonization is not helpful. I rather choose to contextualize their masculinism as possibly as secularist as it is Islamic.[5] Demonization leads us too quickly away from Islam to the West, where it is too easy to think all women should be free like me – whoever the 'me' is.

At this moment the stance of protection toward women is often mobilized on behalf of misogynists in Muslim countries. Protection is a strange and contradictory stance to take toward the individuals who are best at nurturing life and peace. Supposedly, the Taliban seek to protect their women from public display and abuse; and yet the Taliban are also abusive to women. Women of the former Soviet Union decried the protectionist legislation that demanded they work in the labor force, but at lesser jobs, in order to protect them for maternity. Women in the United States have fought protectionism as a violation of equal treatment and equal freedoms. Many women in Muslim countries have been arguing similarly.

A half-billion women in the world are Muslim and they are a potentially significant worldwide gender community. Many of them emphasize and participate in articulating an egalitarian ethics of Islam; they re-appropriate the veil for access rather than seclusion; diversify the meanings of dress codes to express their freedom; and bring out the Qur'an's woman-friendly teachings. There is no one identity to discover here but rather different forms of Islamic gender activism and reformism.[6]

Thinking and seeing complexity is not easy given the polarized war language being used by all sides. The selective use of terms like 'terrorism', 'democracy', 'civilization', 'modernity', 'traditionalism', and 'fundamentalism' complicate the ability to think and see plurally and openly. Words carry their own context and closure. 'Terrorism' is equated with 'jihad' which is equated with holy wars and death. Jihad becomes a pathological fanaticism and terrorism, irrational and uncontrollable. According to Roxanne Euben 'jihad' functions as a repository for contemporary anxieties about death. It also shores up "an idealized Western public sphere in which reasoned arguments and nonviolent practices largely prevail". Nevertheless, jihad means something very different to most Muslims. It involves the constant struggle with the internal self to strive for worthiness; to change oneself for the better, in order to change the world as well. In this reading, virtuous Muslims are obligated to realize human freedom for all.[7]

The Bush administration has a very imperial comfort level. When US officials were asked why they did not work more closely with other countries on the Afghan war effort, they responded that they feel more comfortable with "our boys and our toys". Our president spoke of the war as Enduring Freedom and Infinite Justice; the antiterrorist bill was renamed the Patriot Bill. We are repeatedly told to be careful, but not intimidated. Color-coded alerts are regularly invoked. Alongside these symbolic gestures and elusive language, the political discourses of the moment do not put women's lives and their already engendered meanings in view. As a result I find myself stretching words beyond their usual limits in order to create visibility for the incredible stakes at issue for women across the globe, and democracy alike.

Silences about women at this juncture make it harder to think through and open up the constructs of traditionalism and modernism. This is especially true if we want to think about women's relationship to building democracies that are earnestly humanist. Earnest democracy will be polyversal if written with women's bodies in their different cultural contexts. I wonder why the rape camps of Bosnia or the sexual slavery of women by the Japanese military during World War Two were never called traditionalist and 'backward'. Yet the woman who is forced to veil and/or be covered by a burqa represents the 'backwardness' of Islam – and the naked porn model the modernity of the West. These choices for women are not acceptable, and I do an injustice by using the term 'choice' here. The choice between sexual exploitation (commodification) and sexual repression (denial) is no democratic choice at all.[8]

Thinking critically about the meanings of women's freedom and equality is central to navigating this historical 'terror'-filled moment. But these meanings are not best understood as simply of the West, because the West is not a singular site for these ideas, even if Western appropriation says so. Women's struggle for their independence takes hold in its own way everywhere and elsewhere. No one system of thought can contain or claim 'freedom' as its own; only humanity can do so, human bodies within their plural contexts, with similar needs.

Further, I am not equating all forms of male privilege but neither do I want to allow the Western forms of patriarchy to parade as democratic. Instead, I wish to bring the similarities between the different formulations of patriarchal privilege into fuller view. Neither form of masculinism – bin Laden's terror tactics or Bush's bombs – is good enough for women and girls across this globe. So Bush's bombs in Afghanistan should not be cloaked and wrapped in a defense of women's rights.

If feminisms' meanings are continually redeciphered given the political contexts of struggle, it is important to allow feminism to be named by sites that may use different languages to embrace this varied activity. The multiple languages that women speak across the globe necessitate that one should be extremely careful and hesitant about assuming that there is only one word – and an English one at that – that describes and represents women's struggles to enhance and better their, and their nation's lives. There is no monolithic global feminism; nor can a universalizing language ever encompass a complete accounting of women's activism. Yet human rights language is both liberating even if colonizing for women living across the globe. Uma Narayan cautions that the very idea of transnational gender can lead to overstatement and overgeneralization. But the colonial encounter can also "insist on difference" when it does not exist in order to create the West versus the Other. Cultural imperialism in these cases denies sameness where it exists.[9]

Feminisms are hard to name and therefore see; and hard to see and therefore name. This is why Miriam Cooke says we must be careful not to lose once again the history of women's struggle within Islam. She warns that the foremothers of present-day Muslim women activists have been mostly erased. She recognizes the importance of women's activism today in Arab countries as Islamic discourse takes hold and creates an "unprecedented focus on the importance of women". As religious groups become more visible and vocal, they are placing "women at the symbolic center". And women are demanding more of a say in this process of defining their rights and obligations.[10] Feminism may be rooted in differing religions, or secularisms, so long as woman's identity is never limited simply to the self, or to others.

Whose Rights? And for Which Women?

Given the flux and tensions that reside within the sexual and gendered relations of global capitalism, women are a key part of the messy political imagery of the times. During the Afghan war, on any given day women appeared in the news in an astonishing array of roles: as passive, burqa-covered creatures, fighter pilots (although I think there was only one), bereaved widows of the September 11 carnage, pregnant wives of men who died in the Twin Towers, Pakistanis holding placards against the war, and Condoleezza Rice, national security adviser to Bush. Rice, a Black woman and sometimes called the "Warrior Princess", made her name while on the board of Chevron oil company and as Provost of Stanford University where the tenure rate for white women and African-American faculty declined during her tenure.[11]

Other key women players of the Bush administration's Afghan war included Victoria Clarke as the hardline Pentagon spokeswoman, worldwide advertising agent Charlotte Beers, chosen to overhaul the government's image abroad, and main Bush aide Karen Hughes as the coordinator of wartime public relations. Hughes resigned her post claiming that her family duties must come first. She would telecommute instead. This instigated much talk-show noise of whether (Western) women can 'really' have it all. These women, along with the well-known conservative Mary Matalin, who was chief political adviser to vice-president Dick Cheney, were in charge of shaping the words and images of the Afghan war.[12]

They were showcased as the movers and shakers of the moment alongside the grieving mothers and wives of September 11, 2001, and contrasted to the supposedly nonmodern women in Afghanistan. This US showcase masqueraded as a modernized masculinity in drag. The war room of Rice, Clarke, and Beers distorts the symbolic of power. They shore up white patriarchy for global capital by making it look gender- and race-neutral. Of course they represent change, but for themselves, not the rest of women either inside or outside the US. Coreene Swealty Palm, bomber pilot of an F-14, spoke about her love of flying even while dropping bombs, which she saw as simply a misfortune of war. Here, too, the United States looks egalitarian in terms of its women. In reality, the military simply resexes its masculinist privilege for a few.

The distortion became even more corrupt as these women of the Bush administration supposedly spoke on behalf of women in Afghanistan and their "deplorable conditions" under Taliban rule. Mary Matalin ignored the facts that in 1979 Jimmy Carter played an important role in the destabilization of the very government that brought significant gains to Afghan women: literacy, medical services, prohibition of the bride price, and so forth. This secular government, the Progressive Democratic Party of Afghanistan (PDPA), is credited with promoting the welfare and liberation of women. And it is this socialist government that the CIA targeted and overthrew through its earlier support of bin Laden.[13] Women become easy barter here. First their successes are smashed by US policy, and then they are used in their smashed existence to justify yet another war on their behalf.

Laura Bush, who had never spoken on behalf of women's rights before, found her voice in order to mobilize women for the Afghan war. She delivered the president's weekly radio address – a first for a First Lady – in order to speak on behalf of women's rights in Afghanistan. She said that the Taliban's treatment of women "is not a matter of legitimate religious practice", that the plight of women and children is a matter of "deliberate human cruelty". She further stated that the "brutal oppression of women is a central goal of the terrorists" and is a clear picture of "the world the terrorists would like to impose on the rest of us".[14] But I wonder about the impetus of the administration's targeted focus on women and its real commitments, when women's rights have never been a priority of US foreign policy.

It made no sense for Laura Bush to have thousands of school uniforms sent to Afghanistan as soon as the Taliban were deposed while most children were starving and too hungry to concentrate on school work. More recently, as disorder and pillage have returned to Afghanistan despite the so-called end of the war, many schools have been closed again. But we have heard nothing further from Ms Bush on behalf of women and children. She has remained silent as have the other women of the war room in spite of the return of draconian measures enforced on women by the Northern Alliance. The "war on terrorism" exacerbated misery, starvation and homelessness for most Afghan women despite breaking the Taliban's hold on the country. The US public is told that the Taliban are gone, but religious zealots are still in charge. Afghanistan is ruled by thuggery; Osama bin Laden remains alive in hiding; the Northern Alliance has not improved the economy; US troops remain but they are not remembered much of the time. It is unforgivable to have used women's rights as a pawn in the Afghan war while increasing human suffering, and then forget to remember women's rights once again.

It is worth noting that although US foreign policy has never made the conditions of women's betterment a key concern, our first ladies often speak on behalf of women in other countries. Hillary Clinton was well known for traveling abroad to speak for women's rights in Africa and India. Yet here at home, she never chose to speak as a feminist or develop a women's rights agenda. I am reminded how she always turned the other way when issues of day care arose, or when confirmations for government jobs for women like Lani Guinier or Zoë Baird got derailed.

Bush administration women do the same. Many speak negatively of feminism, and none has spoken on behalf of a domestic women's rights agenda. Neither do they seek to deal with issues like women prisoners, welfare mothers, accessible day care, or reproductive health. None has shown outrage at the religious fundamentalists who bomb and kill women in US abortion clinics. None has spoken out against the terror of domestic violence. I am uneasy with an imperial women's rights agenda spoken for others while it is not used as a critique for our own lives here at home.

I am also critical of a women's rights campaign that chooses to ignore the numerous worldwide women's organizations speaking on behalf of women in these countries as well as the post-Beijing global network working toward women's equality. The Bush administration women should have brought attention to these initiatives that are local and homegrown instead of appropriating these struggles for the West and its exclusionary version of democracy. Nowhere did the Bush agenda address the health of Afghan women, most of whom still are at great risk from radiation poisoning because of the depleted uranium in the bombs the US dropped.[15] Instead, these very bombs were justified by women's rights rhetoric.

The insider women of the Bush administration should caution feminists across the globe of the limits and risks involved in insider status. Much has been made of the importance and difference that women can make from the inside, because they remain in part always outsiders given their gender. But I am not so sure. Although the main early critique of the FBI's deficiencies in responding to information prior to September 11 was leveled by a woman FBI agent, Coleen Rowley, her criticism was not of the agency *per se*, but of individuals within it. I am not sure that Anita Hill is right when she says that Rowley had "insider status and outsider values".[16] Rowley rose within the FBI, a male-dominated institution, despite being female and used the very same skills that had allowed her to advance to criticize what she saw as inefficient bureaucratic bumbling. In her bombshell memo she asked that the FBI update and restructure itself for the changing times.[17]

Globalization and more porous national borders require a more modern FBI. I might say that Rowley just did a better job than her bosses at modernizing a nation-state apparatus for a global militarist stance. She saw the need for 'modernizing' an anachronistic system; and is the insider par excellence in this instance. Maybe women are better at change and seeing the need for it. Clearly, most of the women in these high-status leagues use their talents as women – adaptability and multi-tasking – to sustain institutions that are structurally misogynist. These women are not embracing democracy but rather seek to reform institutions that wreak havoc on much of the world. What this portends for women on the outside, and for Afghan women as they enter Afghan politics, is fraught with tension.[18]

We must look elsewhere to find an honest embrace of democratic imaginings for women, like the "Proposal for UN Women's Strategies for Civil Conflict Resolution" drawn up by the Ugandan women's delegation to the UN. The delegation asks for an end to all terrorism and a worldwide culture of tolerance, for better conflict resolution and a de-escalation of conflict, for an elimination of rich and poor, that each life be accorded the same human rights as all others, for the creation of a World Security Council of Women, and for the elimination of all forms of discrimination against women. The delegation asks the world to embrace the Universal Declaration of Human Rights, which presumes global pluralism and diversity. A twelve-point statement committed to peace was e-mailed to individual women and women's organizations all around the globe, and over a thousand individuals and organizations endorsed the statement.[19] Earlier, on October 30, 2000, the United Nations Security Council unanimously adopted Resolution 1325, which states that "all actors negotiating peace agreements need to adopt a gender perspective which recognizes the special needs of women and girls".[20] It is significant that the Bush administration women do not speak on behalf of these international women's groups but rather as women of the West.

Women in the aftermath of September 11 are captured as both actors and passive receptors of historical moments. And there is little clarity on what a democratic and freely chosen femaleness and womanhood should mean. US policy spoke against the Taliban's mistreatment of women at this historical juncture, but condoned it earlier. The United States supports Saudi Arabia, Egypt, and Pakistan, which all regularly violate women's rights.[21] So what exactly is US foreign policy toward women's rights, the very rights that the United States parlays as central to so-called Western democracy? At least one senior administration official early on in the "war on terrorism" said that the US could not make women's rights a part of the post-Taliban package because we have to be careful not to look like we are imposing our values on them.[22]

The official went on to say that the championing of women's rights goes well with a domestic audience, but that we must be careful how it sounds abroad. But who exactly is this official thinking of here? Hundreds of thousands of women, as well as men, abroad applaud the rights of women. Afghan women were active contributors to and participants in everyday life before the Taliban. The 1964 Afghan constitution guaranteed equal rights and the vote for women; and four women were elected to parliament during this Soviet-run period. As well, 70 percent of schoolteachers and 50 percent of civilian government workers were women. And by some readings of the Qur'an, it too gave women rights of inheritance and divorce before Western women had such status.[23] The anti-Taliban Northern Alliance even had a female lobbyist in Washington and a position paper on women's rights, despite criticism by some Afghan women's groups that the Alliance has not been a friend to women in the past.[24] The divide between "us and them" is no simple divide and should not be used to occlude the similar patriarchal roots/routes of global capitalism. Also, if US policy makers aggressively think they have a right to orchestrate aspects of a new Afghan regime, why exclude women's rights for fear of seeming too pushy? Obviously, these Western officials do not see women's human needs as essential to the transition toward and construction of democracy.

There is no one position on women's rights to analyze because the government's stance has shifted and changed. The State Department released a report, "The Taliban's War against Women", which stated that "Islam is a religion that respects women and humanity", while the "Taliban respects neither". The report then advocated a role for women in a post-Taliban Afghan government.[25] Although several women became a part of this new government the government itself has not been able to establish any semblance of order. President Karzai can travel nowhere without US bodyguards.

In interesting contrast, at home in the US, the period after September 11 became a very manly moment. The new heroism celebrated the American male worker, be he firefighter or policeman or welder. As stated in the *New York Times*: "The operative word is men: brawny, heroic, manly men. The male hero expresses the new selflessness of masculinism. Physical prowess is back in vogue along with patriotism."[26] New York City police, the same police who have been repeatedly charged with racist violence towards people of color and the violation of their human rights, embodied the new heroism.

In the early aftermath of September 11 there was little if any talk of women firefighters, or heroic women in general, for that matter.[27] Women, who were busy trying to rebuild the lives of their shattered families while they scrambled to get to their jobs as well, were shunted to the side – seen only through the veil of motherhood and wifely duty. There may be a few women in the Bush White House, but it is men who make the system work. They are the heroes and patriots. Ironically, amid all this, it is the Taliban that were viewed as "living in a world without women", not us.[28]

September 11 ignited a renewal of masculinist patriotism. Jashur Piar and Amit Rai describe this disciplining of the docile citizen as a "heteronormative patriotism". Bin Laden the terrorist is made into a "monstrous fag"; and anyone who does not support the war is a fag as well. The "terrorist fag", as the "queered other" is "both a product of the anxieties of heteronormative civilization and a marker of the non-civilized".[29] The nation is once again renewed through an exclusionary, antidemocratic 'othering' that smashes the very freedom that it supposedly honors.

Afghan Women and Their Feminism

Establishing a context for thinking about the universality of humanity is hard while the wars of/on 'terror' rage. A sense of genuine universal humanity is always the chief casualty of war.[30] When Islam is named as an enemy at the same time that the rights of women are used to define the war against bin Laden and the Taliban, Islam and democracy are positioned as oppositions. But I want to create a dialogue between the democratic promissory within Islam as it is articulated by Muslim women and feminists in Islam, and feminisms in the West.

The Qur'an, which is the text for Islamic practice, has multiple interpretations and interpreters. Much of the interpretation is done within and through a misogynist rendering of patriarchal privileges. Women are then read as less than men, different from them, in need of protection, to be veiled and hidden away. This patriarchal reading matches similar readings in fundamentalist Judaism and Christianity. West and non-West can share misogynist fundamentalism and patriarchal privilege. All religions can be read for the sinfulness of women, the contamination of their blood, their lust, and the need for their seclusion. The Taliban took this fear and rage toward women to a horrific extreme but this should not occlude the recognition of the universalizing practices of masculinist privilege, nor isolate them to the likes of the Taliban.

A problem with calling the Taliban fundamentalist is that it implies they actually know the authentic fundamentals of Islam. But there are many feminists in Islam, both religious and secular, who argue that the Qur'an is potentially democratic for women. The text itself has democratic capabilities. According to Asma Barlas, the Qur'an is filled with open meanings for what equivalence can and should mean for women and men.[31] According to Azizah Y. Al-Hibri, nowhere does the Qur'an say that Eve was crafted out of Adam. Instead it states that males and females are created by God from the same soul or spirit (*nafs*). The founding myths are not inherently patriarchal when read in this way.[32]

Leila Ahmed chooses to think of at least two Islams: one of men, another of women. Men's Islam – an official, textual Islam – is interpreted with several authenticities that are misogynist. Women's Islam evolves in practice through oral traditions that are always changing and developing as women sort through the meanings of Islam in daily life.'[33]

The struggles between differing sectors of mainstream Islam, Islamic misogynist extremists, and the Western culture of global capital with its discourse of freedom have become more visible. Established practices of patriarchal culture are unsettled as the universalizing practices of global capital redefine the secure divisions between public and private life, family and economy, men and women. The lives of women in the Islamic world are at the center of this flux and change, and they become the touchstones for defining and establishing cultural autonomy and nationalist identity. Yet many of these women, some who call themselves feminist, are not obedient and docile. Their democratic readings of Islam have not gone unnoticed by fundamentalist misogynists of all sorts. Women in countries throughout the Muslim world have been unsettling the masculinist divide in ways that make sense to them while global capital colonizes as well as instigates women's freedom.

Women in Turkey are twice as likely to kill themselves as men, in acts of desperate defiance.[34] In Tehran, Iran, although the law now requires women to cover their hair and conceal their bodies in loose clothing, women still perform their individual acts of rebellion. Upper-class women have nose jobs and wear their post-surgical bandages as badges of honor. Others, wealthy enough to do so, work out aerobically in their women-only gyms and wear long nail implants. Others wear their long coats and scarves over black miniskirts imported from Italy. And these acts should not be seen as simply 'Western'. A few teenage girls cut their hair short and dress as boys to rebel against the restrictive dress codes.[35] Meanwhile Iran's reformist parliament has approved a bill that grants women the right to seek a divorce, the same as a man.[36] And so far, it is the women's vote that has kept the relatively moderate government of Mohammed Khatami in power. In Morocco hundreds of thousands support the government plan to reform women's status in terms of literacy and divorce law. Prince Saud Al-Faisal of Saudi Arabia says that necessary reforms for women will soon take place because "women are going to take their rights, whether we want it or not".[37]

Little of this cultural complexity comes through in the post-September 11 antiterrorist war rhetoric, polarized as it is between modernity and the West and religious fundamentalism and the East.[38] Women's rights, as though this issue were simply Western, becomes the rallying cry as women are once again made the pawns of war: the civilized world will have to protect the women of Afghanistan from the Taliban even though there are religious fanatics in the West and secularists and mainstream believers in the East. This use of women's advancement is hardly new to the women of Afghanistan. The Soviets deveiled women and insisted they wear skirts as part of their modernization program. Then the Taliban, as part of their anti-Soviet policy, passed laws enforcing the burqa and disallowing women to work or go to school, laws which affected up to 150,000 working women and about 100,000 girls at school.[39] Clearly, the blue burqa (also called the chad'ri) became the symbol for the Taliban's atrocities, especially toward women. It is that, and, less clearly, it is also part of a complex history of *befores*.

One repeatedly sees the centrality, and yet evasions, of women's rights talk in the discussions of the reconstruction of Afghanistan. In an interview Hamid Karzai, the leader of Afghanistan's interim government and then president-elect, unwittingly exposes the contested nature of women as a symbol of Muslim nationhood. He reiterates his commitment to women in general, and sees their education as "the highest priority for us". He says that women in Afghanistan will enjoy rights like women in other countries, like Iran, to choose their own profession. When he is asked about the veil, he responds, "We are a Muslim country". When asked if this means that the veil will be obligatory he again responds, "We are a Muslim country".[40]

Before September 11 2001, the Iranian filmmaker Moshen Makhmalbaf made the film *Kandahar* in order for the world to 'see' Afghanistan and break the silence and invisibility of the crisis it faced alone. He wished to bring attention to the pending deaths of at least one million Afghans from starvation. He wanted the world to see the faces of these people and the countryside they inhabit. Afghanistan's tragic war fate was faceless and he would give it a face filled with its people. His film brought the world the human tragedy of the Afghan war and the plight of the Afghan people through the lens of one woman's life – through the eyes of a woman journalist who tries to find her sister who threatens to commit to suicide rather than continue to live under Taliban rule. It is a woman's story about the human love of freedom. But as Makhmalbaf uses women as a symbol of humanity he also uses women to embody the authentic needs of Afghanistan. Women's facelessness – behind the burqa – is used to critique the Taliban and also exposes Makhmalbaf's own patriarchal viewings of women. His women are seen less as sites of resistance and more as mirrors of human hope as they cross the screen in flowing burqas in their gorgeous rainbows of color. Yet, the film indicts both the Taliban and the US for their inhumane cruelty, and the burqa is used to translate across cultural divides to uncover this barbarism.

With the end of the war and the lifting of taboos on work and school for girls and women, the Western press claimed that Afghan women would provide the greatest promise in the post-war phase of reconciliation and the rebuilding of communities and civil society.[41] But the changes affected a small number of women living in the cities, rather than the masses of poor women. And instead of these changes halting the use of the burqa, wealthy women briskly bought newly designed burqas.[42] Besides, huge numbers of Aghan women were refugees, or becoming so. Between September 11 and October 16, 2001, one thousand refugees a day fled Afghanistan to Pakistan. Up to one-third of all Afghan women are widows suffering hunger and desperation while also struggling for their families' survival in amazingly creative ways.[43] Civil society grows here too. Feminists in the West must enlarge their viewings to encompass more than a few privileged women, abroad, and at home.

Feminisms' Dialogues

The Feminist Majority, a US liberal feminist activist group, was crucial in first bringing the plight of Afghan women to the attention of the world. It might be more accurate to say that they brought this plight to the attention of women of the West, and that other women throughout the world were already cognizant of the offensive treatment of Afghan women by the Taliban. Nevertheless, the Feminist Majority's work was tremendously important. Its access to global media allowed it to make a formidable indictment of the Taliban on behalf of Afghan women. But there were serious deficiencies in the exposure they brought. The Feminist Majority did not criticize US policies for past support of the Taliban during Afghanistan's war against the Soviet Union. And the Feminist Majority ignored women activists in Afghanistan and in exile, as well as the wide swath of ferninisms that exist within Islam and the Muslim world. It was thus too easy for the Bush administration to take hold of the Feminist Majority's women's rights initiative for its own purposes of war. The Feminist Majority's earnest attempt to assist Afghan women was redesigned and realigned in Western imperial fashion whereas most feminisms in Islamic countries, are anti-colonial/ anti-imperialist at their core.

Most Muslim feminists who speak against the Taliban also speak out against US foreign policy. Fawzia Afzal-Khan, for example, states clearly that Muslim feminist voices speak simultaneously against "Islamic extremism" and the "unjust foreign policies of the United States that have contributed and continue to contribute to the 'hijacking' of Islam for terrorist ends". Most Muslim feminists argue that the US must rethink its foreign policy as a whole, particularly in the Middle East.[44] The feminism that is publicized in and by the West largely silences these complex relations between imperial politics, militarism, and women's rights.

Other scholars, like Charles Hirschkind and Saba Mahmood, argue that singular focus on the Taliban rather than on the Northern Alliance too, as well as the US foreign policy that instigated Taliban rule in consequence of US support of Afghan extremists, distorts the real challenges that Afghan women face. They view the issues of extreme poverty, unexploded land mines, the huge numbers of refugees, and the militarization of the region as no lesser a problems than the Taliban's enforced dress code for women.[45]

Sonali Kolhatkar, vice-president of the Afghan Women's Mission, is bothered by a continual media barrage depicting barbaric Afghan men and their helpless, dominated women. Many Afghan women activists wonder why US women, even progressive ones like Helen Caldicott, are more interested in "why Afghan men treat women like dirt" rather than why Western male-dominated governments foster "misogynist religious extremism at the expense of women's rights". Kolhatkar thinks that the Feminist Majority's campaign against "gender apartheid", represented by the blue mesh ribbon pin (of the burqa), only represents Afghan women as passive creatures, rather than the resistance fighters that they also have been.[46]

Many Afghan women activists say they are tired of being saved by others. After all, the Russians, the Taliban, and now the US government have all claimed women's 'protection' as their agenda, and then quickly forgotten that they have done so. Nowadays, still, even after the US declaration of 'victory' in Afghanistan, women there continue to suffer the highest infant mortality rate in the world (2,000 maternal deaths per 100,000 live births) in consequence of inadequate medical care, no prenatal or preventative health care, poor nutrition, lack of education, and so on.[47] Yet President Karzai requested no funding for programs for these women in his 2003 budget. Renewed attacks on schools for girls show that powerful remnants of the Taliban remain in place alongside the masculinist extremism of the Northern Alliance.[48] But Laura Bush is silent. There is no remembering here. And no staying power.

Criticism of the Feminist Majority has also been leveled by members of the Revolutionary Association of the Women of Afghanistan (RAWA) in response to *Ms* magazine's depiction of feminist politics in Afghanistan which makes no mention of the important role of RAWA in challenging Taliban rule. In a letter to the *Ms* editor, RAWA accuses the Feminist Majority of ignoring RAWA because RAWA has always been critical of the US-backed Northern Alliance, and especially of their abusive actions towards women during 1992–96. RAWA has never viewed the Northern Alliance as liberatory and instead feared its misogynist fundamentalist tendencies.

Formed in 1977, RAWA stands against all forms of 'fundamentalism' which cause the pauperization and plunder of women; it calls fundamentalism the "enemy of all civilized humanity'. RAWA works for the decriminalization of abortion; for an end to dowry killings, rape, domestic violence, and sati; for the elimination of pornography and trafficking of girls and women for sex and domestic slavery. RAWA demands equal opportunities in wages; it wishes for women to be able to choose the clothing of their choice; it wants to establish lesbian rights; and it wants an end to prenatal sex selection and forced sterilization. RAWA concludes that men and women should be partners in the struggle to create a democracy free of any and all discrimination. They only condemn those men who regard "women as chattel and deprive them of essential rights" and do not regard all men as the enemy, or the cause of all ills that befall women. The struggle to develop full equality for women is a job for the whole of humanity, they say.[49]

However, the Feminist Majority, as RAWA sees it, is allied with Afghan women who have strong ties to the Northern Alliance. Some in RAWA also had significant reservations about the US-backed Sima

Samar because of her ties to the minority Shi'ite party Hezb-e-Wahdat and its known conservatism towards women. Feminist politics in Afghanistan is sophisticated enough to suffer the divisive differences that are part of any process of reform.[50] RAWA claims that it is too independent and too politicized for the Feminist Majority, and that it therefore has been marginalized in post-war discussions. It is only once Afghan women, in all their variety, are allowed to speak for themselves, that it becomes clear that no one politics encompasses Afghan women's struggles at this point. As always, it is vitally important to ask which women are representing whom and for what ends.

Fifty-seven men and five women – all of whom had been exiled activists – attended the Afghanistan peace talks in Bonn.[51] RAWA, which was at first excluded from the proceedings, was critical that the women chosen as negotiators were compromised by their husbands' and/or fathers' allegiances to the Northern Alliance. After the fall of Kabul, the members of RAWA appealed to the United Nations. They stated that the people of Afghanistan did not accept domination by the Northern Alliance, and they 'emphatically' asked the United Nations to send a "peace-keeping force" before the "Northern Alliance can repeat the unforgettable crimes committed" from 1992 to 1996. They pleaded for the UN to "withdraw its recognition of the so-called Islamic government of Rabbani and establish a broad based government based on democratic values".[53] Amnesty International concurred, making a public statement that the Northern Alliance had previously oppressed women, and should not be allowed to dictate their lives again. Naeem Inayatullah argues that the Mujahideen parties are all fundamentalist misogynists and believe in the public and legal devaluation of women. The US will have its hands full when the Northern Alliance fully clamps down on women's rights, although as early as spring 2003, the US appeared to have forgotten about any and all its promises to Afghan women.

An Afghan Women's Summit for Democracy was next held in Brussels in 2001, and Senator Hillary Rodham Clinton hosted a Forum on the Future of Women in Afghanistan along with the Feminist Majority on the importance of women in the reconstruction of their country.[54] At the hearings, many of the Afghan women present spoke about the importance of support from US women's groups and yet raised their fear of a cultural imperialism that does not fully understand Afghan women's particular situations.

It did not take long for Afghan women to demand seats and representation on the Loya Jirga, the grand tribal council, which was supposed to determine the future of Afghanistan.[55] Many of these demands came from women living in remote villages with no electricity and still wearing the burqa. They demanded representation from their all-male local councils, and they got it. Initially, some 50,000 women went back to work as teachers, and tens of thousands as health workers. And President Karzai signed a "Declaration of Essential Rights of Afghan Women" which was supposed to guarantee equity between men and women, equal protection under the law, equal rights to education in all disciplines, freedom of speech, and the right of choice about the burqa. Yet it remains highly unlikely that these so-called newly won rights will amount to much given the stagnating economy, and the daily unrest of a country without rule.[56]

The future of Afghanistan and its women remains deeply unstable. The renewed and furthered demands for women's rights are set within a context of a ruined war economy and a devastated countryside. It is significant that women were players in writing the new constitution, but it is less clear how this can have effect. Some Afghan women welcome the changes of postwar society, others do not and still live with enormous fear.[57] All women, however, wish never again to hear the sound of one more bullet; they want their humanity to be recognized; they want an end to all war.[58]

When Dr Sima Samar, the physician and exile who headed the Ministry of Women's Affairs in the new Afghan government, was asked whether a liberated Afghanistan is a Western one she answered: "Why should everything be Westernized? Liberation is not just a Western idea. Everyone wants it." The liberated Afghan woman will have access to education, the right to vote, the right to work, the right to choose a spouse. But these are rights of all human beings, not just Western ones.[59] Yohra Yusuf Daoud, a former Ms Afghan beauty queen, who is a radio talk show host in Malibu, California, speaks of her mixed views on women's liberation. "If a woman has to wear a burqa head to toe but can go to school, then that is something I approve of."[60]

Another viewpoint is expressed by the American journalist Amy Waldman, who says that she could not get used to speaking to women through the burqa. You don't see a person, she complains: "it feels like talking to a voice box". It distorts the woman; it is "an impenetrable wall of pale blue polyester where a human being should be."[61] She could not make sense of the contradictions she witnessed: the Taliban would trade sleazy pictures of Indian women and cover and seclude their own women, while treating Waldman with respect.

The burqa and or the veil must be seen from inside the thoughts of the woman who wears it. In 1959 in Afghanistan the burqa (chad'ri) was declared un-Islamic by the King's cousin. Because for the West it has become so much the symbol of a traditionalist patriarchy, it is almost impossible to hear and see fully the complexities and histories in which it is worn by women themselves. For some women the burqa has meant freedom from rape. For others it has meant enforced oppression. Veiling today is sometimes a fashion statement; involving designer labeled hijabs; other times a veil can be a sign of piety and self control; other times an unveiled woman can be as 'believing' as the veiled. Some who veil say that it frees them of the "shackles of femininity and demands for sexuality" and allows them to just be human beings.[62] Others say they sometimes wear it, depending on their daily activities. From inside these Muslim countries there are a variety of meanings to be understood.

But complex meanings for and of the veil are not limited to Muslim women. Lieutenant-Colonel Martha McSally, the highest-ranking female fighter pilot in the US Air Force, challenged the military ruling that required her to wear the *abaya* – the long headscarf and black robe – when she left her base in Saudi Arabia. She argued that no such ruling applied to men regulating their local dress, and that she should not be forced to obey another country's social custom. She won her challenge, although another female lieutenant says she will continue to wear it, although she is glad that it is her choice now. However, interestingly, the US State Department forbids the wearing of the *abaya*.[63]

Veils and veiling bespeak the crucial site of female bodies in and for expressing relations of power. Veils express an inside and outside, the forbidden against the seeable/knowable. A veil creates a private space against a public other. Veils, like any piece of clothing or drapery, cover over; they create both fantasy and fetish at the same time. All clothing is used to cover over desire – to repress it by putting it out of sight. But the covering also is always a reminder of what is covered, of the desire itself.[64] The denial of desirous pleasure remains always unstable; to repress it is to simultaneously expose it. So the pornographic woman – all in view – supposedly controls the very desire because it is already exposed, and known; there is nothing more to see; or to fantasize. The West's obsession with the veil – in colonialism or in decolonization – is a preoccupation with women's bodies (and hence their struggle to be free) as an enduring site of democratic possibility. The veil covers over, and porn uncovers, exactly what the West wishes to dominate. Whether covered, or displayed, female bodies continue to speak fantasies tied to human freedom.

Complexity and contradiction are part of the context of a transnational women's rights discourse. The US supports regimes that greatly limit women's rights when other more pressing policies are at stake. President Bush has allowed the Women's Rights Treaty, which endorses the elimination of all forms of discrimination against women, and which has been ratified by 168 countries, to languish here at home. He continues to endorse the rights of fetuses more than the rights of pregnant women. He called for women's rights in Afghanistan while he eliminated several federal offices charged with protecting women's interests here at home.

Ten regional offices of the US Labor Department of the Women's Bureau were closed; offices on women's health in the Food and Drug Administration and Centers for Disease Control and Prevention were consolidated. Moreover, Bush did not continue the White House Women's Initiative and Outreach post created by Clinton in 1995. As a result, many programs assisting working women were jeopardized.[65] One senator, claiming anonymity, says of Bush's Afghan women's policy: "I think this is a great chance for them to do a gender gap number without rubbing up against the right wing."[66] Further, Bush pushes his "pro-family" agenda every chance he gets. John Klink, former chief negotiator for the Vatican, has been appointed by Bush to almost every United Nations US delegation. Bush sent right-to-lifer Jeanne Head as the US delegate to the annual World Health Assembly and has campaigned against any mention of "reproductive health services" and "reproductive rights" in all international agreements. In 2002 Bush withdrew US support for the landmark agreement of 179 countries in 1994 at the International Conference on Population and Development that established the rights of women to contraception as a means towards women's empowerment.[67]

This hypocrisy makes the work of women everywhere all the harder. Afghan women walk the tightrope between being too traditional and too modern while neither choice is one of their making. They have to try to find a balance that works for them. As Rina Amiri, a senior associate in the Women and Public Policy Program at Harvard who was born in Afghanistan, says: "If we push the gender agenda too blatantly, and we push it too forcefully, not only will Afghans define their attitudes toward gender in defiance of the Taliban but also in defiance of the West."[68] Yet one should not see simple domination here because Afghan women defied the Taliban while wearing the burqa. Many women taught their daughters to read; others organized secret schools at great risk to themselves and others.[69] They negotiate life with an incredible resilience, which is neither simply patriarchal nor Western.

Afghan women have suffered greatly from the selective interpretations of Islam. Many Muslim women believe that the Qur'an gives rights to women for education, health care, and paid employment. Yet they also know the practice of honor killings and acid burnings. Pakistan's woman's commissioner, the lawyer Sardar Ali, remarks that the interpretation of religion is key to this moment and therefore women must "jolly well have the right to interpret it".[70] Barlas argues that many Muslim practices wrongly interpret the Qur'an; that the Qur'an allows for equivalence between men and women with no oppositional notion of gendered meanings.[71] Struggles continue, and while in some places, like Nigeria, the Qur'an is used to justify the rollback of women's civil rights, in many Muslim societies, women's rights to education and public participation are readily accepted. This terrain has also become a battlefield described by an East/West divide. The divide exists within the East itself and is best understood as differing notions of extremist masculinisms that flow both to and from the West.

As the US wars on/of 'terror' continue I remember back to the extremism of Osama bin Laden, the 9/11 planner Mohamed Atta, and the Taliban. It is interesting how seldom these names appear now and how central they were to the start of the US war on Afghanistan. Their extremist misogynist positions were used to mobilize the US for war. Supposedly Atta, in his will, requested that no women attend to his body or participate in his funeral. This spoke his fear of women, his denial of their shared humanity, his need to separate and exclude them.[72] Bin Laden was quoted in an interview with al-Jazeera television stating, "Our brothers who fought in Somalia saw wonders about the weakness, feebleness, and cowardliness of the US soldier. ... We believe that we are men, Muslim men, who must have the honour of defending Mecca. We do not want American women soldiers defending [it]. ... The rulers in that region have been deprived of their manhood. By God, Muslim women refuse to be defended by these American and Jewish prostitutes."[73] Ahmed Rashid, writing on the Taliban, says that most of these young men grew up in refugee camps without the love or camaraderie of mothers or sisters.[74] Yet, bin Laden has five wives and some fifteen children.[75]

It is important at this particular historical moment, when women are arguably more politically and economically active across the globe than ever, that they are denied equality by misogynist interpreters of Islam. The terrorists are named for us in the US as Arab, or Muslim, but there is no accounting for them as men. There is too much silence on this point for it not to be important. And although the Bush administration is not one and the same with the Taliban its misogynist policies punish women in the US and abroad as well.

The policies of the Taliban toward women reflect the centrality of women's lives in defining culture. The Taliban declare themselves the sole interpreters of Islam against women's changing demands. If Afghan women had not been changing and demanding recognition of their rights as they understood them for themselves, there would have been no need to re-articulate their repression in Taliban form. It is the dynamism of women today, not their passivity, that instigates this democratic struggle. And this struggle is also at play in the US.

On Antiracist Feminisms

Women, especially feminists of all kinds, are often eager to find ways to build bridges across difference, rather than blow up the bridges, deny crossings, and find safety by securing border crossings. Yes, there was Madeleine Albright, who was one of the biggest hawks during the Gulf 1991 and Bosnian wars; or Golda Meir, who was an early architect of Israeli militarism; and there are the imperial feminists of the Bush administration. Nevertheless, I believe there are more people than ever, and more antiracist feminists than before, who can make the difference that we must make. Women all across the globe who move and shake these times – the haulers of water and firewood, the leaders in protecting the environment, the activists dealing with AIDS in Africa, the leaders in nongovernmental civic organizations – must mobilize a peaceful voice against all uses of terror.

The globe needs antiracist feminist voices speaking more loudly here: for peace, for our cities, for our schools, against prejudice and discrimination, for protecting the environment everywhere, for the needed freedoms to speak and think and discuss and find new ways of finding coalitions across the differences that make this hard. Women are of all colors and classes, just like the people who died on September 11, 2001, and who die daily from terror-filled politics.

If people were listening to *women* across the globe, there would be much greater focus on the need to end militarism, war, and poverty. Many, from both inside and outside the US, are asking for negotiation rather than aggression; they are asking for an end to the warrior mentality.[76] Feminists in countries throughout the world are asking how we can come to recognize a notion of a global public good that counters the nationalist rancor of hatred and death. Women's rights activists are demanding inclusion in human rights agendas. Human Rights Watch asks that there be an end to the violations of women's human rights, especially in Afghanistan.[77]

As women in poor countries are dragged into sweatshop factories, as women are called away from their families in the US as reservists, as women hold high office in the Bush administration, as Western feminism for export is sold abroad to build new markets for cosmetics and porn, as girls and women are sold into prostitution in Thailand and elsewhere, as women drop their chadors in Iran as soon as they are in the privacy of their homes, as women protest their subservience in myriad acts of defiance, as more and more women become refugees and migrants, as Muslim and secular feminists demand human rights, women remain and become anew both the terrain and the symbols of political struggle.

On one hand, the misogynist despotism of the Taliban was represented through continual imagery of the confined and passive woman; on the other, it was women's *activism* in public arenas that silenced women's progress right at this site. Pre-Taliban, Afghan women were participating in government, schools, and other civic institutions. Pre-Taliban, Afghan women were active in most parts of life, much like women in Iran and Algeria, before the takeover by misogynist fundamentalists.[78] But after years of war, Kabul is home to some 70,000 war widows who live in abject poverty. Pregnant women throughout Afghanistan continue to face the grave risk of miscarriage and other obstetric problems.[79]

The aftermath of September 11 must be used to uncover the similar and yet specifically different patriarchal politics practiced toward girls and women across the globe. This is about the politics of patriarchy and masculinist privilege and the way it comes up smack against the contradictions of global capitalism's promise of democracy for all – for women in Muslim countries and for women in the West. Neither the West nor Islam are humane democratic regimes for women. Traditional patriarchy, as it is defined by misogynist fundamentalists of all genres, does not respect women's freedom or equality. More modem forms of patriarchy refine and revise male privilege in relation to the new needs of global capitalism, but women's freedom remains elusive here too. The newest needs of US global domination pose further challenges to the construction of a nonmasculinist democracy. I dream of an end to the hate-filled politics of fundamentalist misogyny, global capitalist patriarchy, and the newest US imperial militarism.

Women's antiracist feminist activism must become a larger presence in this political moment. Much of the discourse of human rights across the globe has been brought center stage by women's groups, very often not of the West, demanding equality as well as freedom, specifically for women. This has been done in the context of women's growing consciousness of themselves in war, as refugees, as laborers in the fields and sweatshops of the global economy. War rape, acid burnings, honor killings, sex trafficking and prostitution, should put terrorism toward women on the global map.[80] Let us *all* end this terror.

Women's demands for their rights and their freedom from oppressive religious fundamentalist regimes is very often blamed on the West and its excessive self-indulgences. It is important to be critical of the US for its excesses, while recognizing that women's rights are not a Western plot. Women from across the globe demand their rights on their own terms, from their own understandings of what Islam means. Sometimes there are dialogues with the West; sometimes not.

Some young Muslim women who live in the US choose to wear the hijab. A student at Wellesley College says: "We have more freedom being American Muslims because we don't have the cultural baggage from the countries our parents are coming from."[81] No one tells them they must wear the hijab – they choose to do so as an expression of their faith and identity. It is therefore crucial that feminists formulate ways to think through the complex politics of global capital with its racist and sexist formulations as well as the promissories of an antiracist feminist democracy that allows us to build a socially just globe.

The massacre of September 11 reminded me of how devoted I am to the human body. September 11 also brought Americans into the real globalized world of fear and misery. We must take this painful perspective and see more of the world from other locations than our own. We must look at ourselves and come to know others more deeply as we do so. We are more similar to each other than we are different. We must look for this polyversal inclusivity.

The true subversiveness of women's rights discourse is that it speaks from the female body – from the urgings of women's humanity everywhere. The female body desires freedom from war, rape, unwanted pregnancy. It desires control over the self. One does not need to learn this from someone other than oneself. I therefore wish to foil each and every attempt of terrorist actions, but not simply by the use of more terror. This tactic of 'more' simply means the mightiest wins – with no judgment of who and what the mighty demand. My allegiance to the human body – not the nation – defines my struggle to see the complex negotiations necessary to really thinking our way through this moment.

I want to pluralize seeing so that it exists without the opposition between Islam and the West. As an antiracist feminist, I need to slowly bring into view the biggest picture I can of humanity. I am reminded of Sa'adi's poem: "All people are limbs of one body."[82] And that one body begins with a woman's. Let this body speak for peace and justice and freedom for us all.

Notes

1. Kumari Jayawardena, *The White Woman's Other Burden: Western Women and South Asia During British Colonial Rule* (New York: Routledge, 1995), pp. 2, 3, 5.
2. Catherine MacKinnon, "State of Emergency", *Women's Review of Books*, vol. xix, no. 6 (March 2002), pp. 7, 8.
3. Jane Mayer, "The House of Bin Laden", *New Yorker*, November 12, 2001, pp. 54–65.
4. Sunila Abeysekera, "Paying the Price for Ignoring Women's Calls against Fundamentalism", *The Island*, October 31, 2001, p. 12.

5. I am indebted to conversations with Asma Barlas for much of my thinking here, although she differs with my use of the term 'fundamentalist'. See her "*Believing Women" in Islam: Unreading Patriarchal Interpretations of the Quran* (Austin: University of Texas Press, 2002).
6. Nayereh Tohidi, "The Issues At Hand", in Herbert Bodman and Nayereh Tohidi, eds., *Women in Muslim Societies* (London: Lynne Rienner Pub., 1998), pp. 284, 285, 287.
7. Roxanne Euben, "Killing for Politics", *Political Theory,* vol. 30, no. 1 (February 2002), pp. 5, 12, 19, 22.
8. The same day network news programs broadcast Afghan women removing their burqas, the Victoria's Secret fashion show was first broadcast on television. See Alex Kuczynski, "Victoria's Secret on TV: Another First for Women", *New York Times,* November 18, 2001, p. 1, section 9.
9. Uma Narayan, "Essence of Culture and a Sense of History: A Feminist Critique of Cultural Essentialism", in Uma Narayan and Sandra Harding, eds., *Decentering the Center* (Bloomington: Indiana University Press, 2000), pp. 81, 83.
10. Miriam Cooke, *Women Claim Islam* (New York: Routledge, 2001), pp. vii, viii.
11. Evan Thomas, "The Real Condi Rice", *Newsweek.* vol. CXL, no. 25 (December, 2002), pp. 26–35.
12. Peter Marks, "Adept Politics and Advertising: 4 Women Shape a Campaign", *New York Times*, November 11, 2001, p. 4.
13. I am indebted to Minnie Bruce Pratt's statement: "Dear Friends of Women's Liberation", November 12, 2001 (mbpratt@earthlink.com), for this discussion.
14. David Stout, "Mrs Bush Cites Abuse of Women and Children by the Taliban", *New York Times*, November 18, 2001, p. B5.
15. Sarmad Sufian, "US Used Nuclear Waste", *Weekly Independent* (Pakistan) vol. 1, no. 23 (Nov. 29–Dec. 5, 2001), p. 1.
16. Anita Hill, "Insider Women With Outsider Values", *New York Times*. June 6, 2002, p. A31.
17. "Coleen Rowley's Memo to FBI Director Robert Mueller", *TIME*, June 3, 2002, pp. 12–21.
18. Jill Abramson, "I am Woman, Hear Me Roar in the Enron Scandal", *New York Times,* January 27, 2002, p. Wk3.
19. See the "Proposal for UN Women's Strategies for Civil Conflict Resolution", www.cwgl.rutgers.edu.
20. Lynette Dumble, "In the Name of Freedom: Terror, Death, Hunger, Misogyny, and Genocide in Afghanistan", Znet, www.ZMag.org.
21. Mona Eltahawy and Kalpana Sharma, "Commentary: US Should Heed How Our Allies Treat Women," www.womensenews.org/join.cfm
22. As quoted in Alessandra Stanley, "Walking a Fine Line in Showcasing Women and Dealing with Muslim Allies", *New York Times,* October 27, 200 1, p. B9.
23. Sunita Mehta and Homaira Mamoor, "Building Communities Across Difference", in Sunita Mehta, ed., *Women for Afghan Women* (New York: Palgrave, 2002), p. 24.
24. Alessandra Stanley, "Walking a Fine Line in Showcasing Women and Dealing with Muslim Allies", p. B.9.

25. US State Department, "The Taliban's War against Women", www.state.gov
26. Patricia Leigh Brown, "Heavy Lifting Required: The Return of Manly Men", *New York Time* October 28, 200 1, p. 5.
27. For interesting discussions of the aftermath of September 11 see Susan Hawthorne and Bronwyn Winter, eds., *September 11, 2001: Feminist Perspectives* (Australia: Spinifex, 2002); William Heyen, *September 11, 2001: American Writers Respond* (Silver Spring, MD: Etruscan Press, 2001); and "Roundtable: Gender and September 11th", *Signs,* vol. 28, no. 1 (Autumn, 2002), pp. 431–79.
28. Barbara Crossette, "Living in a World without Women", *New York Times,* November 4, 2001, p. B1.
29. Jashir K. Puar and Amit S. Rai, "Monster, Terrorist, Fag: The War on Terrorism and the Production of Docile Patriots", *Social Text,* vol. 20, no. 2 (Fall 2002), pp. 126, 139, 140.
30. Mohsen Makhmalbaf, "Limbs of No Body: The World's Indifference to the Afghan Tragedy", *Monthly Review,* vol. 53, no. 6 (November 2001), p. 29.
31. See Barlas, "*Believing Women*" *in Islam,* especially Chapter 5.
32. Azizah Y. Al-Hibri, "Is Western Patriarchal Feminism Good for Third World/Minority Women?" in Susan Moller Okin, ed., *Is Multiculturalism Bad for Women?* (Princeton: Princeton University Press, 1999), p. 42.
33. Leila Ahmed, "The Women of Islam", *Transition.* vol. 9, no. 3. Issue 83, pp. 78–96; and her *Border Passages* (New York: Farrar, Straus & Giroux, 1999). Also see Margot Badran, "Islamic Feminism: What's In A Name?", Al-Ahram. Weekly Online, 17–23, January 2002, Issue No. 569, www.ahram.org
34. Douglas Frantz, "Turkish Women Who See Death As a Way Out", *New York Times* November 3, 2000, p. A10.
35. Elaine Sciolino, "Iran's Well-Covered Women Remodel a Part That Shows", *New York Times,* September 22, 2000, p. AI.
36. Nazila Fathi, "Iran Legislators Vote to Give Women Equality in Divorce", *New York Times,* August 27, 2002, p. A9.
37. Stated in an interview on NBC *Today Show,* January 13, 2003.
38. Rina Amiri, "Muslim Women As Symbols and Pawns", *New York Times,* November 27, 200 1, p. A19.
39. Pankaj Mishra, "The Afghan Tragedy", *New York Review of Books,* vol. XLIX, no. 1 (January 17, 2002), p. 43.
40. From an interview run by Eurasianet. See: www.eurasianet.org (2/7/02)
41. Masuda Sultan, "Hope in Afghanistan", in *Women for Afghan Women,* p. 203.
42. John Bums, "Relishing Beautiful New Freedoms in Kabul", *New York Times.* September 15, 2002, p. A10.
43. Ayesha Khan, "Afghan Refugee Women's Experience of Conflict and Disintegration", *Meridians,* vol. 3, no. 1 (2002), pp. 89–121.
44. Fawzia Afzal-Khan, "Here Are the Muslim Feminist Voices, Mr Rushdie", www.counterpunch.org/fawzia1.html
45. Charles Hirschkind and Saba Mahmood, "Feminism, The Taliban, and Politics of Counter-Insurgency", *Anthropological Quarterly,* vol. 75, no. 2 (Spring, 2002), pp. 342, 345.

46. Sonali Kolhatkar, "Saving Afghan Women", May 9, 2002, www.zmag.org/content/gender
47. Carlotta Gall, "Afghan Motherhood in a Fight for Survival", *New York Times,* May 25, 2003, p. A3.
48. David Rohde, "Attacks on Schools for Girls Hint At Lingering Split in Afghanistan", *New York Times,* October 31, 2002, p. A1.
49. Weeda Mansoor, "The Mission of RAWA: Freedom, Democracy, Human Rights", in *Women for Afghan Women,* p. 68, 80.
50. "An Open Letter to the Editors of Ms. Magazine". available at www.rawa.org. For the initial Ms. article that RAWA is criticizing see Janelle Brown, "A Coalition of Hope", Ms., vol. xii, no. 2 (Spring 2002), pp.65–76.
51. Fariba Nawa, "5 Women at Table in Afghan Talks", *San Francisco Chronicle,* November 29, 2001, p. 8.
52. RAWA, "The Northern Alliance: The Most Murderous Violators of Human Rights", December 10, 2001, www.rawa.org.
53. This statement is available from portsideMod@netscape.net.
54. See www.feminist.org/news/newsbyte and www.womensedge.org
55. Carlotta Gall, "Afghan Women in Political Spotlight", *New York Times.* June 26, 2002, p.A11.
56. Jan Goodwin, "An Uneasy Peace", *The Nation,* vol. 274, no. 16 (April 29, 2002), pp. 20–24.
57. Barbara Crossette, "Half the Afghans, the Women, Fight to Establish Their Rights", *New York Times,* June 7, 2002, p. A7.
58. Carlotta Gall, "Afghan Women in Political Spotlight", *New York Times,* June 26, 2002, p. A11.
59. Sima Samar, "Meet the Boss", interview by Gayle Forman, *New York Times,* December 23, 2001, p. 15.
60. Quoted in Sara Austin, "Where Are the Women: Debating Afghanistan's Future", *The Nation,* vol. 273, no. 22 (December 31, 200 1), p. 12.
61. Amy Waldman, "Reporters in Afghanistan: Fear, Numbness, and Being a Spectacle", *New York Times,* December 29, 200 1, p. B6.
62. Haleh Afshar, *Islam and Feminisms, An Iranian Case-Study* (New York: St. Martin's Press, 1998), p. 15. Also see Susan Muaddi Darraj, "Arab Feminism", *Monthly Review Press,* vol. 53, no. 10 (March, 2002), pp. 15-25; Yvonne Yazbeck Haddad and John Esposito, eds. *Islam, Gender and Social Change* (New York: Oxford University Press, 1998); Lila Abu-Lughod, *Remaking Women: Feminism and Modernity in the Middle East* (New Jersey: Princeton University Press, 1998); and Sherifa Zuhur, *Revealing Reveiling* (Albany: State University of New York Press, 1992).
63. Elaine Sciolino, "Servicewomen Win, Doffing Their Veils in Saudi Arabia", *New York Times,* January 25, 2002, p. A6.
64. Joan Copjec, *Read My Desire: Lacan Against the Historicists* (Boston: MIT Press, 1994), pp. 106–16.
65. Tamar Lewin, "Bush May End Offices Dealing with Women's Issues, Groups Say", *New York Times,* December 19, 200 1, p. A23.

66. Quoted in Elisabeth Bumiller, "The Politics of Plight and the Gender Gap", *New York Times* November 19, 2001, p. B2.
67. Jennifer Block, "Christian Soldiers on the March", *The Nation,* vol. 256, no. 4 (February 3, 2003), pp. 18, 21.
68. Quoted in Barbara Crossette, "Hope for the Future, Blunted by a Hard Past", *New York Times* December 2, 2001, p.wk3.
69. Amy Waldman, "Behind the Burka: Women Subtly Fought Taliban", *New York Times,* November 19, 2001, p. Al.
70. As discussed in Frances McMorris, "Lawyers Argue Laws, Not Quran, Repress Women", www.womensnews.org/article.cfm/dym/aid475
71. Barlas, "*Believing Women*" *in Islam*, pp. 152–66.
72. I use this cautiously because the authenticity and translation of the will are questionable.
73. Quoted in Tony Judt, "America and the War", *New York Review of Books,* vol. XLVIII, no. 18 (November 15, 2001), p. 4.
74. Ahmed Rashid, *Taliban, Militant Islam, Oil, and Fundamentalism in Central Asia* (New Haven, Con.: Yale University Press, 2000), especially Chapter 8.
75. Yossef Bodansky, *Bin Laden* (New York: Forum, 1999), p. 1.
76. Katha Pollitt, "Where Are the Women?" *The Nation,* vol. 273, no. 12 (October 22, 2001), p. 10.
77. "Afghanistan: Humanity Denied," *Human Rights Watch,* vol. 13, no. 5 (October 2001), pp. 1–25.
78. Kalpana Sharma, "A War ... by Men", *The Hindu,* October 21, 2001, www.hinduonet.com/stories/13210618.htm; and Jan Goodwin and Jessica Neuwirth, "The Rifle and the Veil", *New York Times,* October 19, 200 1, p. AI9.
79. Judith Miller and Carlotta Gall, "Women Suffer Most in Afghan Health Crisis, Experts Say", *New York Times*, October 27, 2002, p. A3.
80. For important information on discussions for peace among feminists and women's human rights activists in New York, Asia, and Latin America, see www.whrnet.org
81. As quoted in Laurie Goldstein, "Muslims Nurture Sense of Self on Campus", *New York Times*, November 3, 200 1, p. B 1.
82. I am indebted to Mohsen Makhmalbaf's discussion of this in his "Limbs of No Body" (see note 30).

8 Feminisms from Elsewheres: Seeing Polyversal Humanity

It is a hard time to write about feminisms. There is too much to know to be able to do this right. So I risk myself because I cannot know enough. I am trying to build a public intellectual and political space in order for feminists to both spark anew and continue the struggle for a just democracy for all people. I return to women in Africa both because of the US debt to slaves and because of women's incredible activism there against neoliberalism. I return to women in Islam because the historical struggles of the moment locate me here. There are also many other feminisms: in Korea, Argentina, Thailand, China, Brazil, Chile, India, and on and on. So I do not mean to create silences here, but I do.

If context – historical and of the moment – always matters, then I must locate today's feminisms in ways that respect their many differences and varieties, across time, geographical space, and culture; along with race, class, ethnicity, and sexual preference.[1] But language is not helpful here. I think feminism is always plural and always has been. Yet when I write feminisms and refer to them as one, I risk people thinking that I am writing of a homogeneous politics. Yet if I refer to feminisms and write of them as plural, it appears that I see many different kinds of feminism rather than their co-equal pluralism and singularity. So I will sometimes refer to feminisms as singular – 'it' – and other times as plural – 'they', because it/they is/are both. Multiplicity and cohesion exist simultaneously.

Is feminisms – the belief that women should define the contours of their own creativity – more at home in one place than another? Who gets to answer these questions in the first place? It has never felt more urgent to clarify and answer these questions given the way that women's rights discourse has been appropriated by the Bush administration for making war instead of peace. In the aftermaths of September 11, 2001 neoliberal democracy has become even less democratic. I wish to unwrap and distinguish the progressive use of women's rights discourse by women in places 'elsewhere' from the imperial feminism of the Bush administration. And I wish to differentiate between the right-wing takeover of feminist discourse and other progressive feminisms which also exist within the West. These dialogues will hopefully recapture and create anew the humanely democratic and thriving complex communities of women and girls across the globe.

'Feminisms', as a term, identifies women politically. The name as such puts the patriarchal and misogynist structures of power in view no matter how variously. It breaks the silence of male privilege by denaturalizing and denormalizing it. Because power and oppression are never static, but rather dynamic, feminisms are always changing to address these historical and newly formed systems. Feminisms develop the possibility of seeing theoretically how women's oppression has newly formed sites. Theoretical means seeing the connectedness between women, between them and the multiple systems of power attempting to harness their creativity. Feminisms always requires new dialogue to unfreeze the varied constructions of womanhood. Women's struggle for self-determination is always defined within the cultural contexts and structures of power that women inhabit.

Feminisms recognize the collective life of women defined by child-bearing and child-rearing and the layers of labor connected with this, and also critiques these burdens, and also demands freely chosen options structured by equality of race and class. Such a rendering must accept diverse understandings of these meanings. But the respect for woman's need to define her own body's integrity is always crucial, whether it be covered, or exposed. I am opening feminist practices to the widest range of possible meanings without undermining their completely revolutionary stance: that feminisms fundamentally reorder the way 'natural' is seen, spoken, and lived. In this reordering women's lives are seen as crucial to life's daily rhythms but not as static or inevitable. The abuse of women's bodies – whether the sex/gendered structuring of the slave trade and racial apartheid, or the sexual terrorism of the trafficking of women, or their exploitation in the global factory – is no longer silenced. Globalization is then understood as a systematic patriarchal structuring of racialized, sexualized, global exploitation.

Feminisms, especially of the West in the US, must be ready to speak against the cultural and economic domination of their home country that creates such impossible sadness and pain to people at home, as well as elsewhere: Afghans, Iraqis, Rwandans, Palestinians, Israelis, and so on. Today, at this moment, given the ascendancy and arrogance of the US, US feminism is too easily equated with the West. Historically this has equated European politics with 'democracy', and 'modernity'. Yet, these early forms were colonialist and racist. As well, today's brand of ascendant feminism articulates a neoliberal agenda which advertises an imperial feminist agenda, even though other marginalized feminisms exist in the US that are silenced in this reading.

Much that is said to be Western and therefore democratic and or/feminist has local sites 'elsewhere' where feminisms also thrive. Feminisms are not simply Western, or non-Western, but embrace women's activism in places elsewhere whether named as such, or not. A polyversal feminism – multiple and connected – expresses women's potential shared humanity wherever it exists. When women are subordinated and not allowed the lives they wish to live, they respond with resistance. The plural acts of resistance are what women do to survive and thrive in multiple and yet connected ways. I am locating a human response to suffering, although it will always be articulated through localized meanings.

West and non-West are both real and made-up as coherent geographical/ cultural locations. The flows between empires and their colonies, between colonizer and colonized, between slave and slave-master, between colors of the skin, are misread as separateness and opposition. Feminisms have palpably suffered from this overdrawn divide. They have been wrongly homogenized as a unity, and then defined as of the West. This negates multiple forms of feminisms in the West *and* the multiple forms of feminisms outside the West. As such, feminisms lose their plurality of meanings which also express the similarities among women.

A similar reductionism has been made between liberal (as western) feminism and feminism *per se*. The US feminist movement is depicted, by both Western and non-Western discourses alike, as white and middle-class. Although this often accurately describes the mainstream of

US feminisms, it silences the difference between mainstream liberal feminism and its neoliberal/imperial self. Other multiple radical sites are also silenced in this equation which simply furthers a right-wing takeover of Western feminism.

Today, I revise my thought in *The Radical Future of Liberal Feminism*, that "all feminism is liberal at its root in that the universal feminist claim that woman is an independent being (from man) is premised on the eighteenth century liberal conception of the independent and autonomous self."[2] There are other locations for this thinking about woman's freedom. It is wrong-headed to assume that the notion of feminist individuality and autonomy is always an extension of liberal individualism. There are other notions of autonomy that are not simply liberal individualist at their core. As such, the notion of autonomous woman comes from other locations besides the West. There are varieties of autonomy besides liberal individuality that are liberatory. If feminisms from elsewhere have a debt to the West, it is also true that the West has a debt to women elsewhere.

Woman's autonomy, though essential to feminist thinking, has differing contextual routes/roots. There are a variety of meanings of woman's autonomy and independence. When Inji Aflatun, an Egyptian feminist, says in 1949 that the enemies of women are the enemies of democracy; and that women's struggle for themselves will strengthen democracy in Egypt, her meaning is not simply Western, or liberal, but rather uniquely human *and* creatively dialogic.[3] Rich, glocal mixtures emerge: local expressions of the global/universal leave neither as they were separately. This notion of the simultaneity of localized life and global context needs its appropriate translation.

I also previously argued that the creative tension of liberal feminism exists between the individualism of liberalism, and the collectivity of feminism; that "the contradiction between liberalism (as patriarchal and individualist in structure and ideology) and feminism (as sexual egalitarian and collectivist) lays the basis for feminism's movement beyond liberalism".[4] Sadly, much of this creative possibility has been captured by neoliberal/imperial feminists in the US. Yet much of the creative liberal feminist agenda has also been adopted by human rights activists and feminists in places elsewhere. In these transnational dialogues, sexual equality is embraced but with recognition of a complex diversity. Equality is needed for the similarities, rather than the sameness that women share. Hence, there is a tension in all feminisms between the patriarchal structures of women's lives and their understanding of their own potential for democratic life. As I wrote in *The Color of Gender*, women need freedom for our uniqueness, and equality for our similarity.[5]

Feminisms, like any politics, should always be in process. I do not want to freeze the meaning of feminisms, nor can I. It is a series of political understandings that develop given the demands and uniqueness of the moment. The flux and change elucidates feminisms, rather than denies their status as a coherent politics. I continue to use the term, problematic though it is, because it is the only term I know that translates across time and culture to put women in view politically – as more than isolated individuals living in disparate political moments. Feminisms continue to name patriarchy and misogyny as a global problem for the times we live in. English privileges women in the West, so I gladly translate feminism into its home language whatever this is. And we shall all speak and write of feministe, feminismo, and so on.

Feminists in Islam allow feminists in the US to see secular and believing Muslims in their political struggle for democracy against their own home-grown patriarchal regimes, and against US hegemony. This positioning, along with Africana feminisms, necessitates a self-critique of US feminisms' privileged status within globalized discourses. Feminists in Islam who are re-reading the Qur'an also query in a variety of ways their understandings of women's equality, which are not hostile to ideas of sex difference as well as obligation. Africana womanists demand that Africa be seen as a resource for enriching feminism's notion of liberation. Given the extraordinary hegemony of US neoliberalism, and my own place/consciousness in the US. I attempt as best I can to create dialogue, rather than misappropriation. My hope is that progressive feminists in the US will assist in building an anti-globalization movement that will successfully challenge the Bush wars on/of 'terror'.

What Is in a Name?

I find it nearly impossible to name the past three decades of women's activism. US feminists in the early 1970s of all stripes spoke of women's rights or liberation; reform and/or revolution. Although civil rights and anti-Vietnam War activists initiated much of what was called feminism at the time, the mainstream women's movement was predominantly white and middle class. At this same time, there were many other women activists – in Algeria, Iran, Egypt, Chile, Argentina, South Africa, and so on – struggling for democratic lives, but they were treated as invisible by the West. It easily followed, through this silencing, that feminism was depicted as *of* the West. And much of women's activism elsewhere, was subsumed under the rubric of anticolonialism and anti-imperialism, even by women themselves.

US Black and Latina feminists, by the late seventies, played a crucial role in critically pluralizing feminism beyond the liberal individualism of the mainstream white women's movement. Antiracist feminists embraced differences in order to build a larger collectivity and inclusivity of 'women'. Black feminists like Audre Lorde, Barbara Smith, and bell hooks were crucial to this process. Despite the conservative Reagan-Bush decade of the 1980s, antiracist feminists articulated a more honest viewing of women as a sexual class, divided by economic class, race, and sexual preference. At this time feminisms were pluralized to different socialist, anarchist, cultural, liberal, lesbian, environmental, radical, Black and Latina agendas. Such naming was necessary, and yet these borders dividing one feminism from another were only partially accurate. A Black feminist also has other identities, like socialist, or lesbian or … or … At this time, horizons, though, were not often global. There was little mention of Muslim feminisms, and little recognition of the feminisms abroad elsewhere.

During this period I identified as a socialist feminist to distinguish myself from the mainstream/white liberal movement in the US. Then came the revolutions of 1989, and Eastern European women's indictment of the misuses of feminism by statist socialism. Socialist feminist no longer felt like an effective identity. I began just to say I was a feminist. But the more this term was being appropriated by neoliberals for global capital, the more I felt uncomfortable with this as well. I began to think I needed to reclaim socialism again; and as a white woman of the globe, I needed to name my antiracism.

My process of seeing and naming a more inclusive feminism has been a process of recognizing the growing power differentials between the US and the rest of the world and also of looking to see more kinds of women across the globe. My viewing from the US may be less encompassing than other women's standpoints from their sites elsewhere because colonialism and imperial capitalism have demanded that they know more and see more in order to survive. Because hegemony of and by the West appropriates and narrows vision to its own visor I must work at deconstructing the universalized gaze and not see through its distortions as I look elsewhere. There are glocal polyversal feminisms to unveil and learn about. These local sites of women's activism are the locations from which to recognize and give voice to a cacophony of feminisms.

Despite globalization's attempts to homogenize cultures, it also puts other cultural practices in view. Global markets create a broader lens through which the world is seen, even if it distorts the world's unique multiplicity while doing so. The UN-sponsored Fourth World Conference on Women in Beijing, 1995, mobilized and publicized various women's movements around the world to the world. It was the time that many across the globe first came to know of Muslim feminists who had been reading the Qur'an in nonpatriarchal ways for a long time before; or to know of women's organizing in Nigeria and Ghana on behalf of sustainable development.

Feminism emerges as women become able to see their own identity as at one with other women in like and different situations. The naming as 'feminism' is part of the process of coming to consciousness of one's shared identity, and this identity forms more readily the more one's life activity criss-crosses contradictory locations: slave women committed to their own humanity; Arab women working in the fields and market and relegated to the home; middle-class professional women in Iran and India and the US circumscribed by their dutiful roles as wives and mothers.

Women activists need to pluralize radically, rather than liberally, the concept of feminisms. This means that differences will not be silenced in some hierarchically privileged order against a singular standard, or set up oppositionally against each other. This means that differences of power must be recognized and challenged. The structures of power have to be dismantled so that differences simply express variety and can be earnestly embraced as such.[6] There will be a variety of ways in which women's equality, freedom, and justice are expressed and defended: as long as self-determination – which encompasses individual choices and access (equality) to them – exists as part of this process.

So, feminisms belong to anyone who is committed to women's ability to choose their destiny; to be the agents of their own life choices so long as they do not colonize another. As such, no one simply owns feminism's particular meaning. Naming acknowledges the thing named so that it can be seen. Naming ends silence. Naming also expresses the power of those who get to name. It is part of the very process of self-determination that is so central to feminism itself. Toni Morrison in *Beloved* writes: "Definitions belonged to the definers – not the defined."[7] Feminism locates the sites of women's oppression as visible. There are differing notions of what oppression means, yet 'feminism' gives coherence to the variety. Women, especially in the West, need to multiply the versions/visions of women's oppression and liberation; and to find multiple ways to understand the varieties of feminisms.

The contested domain of feminisms is not understood best as a clear West/non-West divide. Instead I look to see plurally in 'other-than-Western' varieties.[8] Yet to the extent a West is spoken in this phrasing, it is still privileged in this site. I recognize that there has been much of the West written into feminist theory, but I also believe that the West has simply claimed much of feminism as its own that is not. My queries and condemnations are not meant to deny the enormously rich history that feminisms of the West have provided women across the globe. Maria Stewart demanded women's rights for slave women in the 1820s. Working-class feminisms with communal notions of rights go back to at least the seventeenth century in Europe. Yet feminism is not simply of the West. Many women from elsewhere already know this so my inquiry is hopelessly slanted by my own start.

Miriam Cooke, a Muslim feminist living in the US says that feminists are "women who think and do something about changing expectations for women's social roles and responsibilities". She calls attention to the journal *Zanan* and the women who are reading the Qur'an from a women's viewpoint and "demanding equal access to scriptural truth at a time when Islamic discourse is on the rise". For many of these women, Islam does not presume gender inequity, and feminism the opposite. Rather, Islam itself, at its most democratic reading, requires women's equality. These women seek to subvert and adapt Islamic practices to recognize justice and citizenship for Muslim women. Cooke sees Islamic feminism, not as singular but as a politic with no one 'fixed identity' and a series of subject positions. And she also recognizes that some Muslim feminists, like Haideh Moghissi, are radically opposed to the idea that there is any room in Islam for women's rights.[9]

To the extent that English has been predominantly a white/Western woman's language it also is attached to white women's identities. This does not mean that most white women readily claim the term 'feminist', nor does it mean that women of color do not utilize it frequently. But nuanced differences exist within these choices. US Black women have been uncomfortable with the term given its racist history, its exclusionary focus privileging white women, Black women's own multiple oppressions which made feminism's singularity feel too narrow, and the hostility towards feminism as a white woman's thing expressed by Black men. Jill Nelson, who often identifies as feminist, also says that although naming is important, so "is anonymity and adroit warfare". She says Black women know "the efficacy of stealth", of "communicating indirectly", of the "amazing art of passing on information via metaphor" as spirituals do.[10]

Women activists in Egypt in the early twentieth century like Huda Shaarawi wrote and spoke from their own experiences; no one term directly translated into 'feminist'. The problem of translation is so often why Arab feminisms have been invisible to the world outside Lebanon, Iraq, Palestine, and Syria. Shaarawi was an upper-class Egyptian woman who was brought up in the segregated world of the harem, and resisted this life because it constructed her femaleness as a barrier to her freedom. She criticized social custom, rather than the Qur'an, for holding women back.[11] The autobiography of Fay Afaf Kanafani chronicles her sexual abuse as a child at the hands of her father; and her difficult refusal of sex with her husband for years. As a Muslim/Arab woman her identity is formed by this, and by the tensions between Palestine and Lebanon from the close of World War One.[12] Her activism was polyvocal, and feminist. Their stories are quasi-universal: of wealthy educated women who wish to do as their brothers and husbands do.

Deep inside the very notion of feminism resides this conundrum: the translation of plural meanings and multiple locations into one term that cannot be home-grown in each location. The term 'feminism' – its racist and colonialist past – inhibits an embrace of all women's lives across the globe. And yet it calls attention to women like no other term in any other language. If feminisms means the willingness to both recognize and subordinate differences while recognizing the inequalities of power that divide women, the language of feminisms should not inevitably itself reproduce imperial meaning.[13] And yet again, the term 'feminism' silently authorizes the English language as power-filled.

We, the big 'we' – feminists across the globe – need an identity chosen from women's present activism that opens feminisms to their most democratic promise. This will be more than a Westernized antiracist feminism. De-Westernized does not mean less focus on the gendered oppressions of women's lives, but gender is complexly connected to multiple systems of power. It also requires the denuding of the globalized West's cultural dominance and economic appropriation. It means commitment to the gender rights of women while condemning global imperialism. This is a necessary and powerful combination: women challenging global capital with its racialized patriarchal structures of domination and exploitation while also embracing a democratized gender agenda which will destabilize local/cultural misogynies.

So where does 'feminisms' stand at present? Given feminism's troubled history and incomplete understanding of the complexities always present in defining sex and gender oppression, activists must employ the term skeptically and give it new and insurgent meanings all the time. It is impossible to control and limit the radical dimensions of feminisms as they are practiced by women cross-culturally, so language must specify the practices in relentless detail.[14] It is an enormous challenge to remain open and not assume that you know the limits and meanings of a particular practice beforehand. So women from multiple sites and cultures must remain open to new meanings of feminisms, as each person looks for their particular and plural meanings of selfhood. Feminisms are always changing with new possibilities for democratizing human liberation so we – the big 'we' – must allow them to do so.

Modernity and Feminisms

The language of politics – democracy, socialism, modernity, civilization – is deciphered by Marxists, neoliberals, Islamists in relation to the economic system, which by definition makes the racialized gender system invisible. Bourgeois liberalism articulates the relations of capitalism; socialism writes its critique. Conservatism embraces preservation of the economy. Terms like 'Western' and 'modernity' bespeak the bourgeois layering of economic development. In all this, women's lives are depoliticized as private and not public, and stand outside the contours of political language. Despite this, women remain the symbolic of nationhood.

Women's bodies are clothed to represent the status of the nation: chadors, burqas, saris, miniskirts, spiked heels, eye make-up, facelifts, and so on. Non-modern dress, read as non-Western, is seen as a sign of backwardness or underdevelopment. Modernity exposes the woman's body; the more the body is revealed, the more modern the nation. The more that sexuality is spoken, the more modern the culture. Yet, both rich and poor nations, so-called modern and not, suffer domestic violence, rape, and unwanted pregnancies.

Feminisms put women's and girls' lives in full view as part of the matrix of oppression, and intervene in the simplistic modernity debate. For feminisms, societies where rape and domestic violence are practiced are backward, as well as uncivilized, whether or not these countries are Western or not. Rape camps during the Bosnian War should have put Serbs on a par with the Taliban because rape is no more 'modern' than enforced seclusion behind a burqa is simply backward. The enforced prostitution of women in South-East Asia and the Pacific by the Japanese military during World War Two bespeaks woman as the horrific 'other'. She is not a part of the society, but merely serves it as sex slave. From this vantage point of sexual slavery, there are no nations that are not in some sense 'backward'.

Women who were forcibly rounded up as 'comfort women' for the Japanese military during the Asia Pacific War during 1931–45 were imprisoned in brothels to provide sex to military men. As one officer of the Army Corps justifies the practice: "This desire [for sex] is the same as hunger or the need to urinate, and soldiers merely thought of comfort stations as practically the same as latrines."[15] Young women from Indonesia, the Philippines, Singapore, China, Korea, and Burma, were forced to service military men's needs. Their continued rape, confinement and physical abuse, was a grave violation of their human rights which combined sexual violence against women, racism, and discrimination against the poor.[16]

These sorts of rape camps bespeak inhumanity and 'backwardness'. Rape is uncivilized, and yet stands outside the usual markers depicting modernity and 'civilization', as it did in the eighteenth century and the slave trade. This is simply one example of the unsettling of the modernity/ backward, civilized/ uncivilized divide once one looks at the silenced political arena of sexual violence. And this violence should not be oversimplified or misrepresented as one of simple gender oppression. In Rwanda, 1994, the slaughter and rape of hundreds of thousands of women was done by ordinary people wielding machetes. And many in these civilian mobs doing the killing were women.[17]

Given the silencing of women's lives and struggles in political discourses like modernity, it becomes even more troublesome to connect feminisms with terms like 'Western', or 'modern'. Such identifications often simply reproduce silences which negate the possibility for seeing women's activities and contributions as part of the stuff of political life itself. Instead, women are captured by modernity – and its global capitalist markets – as for sale as in "feminism for export".[18] Glitzy advertisements of beautiful women fantasize the freedom of the West. Well-dressed and fashionable women image the promise of democracy. Women of the West are exported to the rest of the global 'community' as CEOs or porn stars. Mass marketing turns feminism into a consumerist self-help market and feminisms' possibilities are de-radicalized as a marketing device of First World markets. In these instances the radical possibilities of feminisms are truncated and the struggle for humane democracies is vaporized. Meanwhile a majority of the women across the globe – inside and outside the West – are living and working harder than ever.

However, the same exploitative system of global capital that renews the oppression of women and girls in sweatshop labor, prostitution, and cybersystems of power, also provokes and makes visible women's activism across the globe. As former divisions between home and work, and public and private life are challenged, patriarchal controls are exposed and undermined in new fashion because the consumerist culture of capitalism also undermines traditional masculinist privilege. So although global capital, as such, is no friend to women and girls, it unsettles existing gender relations in ways that it cannot simply control. In this sense global capital is tremendously contradictory: it promises freedom and riches to the very people it exploits and degrades, while also putting this contradictoriness in view.

Global capitalism exposes women to new levels of exploitation and also instigates new yearnings for democracy that cannot easily be dismissed as simply bourgeois. Instead, these desires tap the human quest for self-determination. These yearnings rather endorse women's own local feminist desires, some of which are resistant to globalization, and some of which embrace the promissory of globalization: freedom for all.

These glocal feminist formulations bespeak reciprocal flows even though the promise of freedom is too distant for women and girls suffering the gravest inequalities of the global market. Again, none of this is best understood as simply 'modern', or 'backward'.

For Leila Ahmed, the history of colonialism has tainted feminism as 'modern' for most women across the globe. Colonialism's episodic and exclusionary notion of modernity defines a complex set of attitudes here. For some Islamists, this set of attitudes stigmatizes sexual independence and freedoms as Western, but accepts women's education and work outside the home. Wearing the hijab is then not seen as traditional but rather as a modern form of rejecting foreign ways.[19] For Margot Badran, there is no culturally pure location that could be termed simply 'modern'. Instead 'entanglement' creates problems for 'modernity' as a concept.[20] In Egypt, indigenous, local elements mix with external elements. Outside elements are absorbed into the local culture with a variety of secular and Islamist feminisms emerging. Leila Abu-Lughod says that progressives in Egypt choose a "moral modernity" which is not Western, that is, sexually immoral and individualist.[21] Omnia Shakry believes that the women's question in Egypt shows "how a local nationalist discourse, articulated in very complex ways with colonial discourse, seeks to situate itself as *both* modern and Islamic", as both with and against the West.[22] Or, as Zohreh Sullivan says, Egyptian women neither want to return to a past, nor do they wish to mimick Western feminism. She argues that modernism should not be thought to be reduceable to a Western formulation.[23] Haleh Afshar says that women activists in Iran cannot easily be classified as liberals or Westerners. She rather argues that the variations within Islam are 'reconcilable' with a host of feminisms that exist in the world today.[24] There are a variety of feminisms to explore here: secular, Islamist, in-between, communist, liberal, and …

Western feminism, when equated with liberal feminism, as it was articulated in the nineteenth century stood as a critique of the exclusion of white women from the bourgeois revolution overtaking England and France. These women wanted the new freedoms being promised white propertied men. In order to claim these rights, these women first had to see that they were excluded as a sexual caste, as a homogenized collective with no individuality. They then used this ascribed status to challenge the engendered exclusivity of bourgeois right. These feminists did not speak of slave women or slaves in general. They did not speak of nonpropertied women, or colonized women. They were exclusionary by the silences they allowed. They instead utilized the abstract/inclusive promissory of individual rights and demanded democracy for themselves. These were the canonized and commodified voices of feminism which silenced other feminisms in the West: Black, working-class, Quaker/believing Christians, and ... Their radical – though incomplete – moment has long since passed.

Western hegemony equates individuality with bourgeois individualism. In this reading the very idea of an individual with rights assumes a competitive and oppositional relationship between the self and others. However, other notions of individuality exist that are not simply at one with a bourgeois individualism that presupposes that the self flourishes best in autonomous, rather than communal fashion. This 'other-than-Western' notion of individuality premises the self as also interconnected with others, and is not by definition antagonistic to sexual difference, but rather to sexual hierarchy. The self is enhanced by others and the social obligations and responsibilities they entail. Instead of equating the liberal notion of equality with sameness of treatment, an individual woman's particularity can be encompassed without negating fair treatment.

Feminisms of all sorts recognize the complex need to rewrite democratic theory while recognizing both women's similarities and their differences, among themselves, and to men as well. The criteria for equal treatment should be about justice for humanity, which is both male and female. This standard for justice is specified through the divides of rich and poor, and all colors, religions, and cultures. Many Islamic and Africana feminisms imagine a social notion of the individual that is connected to family. It is terribly important to distinguish the progressive and life-enhancing dimensions of collectivity – whether under a veil or a tribal commune or family-life – both from the stifling and hierarchical, lonely and arduous dimensions of individualism *and* from the stifling and arduous dimensions of patriarchal and extended families.

Submission to scriptural canon and/or a degrading collectivism negates the individuality of women. Submission to a rugged individualism negates the connectivity of these same women. The recognition of the communal, familial and interconnected concepts of the self is spoken by feminists and women activists in Mexico, the Philippines, and Malaysia. Familial relations have always been foundational for US Black feminists.

Individuality can imply autonomy and connection: one can choose to act individually while also recognizing obligations and responsibilities. This requires recognition of the self-determining woman and her choices while recognizing that these choices are not utterly free and unrestricted. This sense of self is interconnected with others, although the self is also independent. This reading of the self is other-than-bourgeois individualist (which is masculinist and racialized at its root). This feminist self has its roots/routes from 'elsewheres' where slavery and colonialism have demanded more of the individual than selfish desire, but also more than selflessness. A slave woman runs away and risks death rather than rape for herself and her children. A woman wears the veil while fighting for the revolution she believes will free all women. A woman risks her individual job as she makes charges of sexual harassment.

Connectedness and autonomy are not oppositional stances as they so often have been articulated in both bourgeois individualism and socialist collectivism. The significance of the webbed relations between self and others may be more present in women's than men's lives because most women undertake the burdens and responsibilities of family more directly than do most men. Women's lives – their duties and responsibilities – blend and bleed across the usual political divides of bourgeois and socialist, individualist and collectivist, West and non-West. Feminisms that have developed through the challenges of imperialism and globalization explore new meanings of selfhood in response to the complex power regimes defining their lives.

I cling to the self as 'free' even though I wish to disengage the idea of selfhood from its commodified selfish form. I remain committed to individuality because it can nurture a diverse humanity. Because freedom can allow us our differences it always has the possibility of creating uniqueness. Freedom, then, of the self, allows for the possibility of dissidence and resistance in that it nurtures individuality, rather than deference. But of course this presupposes an individual who already is committed to more than just selfishness. Otherwise, submission rather than unique creativity dominates.

Neoliberal and imperial feminism mass-market a selfish individualism and silence concerns with racial and economic equality. Such feminism destroys its promise of democracy because without equality freedoms cannot be actualized by most women. Freedom to choose must be accompanied by the possibility of having access to one's choices. So feminists, especially within the West, must work to equalize the access to freedoms so that they matter more, and for all people. Democratic feminisms embrace equality as a way to recognize women's similarities as female, and freedom because it celebrates women's multiplicity. And they must also recognize that within the sharedness of being female there exist enormous power differentials which must be remedied by creating differential access. Given power differentials, demands for equality must be specified as they are woven through the differentials of race, class, sexuality, and culture. And it is not enough to have economic or legal equality without equality of sexual choices. New feminisms will emerge as women engage in the pressing challenges of this day.

For new feminisms to thrive as they should, it is important to clarify the various present-day feminisms of the West: a neoliberal/imperial feminist discourse of the US government and transnational capital; a mainstream liberal feminist equal rights agenda articulated inside the US and elsewhere as well; a vocal human rights discourse publicized through the UN; and a mix of progressive liberatory discourses from Black, Latina, socialist, women's groups in the US and Europe.

Women in the West and in the East and women in the North, and in the South; women of the non-West living in the West; and women of the West living in the non-West must move and shake these dialogues beyond these falsely defined divides. These various feminist voices reflect the vital power struggles of the twenty-first century. And it is out of these contested voices that new radically pluralist feminist dialogues can develop.

Although the dominant discourse of global capital reproduces and reifies the notion of the Western woman daily, this image silences too many women living in the West, while also rightly speaking her enormous privilege. So, we – women in the US – have an added responsibility to recognize and critique the obscene power of our own country in relation to discourses of the West, in the hopes that this will allow new trust among women from elsewheres. We, the big 'we' – feminists and women activists across the globe – must carefully listen to each other and learn new ways of seeing and hearing silences and whisperings. This demands a generosity of spirit from the many women from elsewheres living in the US, and the women living elsewheres, suffering the consequences of the US wars of/on 'terror'. Hopefully such generosity will allow all feminists to trust, together, that a better world is possible.

Universalizing Polyversalism

Given the new possibilities for thinking cross-culturally it is critically urgent to rethink the contours of the meaning of 'universal', and pluralize it to other-than-its Western formulation. Universality has been exclusionary of the very thing it is supposed to embrace – totality. Universality operates as an abstracted viewing of humanity when it is articulated by the powerful, for themselves. It implies unity rather than a notion of 'all', or 'everyone'. It is why eighteenth century theorists could write of the humanity, the freedom, and the equality of 'all', and really mean of white propertied men. To them, no one was excluded. The abstract metaphor – the individual – makes it possible to misname and mis-see the totality as one and the same with oneself. Yet this notion of the abstract individual' – which presumes any and all individuals – remains a gift of promise for those who have been silenced.

Universal rights are human rights, humanely given to anyone who is human. As such they are said to be natural rights. They are available to anyone who chooses to claim them. These visions were written by men like Kant, and Rousseau who either never spoke against the slave trade or spoke in metaphor, and never endorsed women's freedom or equality. Rousseau wrote his *Social Contract* because men were born free and yet everywhere lived in chains. But his men who were born free were white, not Black slaves. And the men chained were not Black, but white. No woman was a part of his civil contract.

Given the exclusionary history of universal rights they must be democratized by a previously silenced specificity. The universal must be reinvented by particularizing. If universal rights had been written at the start from the site of slavery there would have been no slaves because freedom would have been envisioned more inclusively. Today, if the universal is written from women's bodies in their polyversal diversity – with their actual needs for food, shelter, love, education, and creative lives – humanity is enlarged. Extend universal rights in actual form to the girl working in the Philippine sweatshop. The universal is specifically multiple, or as the Bengali theorists argue, there is "unity in diversity".

Specificity – especially of differences – critiques and informs an overly abstracted humanism which can be read from the site of power as oneness. 'Human' as a term is already encoded with the colonialist's exclusiveness. Nevertheless, "human rights" is thought to be a more inclusive construct than "women's rights" by many. Feminist UN discourse states that "women's rights are human rights". I continue to query why humanism is thought to be more inclusive than feminism. Instead, why not shift the inclusive standard toward women: that human rights are encompassed by women's rights? Women's rights address the shared human likeness with men *and* the distinct uniqueness of differing needs, in a way human rights at present do not.

A health system that provides women with prenatal and pregnancy care provides an inclusive program for both women and men, even though men will not need this specific care. Men are not disabled in this framework, as pregnant women are within the abstracted masculinist standard of universality. Within that framework, pregnancy becomes a (legal) disability, while women are treated similarly to men. Given the specific needs pregnant women's bodies may have, women's bodies become a more inclusive standard for encompassing humanity. Inclusivity derives from a plural diversity written from women's bodies. And this specificity puts sites of powerlessness in view, for those who see themselves as the universal. When women's specified health needs are met, the silences encoded in abstracted and hierarchically privileged conceptions of humanity are uncovered.

It is therefore troubling that when Martha Nussbaum argues for a cross-cultural notion of humanness, she adopts the liberal notion of universalism. She calls for a universal accounting of human capabilities as shared, even though she recognizes the need of a universalism that is sensitive to plural and cultural differences. Pluralism and respect for difference are themselves universal values, yet they also remain liberal, or of the West, for her. The point I have been making throughout is that these values are not in and of themselves liberal, or simply Western. She says we need a universalist feminism, an abstracted promissory of oneness which is understood as liberal.[25] But what can diversity of implementation mean if unity is premised at the start.

Carol Quillen sees much of Nussbaum's proposals as Eurocentric; arguing that she does not recognize the tension between "European humanism and European imperialism". Whereas Nussbaum is bound by the liberal humanist tradition, Quillen asks for an "other-than-liberal humanist" project. Western humanism is one and the same with

European domination and racist and colonialist practices.[26] Without recognizing these power differentials it is too risky that one will simply think that others should be "free like me". Emancipation is thought to lead to the West – away from Islam, or anywhere elsewheres. Nussbaum needs to interrogate the promissory of liberal humanism to try and find a non-colonialist humanity in polyversal form that can retrieve humanism for liberatory feminisms not limited to abstract universals.

Nussbaum thinks that "any universalism" that has a chance of succeeding in the 'modern' world must be a "form of political liberalism". She herself acknowledges that cultures are not homogenous; that "plurality, contestation and individual variety" exist within all cultures, along with overlap and borrowing.[27] So how does she decipher what she terms "political liberalism"; as well as disconnect it from the mix of other influences of which it is a part? Nussbaum either does not see other-than-liberal notions of humanism as promissory, or her Anglocentrism simply allows her to claim that liberal humanism is the universal. Once again, for me, the uni is also poly; and the global flows have always been dialectical, even if unevenly so.

Nussbaum wrongly privileges the notion of 'humanity' when she writes of women's rights. She starts *Sex and Social Justice* with the qualifier that it is "not really about women at all but about human beings and about women seen as fully human". She simply ignores the exclusionary practices performed in the name of humanity. She authorizes her discussion of feminism by saying her feminism is humanism, namely, that it is more inclusive than just about women.[28] Why this deference to human? Why not reject the framework of an abstracted universal humanism and replace it with a specified viewing of humanity through the lives of its women?

Nussbaum herself repeatedly makes the case, as many others at the UN and World Bank do, that if you improve the lives of women, you improve the lives of everyone. Countries develop in direct proportion to the levels of education and participation of their women. She does not consider why this is the case, just that it is so. However, a plausible reason is that women are usually expected to take care of more than themselves. In fact, women's lives often embrace duties and responsibilities that extend beyond, and sometimes are in conflict with, liberal humanism.

Amartya Sen has influenced Nussbaum's thinking. "The voice of women is critically important for the world's future – not just for women's future."[29] According to Sen, women's empowerment through education, property rights, and employment reduces fertility rates and promotes female literacy. And, when women's lives are bettered, their nations also benefit. Improve women and one simultaneously improves the lives of others. Such statements and findings are not said of men, nor is much made of this as a difference: that it is women, and not men, who readily embrace the work of humanity.

A World Bank study states that "countries which promote women's rights and increase their access to resources and schooling enjoy lower poverty rates, faster economic growth and less corruption than countries who do not". The report continues: "Gender inequality hurts all members of society, not just girls and women."[30] Although it is often noted that women are a main resource for community development it is less often recognized that women's sense of self is more than singular. This notion of development begs one to see more-than-a-liberal view of humanism, one that expresses the interconnectedness of female autonomy.

Nussbaum says she will redefine universalism in radically plural ways but instead universalizes liberal pluralism in its Western form. I find this perplexing given that she argues that feminism should become less insular, more international, and more attentive to issues like inequality, hunger, and health care across the globe. In order to achieve such an agenda she needs to dislodge the dominant discourse she adopts. If she does so she will be more able to see other-than-liberal feminisms, and will less readily homogenize women from non-Western countries.[31]

Liberal humanism cannot envision more-than-Western visions of humanity rich in interconnectedness and diversity because abstract individualism demands a homogeneity that makes multiplicity look chaotic and troublesome. The West does not allow for "unity in diversity"; rather global capital uses a corporatist multiculturalism to domesticate difference into a marketable homogeneity.

Liberalism is readily privileged in the West by many in the academy, like Susan Moller Okin. She also believes that cultures must become liberal to be respected. Okin wants to prioritize women's rights and fears that multiculturalism is bad for women. She positions multiculturalism – as group rights – against women's rights – as individual rights. She sees gender equality as in tension with the "claims of minority cultures" because she assumes that cultural diversity will clash with feminist goals. She says that the rights of the group should not trump the individual rights of its members, and she sees group rights usually as antifeminist. She works from within the tradition of liberalism which posits the tension between the individual and the group at its core. Individualism is bourgeois and autonomous for her. Therefore, a tension always exists between the individual and the group, whether women's rights are part of the equation or not.

Okin makes a mistake here by assuming that feminism is not also about group rights – of women as women – however individually these rights are practiced. She also does not deal with the intersectionality and multiplicity of women of color's lives when she assumes that their culture will always oppose their fair treatment. Clearly, to position multiculturalism as being opposed to women, as Okin does, entails that the women are homogenized in a noncultural/nonracial identity. So she also does not wonder about new ways of thinking about women's rights in multicultural fashion.

Okin needs to re-read the dilemma and see how a different rendering of cultural rights can be used to embrace feminisms. Okin sees women's servitude as written into Islam.[33] But wearing a headscarf or veiling oneself is not *a priori* antifeminist, unless Okin is allowing her liberal feminist notion of sameness of treatment to be her defining criteria of feminism. Okin needs to indict patriarchal practices rather than multiculturalism as the problem. And she needs to rethink how her privileging of the cultural traditions of liberalism creates hostility to the multiplicity of other feminisms within other-than-liberal meanings.

Universalism covers over the normalized forms of patriarchal colonialism in the name of democracy. Multiculturalism calls attention to diverse cultural practices, some of which are patriarchal and some of which are not. It is up to feminisms to struggle with its many formulations to decipher the widest interpretive meaning of women's liberation. Multiculturalism comes clothed in many forms and should not be collapsed into a singularized Westernized rendering. In this sense a liberal feminist critique, no matter what its local home is, is too narrow in its viewing. There are too many other feminisms which are a compilation of their own and other cultural articulations. The globalized language of women's rights is both liberatory and colonizing; maybe more so now than ever given the insidious global webs of power that exploit women and girls everywhere while supposedly championing their newly won freedoms – from the Soviet empire, the Taliban, and so on.

Amidst this flux some Africana womanists and feminists see equality not as meaning sameness (of treatment with men) but rather as meaning respect for who each woman is. And they view liberation as an individual, communal, and national affair.

Africana Womanisms and Their Black Feminist Meanings

Global capitalism and its cyber airwaves make more of the world visible to more people than ever, even while large portions of the globe exist without phone lines and cyber access. Africa remains invisible to the West unless stereotyped as a home to the AIDS plague, genocide, music.... Given its paucity of electric power and the patchy cover of its grids, and the present antiterrorist preoccupation with the Middle East and South-East Asia, Africa's exclusion is remodeled. Blacks inside the US and Africa stand alongside the new alien color, Brown Muslim. Women in Africa continue to struggle to create sustainable lives, fight against and live with AIDS, and are also challenged by misogynist fundamentalists in Algeria, Nigeria, Morocco, and elsewhere.

Black feminisms in the US are almost two centuries old. Black feminist critique of the racist practices of white liberal feminism and radical feminism rejected their singularity of focus and the narrowness of their world view. Black feminists see the intersections between their race, sex, gender, and class oppression. They do not have the privilege to disregard or silence their racialized existence and its webbed connection to their gender. Black women did not know the suffocating "institution of motherhood" that turned white middle-class women into housewives and mothers. They instead were expected to earn wages and care for white middle-class women's homes. So there are different histories and trajectories to explore. Many US Black feminists readily identify with Africana 'womanisms', while others do not.

Women's activism has been a crucial part of life in most African societies. Women were central to the liberation of Algeria in its war for independence, were essential to the struggles against apartheid in South Africa, and have led most of the environmental movements throughout the continent for sustainable development. These African roots/routes of feminisms wind back to the days of the slave trade when Black women suffered an enforced equality with Black men – in bearing the whip and its cruelty. These women built their lives out of degradation and resistance.[34] They seeded African culture in North America and the Caribbean.

These women's struggles have yet to be named as part of feminist history, by Black and white women alike, and especially by neoliberal/ imperial feminists in the West. White women in England and the US first named *their* struggles as feminist even while other-than-liberal feminisms had already existed elsewhere in many indigenous forms. The powerful positioning of English as the dominant language – rather than the actual diverse practices of women's struggle – has facilitated these exclusions.

Clenora Hudson-Weems, writing in the US, argues that it is the "ultimate in racist arrogance and domination to suggest that authentic activity of women resides with white women". Africana women in the US like Sojourner Truth, Harriet Tubman and Ida B. Wells were feminists even if they did not singularly and exclusively focus on women's issues. For Weems the struggles of African women are an originary site for understanding women's movements. White feminists have benefited and learned from abolitionists, civil rights workers, and African women activists. Therefore, "when Africana women come along and embrace feminism, appending it to their identity as Black feminists or African feminists, they are in reality duplicating the duplicate".[35]

There is a history to be remembered here of an "androgynous world born, weirdly enough, not of freedom, but of bondage".[36] Black women have practiced an alternative womanhood, in slavery and in freedom, which nurtures alternative feminisms as well.[37] When Black women ask if they are not women as in Sojourner Truth's famous speech – "Ar'n't I a Woman?" – the directional needs redesigning, away from the query Ar'n't I like a white woman? So although there are similarities between white and Black women, differences within the similarity also exist. Aida Hurtado writes that while white women are seduced, women of color are rejected.[38] Yet the common denominator of phallocratic violence, phallocratic fascism, and the destruction of the human being remains.[39]

Women's embeddedness in other relations – their color/race, their economic class, their cultural identity – demands feminisms that recognize these complexities at the start. Most feminists/womanists in Africa demand this polydimensional understanding and reject the singularity of a feminism focused on gender alone, which silently privileges white women and diminishes the presence of women of color. Alice Walker, speaking as a Black feminist in the US, uses the term 'womanist' to refer to feminists of color who are committed to the survival and wholeness of an entire people, male and female. "Womanist is to feminist as purple is to lavender."[40] She chooses 'womanist' over 'feminist' because Black women need to name women's struggles from inside the West for themselves. Dialogues and flows across continents are a part of this naming, and pluralizing.[41]

Awa Thiam wonders: "'Women are the Blacks of the human race'. Can they tell us then what or who are Black Women? The Blacks of the Blacks of the human race?"[42] She calls for this specificity, while speaking a commitment to African liberation in the tradition of self-reliance and autonomy. Race and class are key issues for people/women of color and must come first – before gender – for some Africana womanists like Hudson-Weems. Liberation is a collective struggle for the entire family. African women, in this instance, are not fighting against the strictures of family because they have not suffered from the protective pedestal of familial womanhood.[43] They want no part of white middle-class women's feminism in this arena.

Hudson-Weems also argues that Africana womanists must name themselves. Her criticism lumps all Western feminism together as imperialist, and therefore Black women's own "self-naming, self-defining and self-identifying" is crucial. Feminism, for her, has been defined by white women, for white women. Africana womanism is utterly distinct from white and even Black (Westernized) feminism. Her particular 'womanist' stance is homogenized and set in opposition to a homogeneous, singular, mainstreamed Western feminism.

For Hudson-Weems, African women's struggle against poverty in its colonial and neocolonial forms shapes the contours of their political activism. Women in Nigeria, Ghana, and South Africa connect with men in this "struggle toward a common destiny". Men are not women's enemy but rather are comrades in the struggle against colonialism. Because men in Africa have not had the "same institutionalized power to oppress as white men" Hudson-Weems embraces a "family pride".[44] She rightly focuses on the commonality of purpose between men and women resisting colonial and imperial power, but wrongly equates Western/radical feminism with gender separatism, and loses keen insights by doing so. Unlike Hudson-Weems's womanism, there are other local feminisms developing in many African countries which critique gender privilege in its specific forms, rather than dismiss it as simply of the West.

When Africa is the contextual site from which feminisms are written, economic class oppression is put in the bold. But if this is done by equating feminisms in the West with white feminists of the middle class, class rather than the racialized and gendered meanings of class becomes the oppositioned problem. US Black feminists come in many stripes. Some speak as neoliberals and silence problems of economic class and poverty. Others speak as humanists and anticolonialists; others as lesbian antiracist socialists. The possibilities are varied, as they are in any African country. Instead of parodying either side, if there are sides, let us earnestly blend the collective strategies and intersectional identities of women in Africa with a carefully honed critique of gender privilege. This careful critique always complicates gender to its racial and class hierarchies but it does not deny the place of gender in the power-filled lives of women on any continent. As such, there are no abstracted enemies, but specified relations of power to be dismantled and rebuilt. Women's oppression is then polyversal and glocal and as complex as their struggles of resistance.

African womanism invites a recognition of the important relatedness of people's being. Hudson-Weems writes about "liberating an entire people", of the importance of a holistic harmony and communalism rather than a simplistic and isolated notion of individuality. African womanism is a collective struggle which recognizes the relatedness of women to their families and communities. It "is a family-centered rather than a female-centered perspective". Hudson-Weems says it is by 'necessity' that the first concern must be with "ridding society of racism, a problem which invariably affects our entire family, or total existence". Racism necessitates a frontal and collective struggle against it and Western feminist individualism alike.[45] Given the colonizing history of Western feminism the bifurcation of communalism and individualism is understandable. But too much is lost here.[46] Hudson-Weems could harvest rich notions of female autonomy in local form: a recognition of the woman as able to choose and define her dreams for herself, her community, and her family if she has one, rather than collapsing woman's selfhood with family.

Individuality and collectivity should not be embraced as opposites, or collapsed into themselves. The tensions between these realms need exploration in new directions. One needs to imagine the Nigerian woman who simultaneously struggles on behalf of her reproductive rights without being seen as antifamily, and who also remains critical of global capital's restructuring policies for her country without being seen as antimodern. Her polyvocal feminism embraces the initial recognition of the self without denying responsibilities to other communities. And the multiplicity of her oppressive identities necessitates a more complex wholeness of the individual. This rendering of feminism or womanism is neither simply Western nor simply African. Rather it is a feminist articulation of individuality which recognizes the autonomy of the woman without imagining her as solely alone, or negating her identity as one and the same with her family or community. There are more and more feminists in Nigeria and South Africa who speak and write for unmarried women, women surviving with AIDS, women as lesbians, and women living alone. These are womanist voices with new promises for women's liberation.

According to the Nigerian Zulu Sofola, African womanism expresses holistic harmony and communalism rather than individual isolation. The African experience of exploitation demands that humans recognize their relatedness even as they build their own resilient communities.[47] South African Julia Wells stresses the importance of maternal politics in political struggle. Women, fighting as mothers against apartheid is a dramatically important part of "black South African women's resistance history". South African "motherist movements" were significant challenges to the extreme effects of apartheid rule "which invaded too deeply into their private worlds".[48] Women's resistance is located from within the site of family life, against the state, and as such the family becomes a location of liberation struggle. Similar stories could be written for women in Mexico, Argentina, and Palestine.

For Ifeyinwa Iweriebor, African feminism is "integrationist rather than separatist". Its tactics use negotiation, confrontation, consensus, and compromise. It is often reformist.[49] Obioma Nnaemeka reiterates this, positioned against a Western feminism which is exclusionary. She looks to an inclusionary feminism which she terms "negofeminism – the feminism of negotiation, accommodation and compromise; no ego feminism".[50] Once again, the positioning is against a Westernized separatist feminism that is used by Nigerian men to describe Nigerian feminists as 'Westernized'. But Nnaemeka needs also to look for the not-so-easy-in-view feminisms within the West.

Glo Chukukere writes that "Nigerian feminism is womanism", meaning a nonviolent and non-confrontational self-determined "ability of women to produce maximum results through cooperative endeavors". If feminism means a "female-oriented consciousness then there is no doubt" that Nigeria has a feminist history. However, Nigerian women's history did not start with colonialism, and before the Western experience some say that Nigerian women were "competent warriors, rulers, and co-administrators with their menfolk".[51] The very concept 'Africa' is a colonial artifact. Besides this, Glo Chukukere writes that not all differences between males and females should be assumed to be hierarchical in parallel ways with the West. She argues that hierarchy can also be diffused and multiple, especially when domestic and public lives overlap with one another.

Some African feminists argue that precolonial Africa was defined by gender complementarity, rather than subordination, and that West Africa still has much fluidity between public and private domains that allows for this.[52] Women in many African countries, depending on the specific region, lost land rights with European colonization. Missionaries brought gender inequality with them as they educated boys, and not girls. Some African women therefore scoff that gender inequality was one of the many 'benefits' of contact with Western civilization. In this rendering, today's gender oppression of African women was initiated and exacerbated by Western colonialist policies.

Many women in Africa see themselves as feminist/womanist although they also deeply believe in partnership between the sexes. This partnership focuses their activism on issues of elementary literacy, and freedom from hunger, poverty and disease for everyone.[53] Their feminism is committed to "each and every person" and as such stretches to encompass a polyversal standard for all. There are complex flows to and from Africa today that push feminisms towards a more inclusive notion of humanity even though global capital makes a more humane world much less likely. However, Taiwo Ajai ironically notes that when

African women speak on behalf of their own equality they are dismissed as being too 'Western'.

The complexity of the cultural flows that travel back and forth between continents was painfully and publically visited in 1992 at the first international conference on "Women in Africa and the African Diaspora" (WAAD). Right at the start of the conference conflict erupted over who should be allowed to participate. The conference organizers, who were all African and mostly Black, had invited a few white women to attend. The African-American conference contingent demanded that white women not be allowed to participate in the proceedings. The Nigerians, as hosts, rejected this position as an act of "feminist exclusion and imperial arrogance". They believed that the conference should embrace a full understanding of inclusion, accommodation and negotiation instead of only seeing "color, differences, and separation".[54] The South Africans attending argued that everyone, regardless of race, should be allowed to participate fully in the conference. They were extremely upset that two of their participants, a Black and a white South African who had co-authored a presentation, had been reduced to tears and sadness.[55]

Many of the African women criticized the US Black women, who thought they spoke in African voices, as Western and imperialist in their actions. Their divisiveness felt like European competitiveness, not African cooperativeness.[56] Many of the African attendees saw these US women as shunting the malignancy of their own angst onto the conference. They disrupted the conference because they had come to "find themselves" and return to the motherland; we were caught up in their frustration and rage at being unable to do either.

The African-Americans came to the conference filled with pent-up anger; the South African delegation, after years of living under apartheid, spoke a different notion of possibility. This may seem unexpected, and yet very telling. South African Dé Bryant has written of her grief about the agony felt by the white women attending and celebrates the fact that she cannot enjoy their pain. If I did, she said, it "would mean I have a hole in my soul through which all that is humane and just and good is leaking out".[57] Fidelia Fouche, also South African, argued that apartheid can never cure apartheid.[58] It is important to recognize the differences of culture over notions of inclusion and exclusion, and over the effects of racism.

Without overstating and homogenizing this divide, African feminists/ womanists are in conflict with African-American feminists over the meaning of inclusivity. African-American women were criticized for their Western readiness to exclude and punish. Rather than looking to build bridges through reconciliation, the women from the West, though Black, chose to retaliate and isolate. Then again, I know Black feminists in the US who would have not taken the position of the US delegation, and who work with white women all the time. So there are Africans, so to speak, in the US and Westerners in Africa. Feminists and womanists must be careful to hear and learn from each other in these contested times, so that we make the most of our possibilities for building another world. The Global Women's History Project (GWHP) 2000 was a more recent and successful set of meetings between African-American and South African women organizing against modern forms of slavery, especially in the global factories.[59]

In Nigeria in August, 2002, about 3,000 Itsekiri, Ijaw and Ilaje women in Nigeria seized the Warri headquarters of Shell and Chevron. They stormed the gates, seized the offices, and demanded a living wage and decent life. They were protesting against environmental degradation and substandard employment and demanding accountability for themselves and their families. There is no single expression of feminism in Nigeria at present. Instead there are multiple activisms developing: civil society feminism, legal feminism, radical feminism, secular feminism, religious feminism.[60] In Rwanda, women's lives have been changed forever since the horrific 1994 genocide. As a result of hundreds of thousands of men's deaths, women are now mayors, and members of parliament for the first time. Alongside this, huge numbers of Tutsi women are living with AIDS due to massive war rape. These same women are raising children, going to school, and working.[61] Their activism, which has developed out of sheer necessity, is an important site for feminists to know. At the same time Pauline Nyiramasuhuko is the first woman to stand trial for genocide, charged as the then Minister of Women's Affairs, with inciting the rape of thousands of Tutsi women.[62]

The other-than-Western African feminisms are potentially more inclusive than many feminisms of the West because they view women as human beings responsible to others, while imbricated within multiple systems of oppressive power. Embracing the connective tissue of women's lives while also demanding women their due, allows African women their home-grown feminism, with its inclusive and humanistic character.[63] Women working hard for gender parity in the Organization of African Unity have won it for themselves, as of 2002. Africa is now the only continent in the world to make an explicit commitment to gender equality within its continent-wide governing body. Although this is little more than a symbolic start, it is as much as any Western country has done for gender equality. Potentials for gender democracy located elsewhere and in locations other-than-the West need to be put in view.

In other-than-Western glocal feminisms there must be dialogue between and across and through: involving women-of-color feminisms, Africana womanism, feminisms in the West, feminisms in Africa, feminisms in Islam, and so on. These dialogues must shake loose the overlap between the very categories I have just named. And these discussions must also challenge the established political language of modernity, universalism, nationalism, globalization, religiosity, and secularism so that women can better see and hear one another. This dialogue still must name gender and put it in clear view, but in nonexclusionary form. It must be honest about class exploitation and privilege. It must be brave enough to speak the silences about sexual freedom: a feminisms/womanism that includes lesbians and gays in Africa and Islam.[64] And it must speak against imperial feminism while doing so.

Feminisms in Islam(s)

When "women's rights" were initially used to mobilize the Afghan war against the Taliban, Islam and democracy were purposefully and inadvertently positioned as opposites. But I want to entertain a feminist and democratic reading of Islam as it is articulated by some feminists in Islam and Muslim women that dislodges this simplistic and distorting opposition.

The Qur'an, which is the text for Islamic practice, has multiple interpretations and interpreters. Much of the interpretation is done within and through a misogynist rendering of patriarchal privileges. Women are then read as less than, different from, in need of protection, to be veiled and hidden away. This patriarchal reading matches similar readings in fundamentalist Judaism and Christianity. All religions can be read for the sinfulness of women, the contamination of their blood and their lust, and the need for their seclusion.

Fundamentalist does not necessarily mean authentic. Salman Rushdie says of many Muslims that they "are not Koranic analysts". They rather believe in their customs and habits which are not very theological in the first place.[65] So-called Islamic practices create enormous suffering for women across the globe. In Karachi, Pakistan, a young woman is raped as a punishment for a crime supposedly committed by her brother. But this enactment of *Jirga* law, which derives from tribal customs and traditions, should not be equated with the Islamic religion, even though women are punished all the time as though it were. As Been Sarwar writes of one of these rapes: tradition does not equal religion and religion does not equal patriarchal practice.[66] In Nigeria Amina Lawal, a single mother, was initially sentenced to death by stoning for adultery in the name of shari'a – Islamic law.[67] And yet Islamic feminists argue that no such ruling is written in the Qur'an. Antagonistic struggles continue between mainstream Islamic scholars, Islamic misogynist extremists, and feminists in Islam.

Some "believing women" and feminists in Islam read and interpret the Qur'an as a potentially egalitarian text.[68] There are also "believing women" and Muslim feminists who think that feminism cannot and should not be framed in Islamic terms. Nayereh Tahidi believes that Islam and feminism are incompatible, that reformists within an Islamic republic are not best described as Islamic feminists. There is little agreement and much contestation among Islamic and Muslim women about the relationship between religiosity and secularism for feminism. The plural feminisms within Islamic countries are as multiple as those within the West.

Valentine Moghadam identifies tensions between the differing feminisms in Islam. She sees Haideh Moghissi as viewing cultural pluralism and the right to individual choice as incompatible with Islamic states. For her, therefore, attempts to reform the Islamic state and democratize Islam are misguided, when secularism is what is needed. Moghissi believes that it will be the Left, and secularists who free women; that feminism cannot be fit into the Qur'an. Yet Afsaneh Najmabadi describes Islamic feminism as "a reform movement that opens up a dialogue between religious and secular feminists". For her, religiosity and secularism are not incompatible but can dialogue with each other. Nayereh Tohidi in part agrees: "Many proponents of Islam are playing an important role in the reformation of women's rights in an Islamic context."[69]

Moghissi sees a remarkable feminist tradition within the Middle East that has been largely silenced by Islamic law. She thinks that traditional Islamic culture is overly romanticized in ways that wrongly allow progressive readings of its practices. She does not see the wearing of the hijab in Iran or Egypt as a positive statement of anti-Westernism. Rather, she sees the gesture as antidemocratic in spirit while embracing Western consumer capitalism: Western clothes are worn underneath the hijab. For her, it is the 're-Islamization' of women pretending to be the authentic Islam.[70]

Out of these struggles new developments in feminist theory are articulated. Mai Yamani describes the present feminist choices as: new feminist traditionalists, pragmatic feminists, secular feminists, and neo-Islamist feminists.[71] They each seek to empower women within a rethought Islam. Saudi women seek their own power "through the basic precepts of Islam", even to the point of "manipulating the Qur'an to their advantage" by using fundamental Islamic concepts. Significantly they use the Qur'an, rather than the rhetoric of Western feminism.[72]

There are attempts to articulate an Islamic politics that recognizes the multiple and plural meanings of Islamic practice. In Tunisia, according to Saba Mahmood and Talal Asad, the Islamic leader Ghannushi, who was banned from Tunis, discussed the need to institutionalize politically the multiple interpretations of the founding texts. Recognizing the distinction between the Qur'an and its interpreters and interpretations, Ghannushi has suggested that the electorate be allowed to vote for or against policies that flow from any given reading. This utilizes the doctrine of *nasiha* – the obligation, more than the right – to criticize and debate. This formulation of the Islamic tradition accommodates a plurality of scriptural interpretations; difference is understood as a blessing according to the *shari'a*. Asad reiterates that *ijtihad* authorizes the "construction of coherent differences", not the "imposition of homogeneity". In this instance pluralism is not foreign to Islam; tolerance is not the same as indifference; and intolerance should not be equated with violence. The richness of Islam lies in its openness rather than oneness with God.[73]

This is not the Islam that is put in view for the West. The Islam of the West remains static, traditional and nonmodern. But Talal Asad asks us to see that tradition need not be fixed and unchanging. Authenticity need not be repetitive and uncreative. He gives as an example the tradition of liberalism, which continues to change and adapt. Traditional practices allow for the possibility of argument and reformulation. Then, traditions can be central to modernity itself.[74] He wonders why "Western culture is thought to be pregnant with positive futures in a way no other cultural condition is". And he wonders why liberalism has acquired such a hegemonic status that all other cultures are seen and judged in terms of a teleological Westernized path to the future.[75]

Although sectors of Islam fight against Westernization and its domination, Ali Mirsepassi is one of many who argues that being anti-Westernization is different from being antimodern. In the case of Iran, he writes of the rejection of a Western-centric modernity in favor of a historically and culturally specific one. Iran has tried to "reimagine modernity" in accordance with an Iranian–Islamic tradition that "articulates a viable modernity". Iran is looking to create its own "authentic Iranian modernity", and much that is happening is both authentic and modern and "grounded in the local".[76] The Iranian revolution which deposed Shah Pahlavi was a rejection of despotic secularism, not secularism itself; and of Westernization, not modernism. Moreover, rejection of secularism is not necessarily the same as a rejection of modernity. The men of Al Qaeda who attacked the Twin Towers used cell phones and computers, and knew how to fly planes. The hard-liners in Iran want investment, modern technology, family planning, and so on.

Abdolkarim Soroush argues that Islamic liberalism is no less authentic than anti-Western fundamentalism. And religion need not be an imposition, but can be democratically embraced. Religious knowledge changes and develops with human knowledge. Creative religion is unfolding and not static.[77] Islamic radicalism was innovative and imaginative in mobilizing the masses and took hold as a result. Today the struggle is renewed to define a modern Iran that does not suffer 'Westoxication'. Jalal Al-I Ahmad says that Iran suffered from 'occidentosis' – the political and economic subordination of Iran to Europe and America.[78] Now feminists need to pressure Islam to become an antiglobalization site which explicitly embraces democracy for women. This is a moment when progressive feminists across the globe should inform themselves about Muslim women's local struggles.

Saba Mahmood also interrogates the way the West thinks in terms of oppositions such as religiosity and secularism, and equates traditionalism with patriarchy and modernity with women's freedom. She asks that religious practices in Islam not be viewed as *a priori* subordination of women. Instead women's agency within these practices must first be explored. Mahmood studies women in the Mosque movement in Egypt as 'reconfiguring' gendered practices within Islamic pedagogy. These women defy the practice of male teaching and instruct women and girls on the meaning of the Qur'an. They have their own rendering of self-realization and autonomous will which cannot simply be read from the West. The women's Mosque movement wants to restore virtue and humility, and embraces "individual and collective practices of pious living". These women "subvert the hegemonic meanings of cultural practices".[79]

Women's agency, for Mahmood, is "not simply resistance to domination" but is also an "action that is created and enabled by relations of subordination". If I understand this point correctly it means that the rigid oppositioning of oppression and freedom is ill-placed and that agency develops from within resistances that are incomplete or less than total. Mahmood re-reads the meaning of docility and humility as the effort to achieve a malleability to be instructed in the ways of Islam, but with women as teachers of this process. *Al-haya*, meaning diffidence and modesty, is seen as a process of learning shyness, not oppression.[80] Mahmood's description embodies the veil with piety and rebellion. She sees agency instead of passivity.

Mahmood asks secular women to revisit their dismissal of religion as oppressive. Cultural and religious practices can be habitually repressive and re-readings are still possible. She does not see secular reasoning and morality as exhaustive of "valuable human flourishings". She asks that non-liberal traditions should be explored for their possibilities for liberation and not be subsumed into a "universalized seeing of subordination".[81] When women teach and study Islamic scriptures this modernizes religiosity and does not limit it to a traditionalist misogyny. Islam is not simply custom and tradition; nor is the West simply modern. Religious women of all sorts – Christian, Jewish, Hindu – have been engaged in similar re-castings of religious texts for years.

For Mahmood, choosing religion can be an act of liberation, as can veiling, if the woman sees it as part of the process of teaching herself humility. The veil means "both being and becoming a certain kind of person"[82] and contributes to the making of the self. These women develop their individual selves, although not in a Western autonomous fashion. I remain unsure why humility, embodied in the veil, is such a privileged construct particular to women. But if humility nurtures a humbleness of who we are in relation to others I am open to learning more of this. Veiling also has a history of misogynist extremism and Western colonialism, meaning different things at different times. Context matters before women's agency can be known.[83] Self-realization is not simply a Western construct. More-than-liberal notions of self-fulfillment are germinating in these instances.

Progressive interpretations of the Qur'an reveal an egalitarian spirit, although there is often no clear position on what equality is meant to mean. Shaheen Ali believes that a human rights discourse exists in the Qur'an for women so that the West and feminisms of the West are not needed here.[84] Haleh Afshar thinks that these new interpretations of Islam are more liberating for women than feminism has been liberating for women in the West.[85]

I still wonder about Mahmood's discussion of the veil. Why veil women? Why not have men veil to learn humility? Maybe I am thinking too much about equality as sameness here. Yet the veil encodes gender difference, and 'difference' remains contested. When I think I would not choose to veil I wonder whether there is something more than my Western acculturation at play here. I do not see the veil as intrinsically more problematic than Western codings of femininity and gender difference. I dress as a female with signs given on my face: make-up, hair in view, jewelry. And even though I think I give these signs my own personal meaning, I am not fully free to do so. The veil has its parallels here. I am thinking/wondering whether oppressive practices – those that encode gender – can ever be wholly recuperable or self-realizing.

What are the hybrid blendings of and between liberal individualist autonomy, selfhood with humility, and woman's connectedness? The concept of self cuts through each, but with differing understandings of fulfillment for the self. In order to see the polyversal status of individuality within these discourses one needs to de-naturalize the concept of the singular, competitive, autonomous self while holding onto the notion of the social, communal self which has obligations to others but rights as well. This is neither an anti- nor a pro-Western/liberal stance. Rather it is a dialogic positioning of an individuality defined in other-than-liberal-individualist frames recognizing women's connectedness to children and family alongside men sharing a colonized location with them, although with gendered privilege. But the woman is self-determining in these connected spaces. The self-determining woman is free but not alone; obligated yet independent; equal and also unique.

A word on sex, which has been too silent here. Homosexuality is often a crime, sometimes punishable by death in Islamic countries. However, the founder of the US-based gay Muslim group Al-Fatiha argues that homosexuality is a matter of interpretation, and not simply forbidden in the Qur'an. Some scholars say that the sin is promiscuity rather than homosexuality. Homosexuality is not an easily accepted identity, almost everywhere, not simply in Islam. In the US, Muslim gays are reviled by mainstream Muslims for their sexual orientation, and viewed as potential terrorists by some Americans.[86] Today GLAS, an Arab gay and lesbian international organization networks gays and lesbians of Arab descent, or those living in Arab countries, worldwide.

Sex, though always present, is almost always silenced in public, and as such creates complex and silenced political fault lines. So it should not be a surprise that the Taliban tried to erase pedophilia from male-dominated Pashtun culture, and now that the Afghan Ministry for the Promotion of Virtue and Prevention of Vice is gone, supposedly the practice has burgeoned again.[87] This cannot help but also remind one of the US scandal-ridden Catholic Church and the sexual predators it too often has for priests. The silences about sex and desire need their glocal theorization.

Ms World and the West in Nigeria

Kaduna, Nigeria, hosted the Ms World contest, 2002. Contestants representing Costa Rica, Switzerland, South Africa, Panama, and Denmark refused to participate in the pageant because of the choice of host country. They thought it was unacceptable for the pageant to condone, inadvertently or not, the practice of *shari'a*, Islamic law, which notoriously prescribed death by stoning for single mother Amina Lawal.

These contestants spoke out against what they saw as the cruelty of Islamic law and its unfair treatment of women. At this same time, Isoma Daniel, a Christian Nigerian journalist, wrote disrespectfully in her newspaper that perhaps the Prophet Muhammad would have liked one of these contestants as a bride. Extremist/Islamist-led violent riots broke out almost immediately in Kaduna. Hundreds of people died, and thousands were seriously injured. The pageant quickly relocated to London.

Let me try and unpack the messy mix of issues here. Before doing so I should say that I have chosen to look carefully at this specific moment because it reveals the insufficiency of established political discourses to represent, without distortion, the tangled webs that map cross-cultural patriarchal and masculinist continuities. The simplistic oppositional frames, which always falsely homogenize complexity, make it almost impossible to see new feminisms and their fault lines as they emerge. The pageant itself is of the West and yet is watched by several billion viewers around the world. It is a globalized site which offers up women's bodies from around the world in Western garb, according to Western standards. But one should not assume, as I think Katha Pollitt does, that this "cattle call" represents secular modernity, while the Islamic extremists who rail against it are simply religious 'backward' fanatics.[88] Neither, by the way, are these extremists standing up for women's rights, as they demand circumscribed lives for women.

So there are partial truths and partial realities here. The contest itself treats women more like pieces of meat than human beings. It reduces women's worth to their bodies. A particular kind of beauty is what counts: high cheekbones, narrow noses, thin necks, slight muscle, long legs, lean bodies. Beauty models of all nationalities try to look like the fashion models of the global cosmetic and fashion industries, and try to mold themselves accordingly to this singular standard. This mold is a Western hegemonized notion of beauty that tyrannizes women everywhere with its power-filled exclusions. Awura-Abena Ansah of Ghana says that women need to carve out a more all-encompassing notion of beauty respecting their home cultures. Long necks with fleshy folds are seen as beautiful by Ghanaians.

But what happens to this critique of hegemonic Westernized patriarchy when the pageant is presented as an expression of women's freedom and positioned against religious extremism? Instead of seeing the pageant as exploitative and 'backward' in and of itself, Islamic fundamentalists are characterized and singled out as such. It is not that I do not think that Islamic extremist masculinism is not 'backward', but that the pageant, in its own way, is 'backward' too. Although women in the West as well as women 'elsewhere' speak out against fundamentalist misogyny, some Muslim women take offense and defend the "true and progressive" Islam against what they see as arrogant Western feminism. On Amy Goodman's radio show, "Democracy Now", Fawzia Afzal-Khan and Azizah al-Hibri criticized Western feminists for 'obsessing' over Islamic violence.[89] Salman Rushdie weighed in and asked why a majority of Muslims in the West, if they believe in this progressive side of Islam, do not speak out against the rioting in Nigeria.[90]

Katha Pollitt, who usually gets it right, has it partially wrong in this instance. She reduces the pageant and the ensuing riots to a religious/secular struggle even though she readily admits that "religious texts mean what people want them to mean, and always have". Women's rights will never be a perfect fit for her in either the Qur'an or the Bible. Yet she also says: "Say what you will about beauty pageants, if it's bikinis versus burkas, you've got to be for bathing suits."[91] But exactly who benefits from this oppositioning? The issue is not about burqas and bathing suits as pieces of clothing, so it is crucially important to flesh out what the problems really are in this instance. Pollitt needs to look inside these choices for the silences and the whisperings inside each.

One last pluralizing of 'seeing' the pageant comes from Zohra Yusuf Daoud, who was crowned the first Ms Afghanistan in 1972. She writes that despite the trivializing of pageants in the US, their role in Afghanistan is different. They mean "we were catching up to the world, working to fit in, joining the global community". Her role as Ms Afghanistan involved promoting literacy, and visiting women's prisons that were filled with women who had run away from forced marriages, killed husbands who had beaten them, escaped from domestic violence. She says that maybe pageants are 'silly' but being Ms Afghanistan changed her life. She notes: "I'm no politician, I'm no activist. I am a mother, a wife, a woman, and a refugee from a country whose glory has long since passed. Like so many other Americans, I am an immigrant with only stories of what my life used to be like in a land far away."[92]

Women's bodies remain a major site of political contestation because so much power is located in women's activism and energy for sustaining life. Even a commercialized and domesticated event like Ms World reveals this contestation. Women themselves must struggle to develop ways of seeing beyond the imperial and masculinist divides that prevent new dialogues for revolutionary action.

Relocating Polyversal Feminisms

Feminisms are humanist theories of inclusivity that attempt to name women in their cacophonous varieties. This variety expresses the standard of polyversality – a connectedness rooted in multiplicity – a sharedness expressed through uniqueness. Self-determination of women's bodies and minds is expressed through local cultural meanings but with a cross-cultural recognition of women's duties and rights. No woman shall be excluded or silenced because of imperial blinders or cultural domination.

Feminisms have a unity which is also simultaneously diverse. It is multiple and continues to multiply. As such, feminisms is the most inclusive theory of social justice I know, but I am not sure that this is the same thing as saying, as feminist and friend bell hooks does, that *Feminism is for Everybody*. Because feminisms are about displacing and rearranging masculinist privilege – with its racist and colonialist roots/routes – there are men and women alike who will not embrace it. The inclusivity is too revolutionary, the power rearrangements too unsettling.

This poly/dimensional origin of feminisms means that liberal, Islamic, and Africana womanists dialogue with each other while challenging the limits of each other's understanding and viewings. The tensions between beliefs about family, religion, secularism, sex, veils, and nudity are not easily resolved. Nor is it clear that they need be in order for us to recognize women's and girls' shared exploitation and oppression. Women's bodies and the life women live because of them create the bridges that are necessary to humanely embrace each other in spite of conflicts. We, the big 'we', must disentangle ourselves from the imagined West/non-West, modern/backward, developed/lacking divide in order to see the panoply of women's activism more fully and creatively. This means challenging US imperial feminism wherever it exists.

We, the big 'we', must also acknowledge that most women want freedom and most women want equality as well. These desires make us similarly human. Women may define these desires differently, and this also makes us uniquely human. Women's polyversality allows us to see one another but not simply as in a mirror. At this moment, women across the globe must find ways to celebrate and blend these different traditions of women's struggle. The process of naming, and seeing, and working together dislodges former barriers. New ways of thinking will allow for more inclusive ways of knowing and seeing so that no one is left behind.

As an anti-racist feminist in the US, I believe it is urgent for me and others like me to work actively towards ending women's and girls' exploitation and oppression at home and all places elsewhere. Alice Walker says somewhat the same thing when she says that "we must see where our tax dollars flow and try, in awareness, to follow them".[94] This anti-globalization position must also be clarified to demand a fair wage for all. The US government must be pressured to make good on its obligations to Afghanistan and allow justice in Iraq; to end the wars of/on 'terror'; to rebuild a just welfare state in the US; to change its policies toward Palestinians. We, the big 'we', need peace, not war; justice not greed; support not competition; health care not insurance companies. For any of this to happen the right-wing takeover of the US, and with it the globe, must be stopped.

The reach of neoliberalism extends well beyond any one nation. It is the major obstacle that women face in their struggles for just and humane democracies almost everywhere. What makes this all even more difficult is that like the wars of/on 'terror', women's rights are now embedded in neoliberalism, as a way of containing them. The UN Development Program's *Arab Human Development Report* says that the lack of women's empowerment and education is a key reason for the poverty of the region. The report advises enhancement of the freedom of Arab women. Interestingly, there is no mention of women's equality, given the report's neoliberal framing. Choices should be increased rather than access. And the state should empower the poor, but not by assuming "the role of direct provider of economic goods and services. This approach has failed."[95] So much for humane democracy: the private sector is preferred.

Nevertheless, hugely viable women's movements throughout the world speak an amazing diversity and heterogeneity that pushes out the borders that each of us inhabit. New bridges are being built as women discover each other in transborder actions across diverse currents. Latin American and Caribbean feminisms have been newly naming their struggles in their Encuentros (encounters) since the early 1980s. Feminists in Arab states lead the struggle for democracy in Iran, Afghanistan, Algeria. Peasant women in Mexico kept an airport from being built in the name of land rights for peasants. Women Reebok workers in India fought for better wages and working conditions and won.[96] It is at each of these locations that the meaning of feminisms and democracies will unfold for this next century.

Ask me a few years from now if my understanding and agenda for feminisms are the same as they are today, and I hope I can say no. I hope that we, the big 'we', will have moved on, beyond neoliberalism and imperial feminism, to humane democracy for us all.

Notes

1. See Estelle Freedman, *No Turning Back: The History of Feminism and the Future of Women* (New York: Ballantine Books, 2002), for an important attempt, although not always successful, to pluralize the very idea of feminism to non-Western moments. Her discussion of feminism embraces sites that are not always readily seen as feminist although, in the end, Western feminism appears dominant.
2. Zillah Eisenstein, *The Radical Future of Liberal Feminism* (Boston: Northeastern University Press, 1981), p. 4.
3. Inji Aflatun, "We Egyptian Women", in Margot Badran and Miriam Cooke, eds., *Opening the Gates: A Century of Arab Feminist Writing* (Bloomington: Indiana University Press, 1990), p. 350. I am indebted to years of discussion with Rosalind Petchesky about this issue.
4. Eisenstein, *The Radical Future of Liberal Feminism*, p. 3.
5. Zillah Eisenstein, *The Color of Gender: Reimaging Democracy* (Berkeley: University of California Press, 1994), p. 173.
6. Ibid., p. 175. Also see my *The Female Body and the Law* (Berkeley: University of California Press, 1988), especially chapters 2, 3, and 6.
7. Toni Morrison, *Beloved* (New York, Alfred Knopf, 1987), p. 190.
8. I am indebted to Carol Quillen, "Feminist Theory, Justice and the Lure of the Human", *Signs*, vol. 27, no. 1 (Autumn, 2001), pp. 87–122, for the phrasing "other-than" in pluralizing feminisms beyond liberalism.
9. Miriam Cooke, *Women Claim Islam* (New York: Routledge, 2001), pp. ix, xv, 60, 61.
10. Jill Nelson, "Call Me Woman", *Ms Magazine*, vol. XI, no. 2 (February/March, 2001), p. 48.
11. Huda Shaarawi, *Harem Years: The Memoirs of an Egyptian Feminist*, translated and introduction by Margot Badran (New York: The Feminist Press, 1986), p. 40.

12. Fay Afaf Kanafani, *Nadia, Captive of Hope: Memoir of an Arab Woman* (New York: M. E. Sharpe, 1999), p. xiii.
13. Zillah Eisenstein, *Hatreds, Racialized and Sexualized Conflicts in the 21st Century* (New York: Routledge, 1996), p. 109.
14. I am indebted to my friend the African historian Sandra Greene for helping me clarify this point.
15. As quoted in Yoshimi Yoshiaki, *Comfort Women: Sexual Slavery in the Japanese Military During World War II*, (New York: Columbia University Press), p. 199.
16. Ibid., As stated by the United Nations Commission on Human Rights, 1996, p. 23.
17. Mahmood Mamdani, *When Victims Become Killers* (Princeton: Princeton University, 2001), Chapter 7.
18. Eisenstein, *Hatreds*, Chapter 5.
19. Lila Abu-Lughod, "The Marriage of Feminism and Islamism in Egypt: Selective Repudiations as a Dynamic of Post-colonial Cultural Politics", in Lila Abu-Lughod, ed., *Remaking Women: Feminism and Modernity in the Middle East* (Princeton: Princeton University Press, 1998), pp. 243, 263.
20. Margot Badran, *Feminists, Islam and Nation* (Princeton: Princeton University Press, 1995), pp. 31, 32.
21. Leila Abu-Lughod, "Introduction", in Abu-Lughod, ed., *Remaking Women*, p. 15.
22. Omnia Shakry, "Schooled Mothers and Structured Play: Child Rearing in Turn-of-the-century Egypt", in Abu-Lughod, ed., *Remaking Women*, p. 158.
23. Zohreh Sullivan, "Eluding the Feminist, Overthrowing the Modern? Transformations in 20th Century Iran", in Abu-Lughod, ed., *Remaking Women*, pp. 216, 236.
24. Haleh Afshar, *Islam and Feminisms: An Iranian Case-Study* (New York: St Martin's Press, 1998), p. 217.
25. Martha Nussbaum, *Women and Human Development* (New York: Cambridge University Press, 2000), pp. 8, 32, 74, 242.
26. Carol Quillen, "Feminist Theory", pp. 88, 89, 100, 120.
27. Martha Nussbaum, *Sex and Social Justice* (New York: Oxford University Press, 1999), pp. 9, 256.
28. Ibid., p.9.
29. Amartya Sen, "Population and Gender Equity", *The Nation*, vol. 274, no. 4 (July 24/31, 2000), p. 18.
30. "Women Key to Effective Development", available at: http://www.worldbank.org/gender/
31. Ratna Kapur, "Imperial Parody", *Feminist Theory*, vol. 2, no.1 (2001), pp. 79–88.
32. Susan Moller Okin, "Is Multiculturalism Bad For Women?", in Susan Moller Okin, ed., *Is Multiculturalism Bad For Women?* (Princeton: Princeton University Press, 1999), p. 9.
33. Azizah Y. Al-Hibri, "Is Western Patriarchal Feminism Good for Third World/Minority Women?" in Okin, ed., *Is Multiculturalism Bad For Women?*, pp. 41–6.

34. Angela Davis, "Reflections on the Black Woman's Role in the Community of Slaves", *Black Scholar*, vol. 3, no. 4 (December 1971), pp. 3–15; and her *Women, Race, and Class* (New York: Random House, 1981).
35. Clenora Hudson-Weems, *Africana Womanism: Reclaiming Ourselves* (Troy, Michigan: Bedford Publishers, 1993), p. 153.
36. Willie Lee Rose, *Slavery and Freedom*, edited by William Freehling (New York: Oxford University Press), p. 29.
37. Deborah Gray White, *Ar'n't I a Woman?* (New York: W.W. Norton, 1999), p. 190.
38. Aida Hurtado, *The Color of Privilege: Three Blasphemies on Race and Feminism* (Ann Arbor: University of Michigan Press, 1996), p. vii.
39. Awa Thiam, *Speak Out, Black Sisters: Feminism and Oppression in Black Africa* (London: Pluto Press, 1986), pp. 124, 125.
40. Alice Walker, *In Search of Our Mothers' Gardens* (New York: Harcourt Brace Jovanovich, 1983), p. xi.
41. I was hesitant to accept this naming thinking that it denied an important historical feminist continuity, however problematic. I have come to understand that much of this continuity is one that I envisioned as a white, and not a Black woman. Today I readily embrace a pluralizing of naming and the seeing that goes with it. See Eisenstein, *The Color of Gender*, p. 212.
42. Awa Thiam, *Speak Out, Black Sisters*, p. 3.
43. Hudson-Weems, *Africana Womanism*, pp. 39, 41, 44, 48.
44. Ibid., pp. 2, 5, 7.
45. Clenora Hudson-Weems, "Africana Womanism", in Obioma Nnaemeka, ed., *Sisterhood, Feminisms and Power: From Africa to the Diaspora* (Trenton, NJ: Africa World Press, 1998), p.149. I wish to thank my colleague Peyi Soyinka-Airewele for introducing me to this volume.
46. Ibid., Clenora Hudson Weems, "Self-Naming and Self-Definition: An Agenda for Survival", pp. 450, 451.
47. 'Zulu Sofola, "Feminism and African Womanhood", in Nnaemeka, ed., *Sisterhood, Feminisms, and Power*, p. 54.
48. Julia Wells, "Maternal Politics in Organizing Black South African Women: The Historical Lessons", in Nnaemeka, ed., *Sisterhood, Feminisms, and Power*, pp. 259, 260.
49. Ifeyinwa Iweriebor, "Carrying the Baton: Personal Perspectives on the Modern Women's Movement in Nigeria", in Nnaemeka, ed., *Sisterhood, Feminisms, and Power*, p. 303.
50. Obioma Nnaemeka, "This Women's Studies Business: Beyond Politics and History (Thoughts on the First WAAD Conference)", in Nnaemeka, ed., *Sisterhood, Feminisms, and Power*, p. 371.
51. Glo Chukukere, "An Appraisal of Feminism in the Socio-Political Development of Nigeria", in Nnaemeka, ed., *Sisterhood, Feminisms, and Power*, pp. 139, 145.
52. Niara Sudarkasa, "The Status of Women in Indigenous African Societies", in Rosalyn Terborg-Penn, Sharon Harley, Andrea Benton Rushing, eds., *Women*

in *Africa and the African Diaspora* (Washington, DC: Howard University Press, 1987), pp. 28–36.

53. Taiwo Ajai, "The Voluptuous Ideal", in Daphne Williams Ntiri, ed., *One is Not A Woman, One Becomes …* (Troy, MI: Bedford, 1982), pp. 78, 79, 81.
54. Obioma Nnaemeka, "This Women's Studies Business", pp. 364, 366.
55. "Statement from the South African Delegation Regarding the Request by Some Participants that Whites Be Excluded from Presenting Papers at the WAAD Conference", in Nnaemeka, ed., *Sisterhood, Feminisms, and Power*, p. 480.
56. Martha Banks, "Bridges Across Activism and the Academy: One Psychologist's Perspective", in Nnaemeka, ed., *Sisterhood, Feminisms, and Power*, p. 390.
57. Dé Bryant, "Reflections on Nsukka '92", in Nnaemeka, ed., *Sisterhood, Feminisms, and Power*, pp. 406–8.
58. Fidelia Fouche, "The Nigeria Conference", in Nnaemeka, ed., *Sisterhood, Feminisms, and Power*, p. 419.
59. Elise Young and Zengie Mangaliso, "South African and African American Women", *Meridians*, vol. 3, no. 1 (2002), pp. 191–200.
60. Hussaina J. Abdullah, "Religious Revivalism, Human Rights Activism and the Struggle for Women Rights in Nigeria", in Mahmood Mamdani, ed., *Beyond Rights Talk and Culture Talk* (New York: St. Martin's Press, 2000), pp. 96–120.
61. Kimberle Acquaro and Peter Landesman, "Out of Madness, A Matriarchy", *Mother Jones*, vol. 28, no. 1 (January/February 2003), pp. 59-63.
62. Peter Landesman, "The Minister of Rape", *New York Times*, September 15, 2002, pp. 81– 132.
63. Filomina Chioma Steady, "African Feminism: A Worldwide Perspective", in Terborg-Penn, Harley, and Benton, eds., *Women in Africa*, p. 21.
64. Robert Worth, "Duality of Gay Muslims is Tougher After Sept. 11", *New York Times*, January 13, 2002, p. 31.
65. Salman Rushdie, "Yes, This is About Islam", *New York Times*, November 21, 2001, p. A25.
66. Beena Sarwar, "Brutality Cloaked as Tradition", *New York Times*, August 6, 2002, p. A15.
67. Norimitsu Onishi, "Mother's Sentence Unsettles a Nigerian Village", *New York Times*, September 7, 2002, p. A23.
68. I am indebted to collegial discussions with Asma Barlas as well as her book *Believing Women, Unreading Patriarchal Interpretations of the Qur'an* (Austin: University of Texas Press, 2002) for much of my understanding here.
69. As quoted in Valentine Moghadam, "Islamic Feminism and Its Discontents: Toward A Resolution of the Debate", *Signs*, vol. 27, no. 4 (Summer, 2002), pp. 1135, 1142, 1143, 1147, 1148, 1149.
70. Haideh Moghissi, *Feminism and Islamic Fundamentalism* (London; Zed Books, 1999), pp. 10, 73.
71. Mai Yamani, "Introduction", in Mai Yamani ed., *Feminism and Islam* (New York: New York University Press, 1996), p. 1.
72. Mai Yamani, "Some Observations on Women In Saudi Arabia", in Mai Yamani, ed., *Feminism and Islam*, p. 263.

73. Talal Asad, interview with Saba Mahmood, *Stanford Humanities Review*, vol. 5., no. 1, pp. 22–36.
74. Ibid.
75. Ibid.
76. Ali Mirsepassi, *Intellectual Discourse and the Politics of Modernization: Negotiating Modernity in Iran* (Cambridge: Cambridge University Press, 2000), pp. 96, 127.
77. Abdolkarim Soroush, *Reason, Freedom and Democracy in Islam, Essential Writings of Abdolkarim Souroush*, translated and edited by Mahmoud Sadri and Ahmad Sadri (New York: Oxford University Press, 2000), pp. xv, 135. Also see Richard Antoun, *Understanding Fundamentalism: Christian, Islamic and Jewish Movements* (New York: Alta Mira Press, 2001). For a traditional Western viewing of Islam see: Bernard Lewis, *What Went Wrong? Western Impact and Middle Eastern Response* (New York: Oxford University Press, 2002).
78. The term 'Westoxication' was coined by Al-I Ahmad (1923–69) who was committed to developing a local notion of Iranian modernity. See: Jalal Al-I Ahmad, *Occidentosis: A Plague From the West* (Berkeley: Mizan Press, 1984 [1947]); and Mirsepassi, *Intellectual Discourse*, pp. 97–113, for an important explication of Ahmad's writings.
79. Saba Mahmood, "Feminist Theory, Embodiment, and the Docile Agent: Some Reflections on the Egyptian Islamic Revival", *Cultural Anthropology*, vol. 16, no. 2 (2001), pp. 204, 205, 210.
80. Ibid., pp. 210, 211.
81. Ibid., p. 225.
82. Ibid., p. 215.
83. Camelia Entekhabi-Fard , "Behind the Veil", *Ms Magazine*, (July/August 2001), p. 72.
84. Shaheen Sardar Ali, *Gender and Human Rights in Islam and International Law* (Boston: Kluwer Law International, 2000), p. 163.
85. Haleh Afshar, *Islams and Feminisms*, p. 6.
86. Robert Worth, "Duality of Gay Muslims Is Tougher After Sept. 11", p. 31.
87. Craig Smith, "Shh, It's an Open Secret: Warlords and Pedophelia", *New York Times*, February 21, 2002, p. A4.
88. Katha Pollitt, "As Miss World Turns", *The Nation*, vol. 275, no. 22 (December 23, 2002), p.9.
89. "Democracy Now", *Pacifica Radio* Archives, "Ms World Riots in Nigeria", November 27, 2002.
90. Salman Rushdie, "No More Fanaticism as Usual", *New York Times*, November 27, 2002, p. A3.
91. Katha Pollitt, "As Miss World Turns", p. 9.
92. Zohra Yusuf Daoud, "Miss Afghanistan, A Story of a Nation", in Sunita Mehta, ed., *Women for Afghan Women* (New York: Palgrave, 2002), pp. 104, 105, 111.
93. bell hooks, *Feminism is for Everybody* (Cambridge, MA: South End Press), 2000.
94. Alice Walker, *sent by earth, a message from the Grandmother Spirit* (New York: Seven Stories Press, Open Media Pamphlet Series, 2001), p. 49.

95. *Arab Human Development Report*, pp. 72, 107. Available from the UN Development Program at 1 UN Plaza, New York, NY, 10017; or email: publication@U.N.org
96. James Russell, "Land and Identity in Mexico: Peasants Stop an Airport", pp. 14–25; and Bernard D'Mello, "Reebok and the Global Footwear Sweatshop", pp. 26–40, in *Monthly Review* vol. 54, no. 9 (February 2003).

Index